MURDER AT
CAMP DELTA

A Staff Sergeant's Pursuit of the Truth
About Guantánamo Bay

JOSEPH HICKMAN

SIMON & SCHUSTER

New York London Toronto Sydney New Delhi

Simon & Schuster
1230 Avenue of the Americas
New York, NY 10020

First Simon & Schuster hardcover edition February 2015

SIMON & SCHUSTER and colophon are registered trademarks of
Simon & Schuster, Inc.

For information about special discounts for bulk purchases, please contact
Simon & Schuster Special Sales at 1-866-506-1949 or
business@simonandschuster.com.

The Simon & Schuster Speakers Bureau can bring authors to your
live event. For more information or to book an event contact the
Simon & Schuster Speakers Bureau at 1-866-248-3049 or
visit our website at www.simonspeakers.com.

Map copyright © 2014 by Jeffrey L. Ward
Jacket design by Marc Cohen
Jacket photograph: Mark Wilson/Getty Images

Manufactured in the United States of America

1 3 5 7 9 10 8 6 4 2

Library of Congress Cataloging-in-Publication Data is available.

ISBN 978-1-4516-5079-2
ISBN 978-1-4516-5081-5 (ebook)

CONTENTS

———◆———

Part I: The Island

Part II: Discovery

Dedicated to Talal al-Zahrani,
father of Yasser al-Zahrani who died at
Guantánamo Bay, Cuba, while in US custody,
June 9, 2006

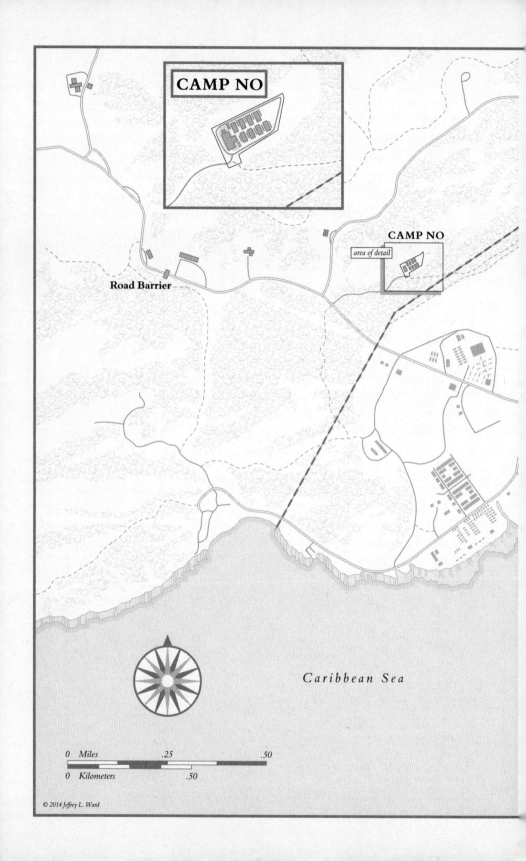

CAMP NO

CAMP NO

area of detail

Road Barrier

Caribbean Sea

0   Miles   .25   .50

0   Kilometers   .50

© 2014 Jeffrey L. Ward

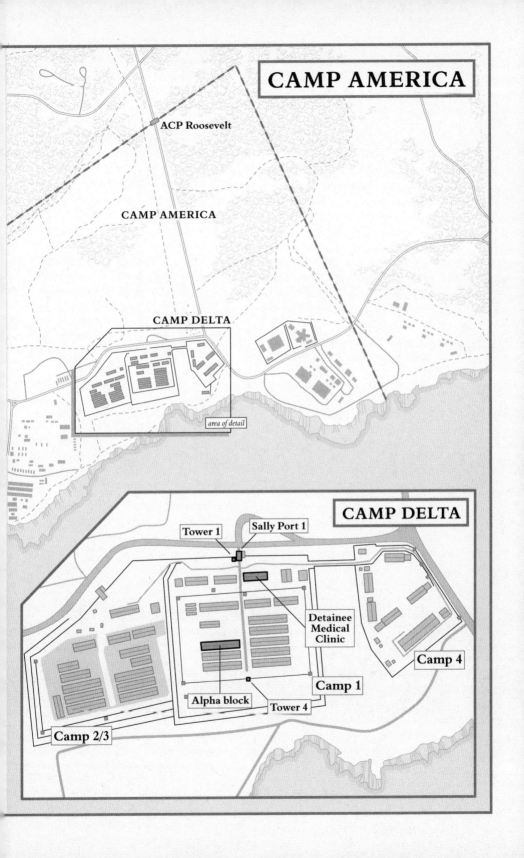

PART I

———

THE ISLAND

Call to Duty

I AM a patriotic American. I grew up in a row house about fifteen minutes south of downtown Baltimore, and I joined the Marine Corps as soon as I could at age eighteen. It was there that I found my place in the world. Aside from the hard training, the military offered me specialized schooling in radio communications and gave me a sense of purpose. I liked the structure, the brotherhood, and the knowledge that I was protecting the land and the people I loved. I worked hard and received high ratings for my job performance in the Marines. I was quickly promoted to a position at Fort George G. Meade, Maryland, where I was assigned to a Marines unit that was attached to the National Security Agency (NSA).

When I left the Marine Corps in 1987 with an honorable discharge, I became the operations manager for one of the largest security and investigation companies in the United States. There I oversaw the operations of many commercial and government complexes in the Maryland–Washington, DC, area: places like Fort Detrick, where the government conducted biochemical research. Some people claimed that a sample of every virus known to man was housed there.

In 1994 I reenlisted, this time entering the army. I was doing well in the civilian world, but I missed the camaraderie you could find only in the military. However, military life in my early thirties was not quite the same as when I was a young man, and in 1998 I once again received an honorable discharge and returned to Baltimore, where I started doing corrections work.

I became a prisoner transport officer for Baltimore and Anne Arundel County. At the same time, I received certification as a private investigator and took a position at Expert Security, Inc., which offered personal protection to corporate executives. Protecting suits paid well, but for some reason—maybe because I grew up in and around a tough city like Baltimore—I preferred my work in corrections. I truly felt that I was helping society. I was in charge of handling dangerous felons, and I always prided myself on treating them with dignity. There were some true animals among them—violent predators with something wrong in their wiring—but many were people who came from backgrounds similar to my own. We just took different turns in life, and theirs took them to a dark place.

Eventually I grew bored protecting high-paid corporate executives and went out on my own. Some of my work was for rich people, spying on their spouses to see if they were cheating. However, most of my clients were just people scraping by who needed help: finding a missing loved one, tracking down an ex-spouse who'd skipped out on child support payments, or protecting strippers who had stalker problems the police didn't think were serious enough to pursue.

The turning point for me was 9/11. When the attacks happened on September 11, 2001, I was glued to the TV. I saw the live broadcast from the Pentagon and was amazed to see Donald Rumsfeld, a sixty-nine-year-old man, in the rubble pulling out bodies. His office had just been blown up, and he was out there in a bloody, torn shirt, tending to people who were hurt, carrying them to the ambulances. I watched that and thought, "That's our secretary of defense. This man is a real American hero."

After seeing that, I couldn't continue working in the private sector. I was thirty-eight years old, and I wanted to do my part. I chose the Maryland National Guard. Six months after that grim day, I was placed in an infantry unit. The idea behind the National Guard is that its units and personnel can be integrated seamlessly into any branch of the army as necessary. The result was that I didn't often know when or where I was going on a deployment, or for how long.

I was initially assigned to an infantry squad that taught urban combat tactics to coalition forces in Germany and Japan. In 2005 I was assigned to a cavalry unit as a scout, and a member of a Reconnaissance Surveillance Target Acquisition (RSTA) team. I also successfully completed air assault school in Fort Campbell, Kentucky, home of the 101st Airborne Division. Instead of deployment to Iraq, where I expected to go, I was assigned to the Maryland National Guard, 629th Military Intelligence Battalion, and told to prepare for a yearlong deployment at Guantánamo Bay prison. Finally, at forty-one, I had my chance to meet the enemy. Guarding him at Gitmo wouldn't be the same as facing him on the battlefield, but I felt that keeping terrorists locked up was an important job.

As I flew to Gitmo in 2006, I knew that because the enemy fought differently than in previous conflicts, our tactics had to change. Gitmo seemed like a legitimate solution for holding nonuniformed enemy combatants in a new kind of war. When I heard people complain about the legality of the place, or the Bush administration's actions, I thought they simply didn't understand the new, harsh realities facing America. I also believed that while the United States's actions might not conform to the letter of the Geneva Conventions, they upheld the spirit. I trusted my government and my military to uphold basic American principles of decency.

I didn't look forward to going away for a year and guarding a bunch of terrorists in Cuba. But my country asked, and I was proud to answer the call.

CHAPTER 1

No Sleep Till Gitmo

March 10, 2006

THE flight to Gitmo from Fort Lauderdale, Florida, should have taken an hour. It was about four hundred miles away as the crow flies. But because of the long-standing hatred between America and Fidel Castro's communist regime, American planes were required to fly the long way around Cuban airspace to prevent an international incident, adding another two hours to the flight. My unit, the roughly 120 men of Company E from the 629th Military Intelligence Battalion, had flown overnight to Fort Lauderdale from Fort Lewis, Washington. None of us slept on the way into Fort Lauderdale. We'd been occupied the day before dealing with our gear, and spent the dark hours at the airport waiting for the four-in-the-morning flight to Gitmo. I'd been up for more than twenty-four hours when I climbed aboard the Boeing 727. It should have been a miserable flight, but I was so excited that I couldn't sleep. Very few of the guys on the plane to Gitmo were able to sleep, either. The sun came up about an hour into our flight, and I could hear the younger men in the unit laughing in the adjacent seats.

"So what do you think the place will really be like?" I heard a voice behind me ask.

"Absolutely nothing like what we've been told," came the reply.

"There's a small seed of wisdom in that," I thought. As a team leader in my platoon, I was worried about what we'd face when we landed. Mine wasn't a top command position, but one thing I learned in the military was a sense of responsibility for the men under me. It's a responsibility I took to heart. As our plane drew closer to the landing field at Gitmo, my heart was not completely at ease. We had all become close during our eight-week training, and I had no worries about any man on my squad not doing his job. We had been briefed repeatedly that we were being given a potentially tough mission, and we were ready for the challenges ahead. We were told constantly in our training that the detainees would take any chance they could to kill us, and that they were highly motivated fanatics. My worry wasn't that any guy on the team would flinch but that someone might get hurt.

Company E was divided into three platoons, with each platoon divided into four ten-man squads, and each squad broken into two five-man teams. I was in First Platoon, second squad, and team leader of its five-man Bravo Team. Everyone from my squad sat together on the plane. Most of them were good soldiers, as far as I was concerned.

The guys in my squad covered an extreme range of ages and experiences.* Phillip Bradley, who was fifty-one years old, was a former Army Ranger, but that was decades ago. He'd spent most of his working life with the coroner's office in Baltimore, picking up and delivering bodies from autopsies and crime scenes. "We tag 'em and bag 'em," he'd say of his civilian duties. The youngest in our squad was eighteen-year-old Specialist Jamal Stewart, whom we all called "Young'n."

One of the guys I was closest to was Private First Class José Vasquez, thirty-eight years old. Vasquez was from DC, where he worked as a private investigator. I'd met him a year earlier in Japan, when he'd deployed there with my unit on a training mission. Everything that came out of his mouth was a joke. Sometimes I had to watch it with Vasquez, because he tended to speak his mind to officers. Even if my guy might

---

*I have changed the names of the personnel at Guantánamo with the exception of the command officers whose names have been widely reported.

be in the right, a blunt-speaking enlisted man could get the whole squad in trouble.

The one person we all had faith in was our squad leader, Staff Sergeant Michael Hayes. When not on guard duty, Hayes was a cop at Morgan State University, a historically black college in Baltimore. Before that he was a marine, and in my experience, former marines tended to be among the best leaders. He was six years younger than me, and though he stood, at most, five feet ten inches, Hayes carried himself like a giant. In my military career, he taught me more than any other leader I ever served under. With him leading our squad, I had as much confidence as possible.

Our squad was predominantly African American. In fact, after two white guys were pulled from the platoon—one because he was needed for another mission, and the other because he couldn't get along with black people—I was the only Caucasian left. Vasquez was light skinned but a proud Mexican. Like most people in the military, race and ethnicity didn't concern me. Soldiers were soldiers. But everybody else in our platoon was white, and that bothered all of us. They had segregated all the black guys and the Mexican into one squad. I guess they figured I belonged because I was from Baltimore. It was wrong, and all of my guys knew it. The military has spent decades integrating its units. For commanders to segregate a unit was almost unheard of in 2006. Worse, it made us very uneasy about the overall wisdom of our company's officers. Despite my positive impression of Staff Sergeant Hayes, the leadership of our company was the biggest concern on my mind. Our training experience at Fort Lewis with our commanders had been, in a word, awful.

CHAPTER 2

Training Days

January–February 2006

O
UR company assembled on January 4 at the Pikesville Armory in Baltimore. The 629th Battalion was based out of Cascade, Maryland, a boondocks area on the western side of the state, inhabited mostly by rural whites. Because the 629th was short of manpower, it took on personnel from guard infantry units based out of Baltimore, such as mine. When we all came together to put together the company, it was basically a case of country boys meeting city boys.

Our company commander was Captain William Drake, who initially struck me as highly disciplined. He was tall, thirty years old, and in top physical condition. He had been through Ranger School, and Drake took this to heart. Ranger School produced the best of the best, and the Captain had that swagger. The first day we met him, he let everybody know he was a Ranger and that he expected the most from us.

But shortly after telling us this, Drake organized the company along racial and socioeconomic lines. Instead of mixing up the country boys and city boys, he kept nearly all the Western Maryland guys from the original 629th in Third Platoon. First Platoon and Second Platoon contained all the guys from the Baltimore units, mostly urban white guys like me from blue-collar backgrounds, along with Latinos, and blacks.

If this had been 1950, maybe that would have made sense, to organize the company along racial lines, but even as far back as 1983, when I joined the Marine Corps, I had never seen any unit deliberately segregated by race. One of the first things they taught us in the Marine Corps, if not *the* first thing, was that we were all brother Marines. In fact, up until my training for Gitmo, my experience had always been that races got along better in the military than in the civilian world.

The next day, I tried to put aside my kernel of concern about Drake's leadership. I focused on the fact that he was a Ranger who carried himself well, so maybe he had valid reasons for organizing the company the way he did. In the military, your life was generally much easier if you gave your commander the benefit of the doubt.

A lot of training we did at Fort Lewis was elemental and much simpler, in fact, than urban assault and the things you learned in the infantry. We practiced how to search bags at checkpoints using metal detectors, what to look for—such as thumb drives, which visitors to Gitmo were not supposed to carry in or out—and how to search vehicles.

The techniques were simple, but I was mostly bothered by our training without real cell blocks. This was bad because we couldn't learn observation techniques, but it was even worse when it came to learning cell extractions: the removal of noncompliant detainees. We were told that cell extractions would be a big part of our job. Because we didn't have mock cell blocks, we had to make do with imaginary cells made from lines drawn on the ground to represent the walls. But even these were useless.

We found out later that command had given us the wrong cell dimensions to practice with, which meant we had learned irrelevant standard operating procedures (SOPs). For instance, they trained us to carry out extractions from a single cell by first sending out "doorman" through the imaginary cell door. Then the rest our squad filed in beside him, forming a line and moving forward toward the detainee. This would have worked great in a large cell—of which there were a few at

Gitmo—but most were so narrow, just six feet wide, that the SOP we practiced would never have worked.

The problem was that many of the noncommissioned officers (NCOs) and officers training us had no experience at Gitmo or doing detention work. They were teaching things they had learned secondhand. The simulations they ran were worthless. They would play the role of noncompliant detainees and hardly put up a fight. From real-world experience, I knew that when an inmate had made up his mind to resist, you could quickly find yourself in a fight for your life. He would use anything to hurt you: sharp pieces of metal, clubs, batons he might have grabbed off other corrections officers, fingernails, and teeth. Once, while I was working at the Jennifer Road Detention Center in Anne Arundel County, an inmate had fashioned a spear-like weapon from tightly rolled magazine pages to stab one of the guards. My guys got none of this in our training.

There was one simulation for which I was grateful, however, because it turned out to be extremely realistic:

"Gentlemen," announced an earnest training officer, "the noncompliant prisoner will use all means at his disposal to make your job unpleasant. This will include hurling his own urine and feces at you. We will be demonstrating such a situation today. For safety's sake, we will *not* be using real human waste. Instead, we will use baby food for this exercise." I was gratified by this particular lack of realism during training, although I was surprised by how much Gerber Strained Beef Liver resembled watery shit.

The gear we had was legit as well. On guard duty, we would wear standard military fatigues, boots, and Kevlar helmets. Outside of the prison camps, but inside Camp America, our living quarters at Gitmo, we would carry standard-issue M16 rifles. In addition, when serving on the quick-reaction force (QRF), we would also wear stab vests, similar to Kevlar ballistic vests but lighter in weight and woven to resist blades and pointed objects. On entering a cell, each man carried a shield. Everybody on QRF would carry flex cuffs and a baton. On a ten-man QRF, two guys would carry Remington 870 shotguns, just like your local police had, but loaded with shells containing rubber buckshot (a somewhat misleading name because the "rubber" buckshot was more akin to hard plastic beads).

Another guy on the QRF carried an M16 rifle with an M203 grenade launcher slung under the main barrel. The 203 fired a small 40 millimeter projectile, sort of like a little rocket tipped with a hard, rubbery projectile. Some of us nicknamed it Evil SpongeBob. We were instructed not to fire Evil Sponge Bob at any distance less than ten yards. At close range, the device was potentially lethal.

Team leaders of the QRF also carried at least one can of capsicum: pepper spray. The spray we used at Fort Lewis and at Gitmo came packaged like an ordinary can of Raid insecticide. Each can was good for about six strong doses. We were taught to get as close to the detainee as possible and aim for his face. Our instructors demonstrated this by spraying our eyes and making us run an obstacle course before we sparred with our squad mates.

"Now, this is a realistic training exercise," I thought as I gasped for breath and tried to ignore the pain searing my eyes.

Even though training lasted thirty days, we were given only one hour of "cultural training." The instructors told us very little specific information about the detainees we would be guarding and mostly said that the detainees all wanted to kill us.

We were told to not call them "hajis," since this was offensive to Muslims (even though among themselves, *haji* is a term of respect for anyone who has made the pilgrammage, or *haj*, to the holy city of Mecca.) At the same lecture, we were given the rundown on hand gestures, the meaning of which could vary from country to country, culture to culture.

"Everyone okay?" our training officer asked as he raised his hand and made a circle with his thumb and index finger. "You'll notice that I have just made a very common, everyday hand signal," he said. "While we think nothing of this type of physical expression, the Muslims will *not* see it as nothing. To them, this means 'Fuck you, asshole.' Avoid using it." There did seem to be one constant, as we were told by the training officer: "Regarding the raised middle finger," he said. "Even the most provincial Middle Easterner will recognize that this is not a friendly gesture."

That was about the extent of our cultural training. Our instructors spent much more time explaining Stockholm syndrome than helping us understand our captives. Stockholm syndrome is when captives start to sympathize with and identify with their captors. Our instructors cautioned us that a sort of reverse Stockholm syndrome could happen to guards. Because we were going to be surrounded by detainees and living alongside them in Camp America, the instructors wanted to make sure we didn't start to develop empathy toward the enemy—or his cause.

I didn't think there was much chance of that happening among the men of Company E. Despite our cultural training, many soldiers continued to refer to the detainees as hajis and other colorful names. I sensed that some of the guys were elated by the prospect of having so much power over other people. That bothered me. It could be intoxicating to have control over men in chains or cages, but in this kind of work, my team needed to keep a cool professionalism at all times. I had seen guards power-trip in civilian corrections work, but at Fort Lewis, I knew we had to be even more careful. I felt the potential for overstepping boundaries was even greater because we all believed the detainees were evil men bent on destroying our country. It worried me to think that some of the men on this assignment might too easily cross a line.

By the end of that first month at Fort Lewis, I had noticed another disturbing trend. It became apparent that our squad was not getting any time off. When we weren't training, we were assigned cleanup duties and other trivial details. I was used to long work hours in the army, but the squads in Third Platoon, made up of the white guys from the original 629th, weren't assigned the same unpleasant tasks as frequently. They even got some weekends off. My squad worked ten- to twelve- hour days and didn't receive a single day off. None of the men in our squad received promotions, either, while members of Third Platoon did. Many of the men in our squad began to feel that these disparities were racially motivated.

In the military, promotions were based largely on the time you served, as well as receiving good fitness reports. Promotions were almost automatic between the ranks of private and specialist. There were guys in our platoon whose time had come to receive promotions, but they were not getting them. Men in the squad started to complain, "You've got to be white to be promoted."

It was pretty insane to me that we were dealing with this problem in 2006. I pulled aside Sergeant Hayes privately and brought this up. "Our guys are losing their motivation, I said. They see they're getting treated differently. We're not even in Gitmo, and they're already starting not to care about this deployment."

Hayes called together everybody in the squad. He looked each man in the eye and told us he was aware of the unfair treatment we were receiving. Then he turned to me and said deadpan, "Now you know what we deal with all the time. Congratulations. You're a nigger now."

Unlike some younger black soldiers, Hayes did not often use the N-word. When it came out of his mouth applied to me, the ugly mood was broken by the sheer ridiculousness of it. Everybody started laughing. I saw then what made Hayes such a good leader. He took the anger and hopelessness we all felt and turned it into something positive. He said, "They're never going to change how they treat us. It's up to us to show them. We're going to outperform all of them in our jobs. We're going to PT [physically train] better than them, and then when we take the final test at the end of this training, we're going to score higher than everybody else. They won't be able to stop us. Even if we work ten hours longer than them every day, when we get our time off, each of us is going to study SOPs for an hour extra on his own time."

From anybody else, this might have been the kind of cornball pep talk that a high school football coach might give. But Hayes had an authority that galvanized the squad, even the smart-asses like Vasquez. We spent our second month outtraining everybody. The command did not offer us a single day off in the second month, but even if it had, we would not have taken it. We were going to be the best, no matter what.

Sure enough, at the end of our training in Fort Lewis, our squad had the highest PT scores and test scores. Despite all the crap they threw at us, we had performed better than every other squad—even though we received no acknowledgment for it.

CHAPTER 3

———◆———

Welcome to Guantánamo Bay

March 10, 2006

As soon as our plane touched the ground at Gitmo, everybody got thrown forward.

"Damn!"

"What the fuck was that?"

The runway at Leeward Point Field was short, so a pilot had to really hit the brakes when landing a big jet. In the bay, across from the landing field, there was actually part of a plane sticking out, from one pilot who hadn't been fast enough.

We were still laughing nervously from the carnival-ride landing when the cabin doors opened. Fierce heat washed over us. The temperature on the runway was about 95 degrees Fahrenheit and layered with an oppressive humidity. After training in the cold, overcast Pacific Northwest, none of us was prepared for the Cuban climate.

Though the temperature was warm, our greeting at camp Gitmo was not. When we climbed down the steps, navy security patrol (SP) guards stopped us on the flight deck. "Form up next to your gear for contraband check," they said as a team with drug-sniffing dogs approached. Around the perimeter of the airfield, I saw more navy SPs on high alert watching us, ready with their M16 rifles, and suddenly it hit me: we had just entered the most secure facility on the planet for America's enemies.

Strictly speaking, our deployment to Gitmo fell under Operation Enduring Freedom: the war in Afghanistan. I would never claim what we did was as dangerous as troops sent into harm's way in the Middle East, but I felt our mission was an important one. Our first battle on this deployment was simply to remain standing and not crumple from the heat. We had on our helmets, our boots, and our army combat uniforms, and were holding our M16s as we stood under the blazing sun, breathing in the fumes of jet fuel and watching the tarmac ripple with heat waves.

Navy SPs knew the drill. They quickly distributed water bottles as the dogs continued their search. The SPs pulled the bottles off of pallets on the back of a Humvee and kept tossing them to us even after we'd each downed a couple. "Drink as much as you can," they told us. "The first few days here will be brutal."

The dogs found no contraband in our luggage, and we were directed onto a bus for a short trip down a winding road to the dock where a ferry would take us to Windward Point on the east side of the entrance to the bay. Standing at the dock, we were surprised by the sight of four-foot-long iguanas skittering along the edges of the road.

The ferry ride was spectacular. We got a cool breeze, and the views of the rolling hills and mountains beyond that were gorgeous. Farther up the bay, closer to the outlet of the Guantánamo River lay the docks for US Navy warships. In the opposite direction, in the sea just beyond the bay, Russian submarines still occasionally poked up from the depths, playing the same cat-and-mouse game that had been going on since the Cold War.

At Windward Point, a bus took us to McCalla Airfield, about a half mile up from the bay. We were dropped off at a massive hangar. Before McCalla closed in 1976, the hangar had housed military blimps. Apparently only a blimp hangar could contain the hot air that was generated in the next four hours of briefings. Some of us were going on thirty hours of sleeplessness when they marched us in to sit on bleachers.

The first to address us was General Jay Hood, commander of the joint task force in charge of detention operations at Gitmo. He was straightforward. "Our mission here is about protecting America from terrorists," he said, "and they have underestimated your courage, your character, and your commitment to do what's right." He talked to us like he was just another "Joe"—army slang for one of the guys. Tired as I was that morning, I felt optimistic that our commander was a good leader.

General Hood was a tough act to follow, and the officers who came after him had about the same effect as a bottle of Tylenol PM. General Edward Leacock portrayed Gitmo as some sort of tropical vacation getaway. He talked up the Morale, Welfare and Recreation (MWR) facilities, the McDonald's and Subway available nearby, and told us that bicycles would be available to us during our free time. Bikes were part of the military's effort to go "green." "Environmental awareness is something all you men should take part in," said General Leacock. "It's something we can all take pride in. Use those bikes." I don't think I rode a bicycle once while I was at Gitmo.

The other officers emphasized a few key rules. When we left the is-land—for the ten-day leave each of us would be given at some point in the year, and on our final return home—we would be searched for hard drives or digital storage devices. Those caught trying to bring any such device out of Camp America would face prison. We were also informed that all of our emails and phone calls would be monitored by the NSA to make sure we didn't talk about our jobs, the detainees, and anything else we might see or hear.

It was no surprise that we were told not to take photographs inside Camp America. But even outside the camp, we had to be careful. We were told that photographing any of the many small windmills that dotted the island was a serious infraction. One could guess that the windmills were used to generate power, but their design, location, and what they might be powering was something we had to preserve as a state secret.

The final and, perhaps, most important rule on the entire island re-garded the treatment of iguanas. The safety of the lizards that ran freely about the naval base was of the utmost importance to the United States. A legal officer gave us a special briefing about them. He was deadly serious as he began: "I'd like to talk for a minute about the Cuban rock iguana, or *Cyclura nubila*. The Cubans on the other side of the fence," he said gravely, "hunt them down and eat them with the kind of reckless abandon that only a food-rationed communist can bring to such an enterprise. Because of this, those iguanas comprise what is considered a vulnerable population. We guard the health and well-being of these creatures to maintain compliance with the Endangered Species Act. Men, the use of deadly force on a detainee can be justified given the right circumstances. There is absolutely no justification for harming an iguana. If it happens, you will automatically be busted down a rank and fined ten thousand dollars. Remember that." This would prove to be a source of constant anxiety for us. The leaf-eating creatures were everywhere in and around Camp America, including the roads we patrolled—and they just loved to dart out in front of our Humvees.

A load of pizzas was brought in at the end of our briefing. Several of the California National Guardsmen whom we were replacing had picked them up at the Pizza Hut down the road. These guys were very professional, very courteous, and overjoyed to see us. Our faces were about the last thing they were going to see before leaving the island and going home.

We were sitting around with the guardsmen, getting the unofficial "sit-rep"—military slang for situation report—on the island when their commander walked over and told us to get some shut-eye. In two days' time, the California Guardsmen had planned to take us around and train us in all of their SOPs. Until then, their commander wanted us to relax and acclimate.

Captain Drake overheard this and told the commander, "My guys got plenty of rest on the plane. They can start their training tomorrow." I guessed he wanted to impress the guardsmen by showing how gung-ho we were, but as he walked off, I could tell they were as pissed off as we were. It meant more of them would have to work tomorrow to train us. A few hours on the island, and Captain Drake already had another platoon hating him almost as much as ours did.

We drove out of McCalla late in the afternoon. The two-mile road leading to Camp America held what were to be our only getaway spots for the next twelve months: McDonald's, Kentucky Fried Chicken, Pizza Hut, and Subway. Farther away were the Navy Lodge Hotel, a bar called the Windjammer—nicknamed the Cockjammer because there were so few women—and the Navy Exchange, or NEX, which was like a mini Wal-Mart. It looked as if a little slice of home had been excised from some random freeway off-ramp and dropped intact here on the island. The only real difference were the watchtowers on the Cuban side manned by Fidel Castro's snipers. Castro's guards weren't there to shoot us. They were there to stop his people from running across the border and trying to get into Gitmo.

After winding a bit past the NEX, the road straightened out, and up ahead we could see the main gate into Camp America. It wasn't much: just a guard shack in the middle of the two lanes where the road split. One lane was for entering and the other for exiting. The guards there—whose boots we'd fill within a few days—were armed with M16s, and one with a 9 millimeter pistol. One came on the bus and inspected the IDs we'd been issued in the hangar. Outside they put mirrors under the bus to check for bombs, contraband, or human stowaways. I was curious about their SOPs, because during our two months at Fort Lewis, we'd never actually trained using a bus.

They let us through, and after going about a half mile down the road, the bus turned right, driving past a jumble of concertina wire, fences, and guard towers. It looked like the site of a half-finished construction project. That was Camp Delta.

Until the California Guardsmen vacated their more modern barracks at the opposite end of Camp America, we were placed in Camp Buckley, a collection of crude wooden huts, each with five bunks for holding ten men. Perfect for a squad.

My squad dragged in and settled down for the night. It wasn't dark yet, but because of Captain Drake's generous offer to volunteer us for duty, we would be up before dawn. Most of the guys crawled into their racks and were asleep by nine. We were so full of pizza, we didn't even go to the chow hall. Sergeant Hayes and I stayed up. At about eleven o'clock, we heard this eerie Arabic wailing. It was the evening call to prayer. I'd never heard it before, and the effect was chilling. Eventually

I would get used to it. The prayers were recorded on tapes and were blasted on loudspeakers five times a day across all of Camp America. But as I lay down to sleep that night, with those sounds still reverberating in my head, a part of me thought, "A prayer is a prayer." I knew I could use as much help from God as the men on the other side of the fence in Camp Delta.

*   *   *

The California Guardsmen didn't know what to do with us when our squad showed up at their office at six thirty the next morning. They weren't happy to see us.

Apparently when Captain Drake volunteered us to work, he never followed up by sending word down the chain of command. Now, squeezed into the cramped Sergeant of the Guard office, the SOG looked at us and said, "Wouldn't you men rather take the day off and acclimatize?"

The temperature was already 85 degrees, and some of the men were perspiring through the backs of their clothes from the quarter-mile walk from the chow hall, but Sergeant Hayes explained to the SOG, "My captain told us to start today."

Even though it was a pain in the ass for them to figure out what to do with us, they understood what we were up against. There were a lot of captains like Drake in the Guard. They overcompensated because the Guard didn't have the same reputation as the full-time military. Most enlisted guys in the Guard would put their 110 percent into it and weren't worried about how they compared with other soldiers. However, the Guard seemed to breed officers with inferiority complexes who made brash decisions to prove themselves. The sad part was that they then lived up to their reputations as being inferior to regular army officers.

The California Guardsmen had created a specific training plan to transition us into their jobs, but it wasn't ready to be implemented for a few more days. The guys at the office were part of a skeleton crew, so they scrounged some extra Humvees and drove us around to the different posts.

As big as they looked on the outside, Humvees were tiny on the inside. They could comfortably fit about five troops, but we could usually squeeze in one more. The ones on Gitmo were from a generation without air-conditioning and were like rolling ovens.

Our first stop was Checkpoint Houston, the observation post on the western side of Camp America, just above the beach. On the way, we passed Camp Iguana, a small facility that once held a couple dozen minor-aged boys scooped up in the Middle East. Iguana contained a couple of enclosed buildings that looked relatively comfortable, like rustic dorms at a summer camp. The teenaged detainees had all been repatriated, and the camp was now used to hold adult detainees who'd been cleared for release and were on hold to be sent home.

OP Houston itself was a small aluminum guard shack that sat atop a small hill—like the kind you'd see at the entrance to any parking lot back home. It was on the most beautiful part of the island. The hill overlooked the ocean, and there was a beach below it. The beach was one of the main R & R spots. The military had put in grills, picnic benches, and a pavilion, and people would often go down there for barbecues.

Of course, OP Houston wasn't positioned there for the recreation. The guards manning Houston had to watch for boats coming in from the ocean. For anyone seeking to infiltrate the camp, the beach was a prime spot. Since Gitmo itself was a US military installation, in addition to a detention camp, the coastline was always watched for Russian or Cuban ships navigating too close. The other side to guarding OP Houston was humanitarian: guards were always looking for refugees from Cuba or Haiti trying to sneak ashore. We were instructed to detain any refugees and render them medical aid.

I was in a hurry to get out of OP Houston, because the smell of charcoal lighter fluid and smoke was curling up from the beach. Someone was starting an early-morning cookout, and I didn't want my men to linger on that image as we went through our rounds of make-work.

But just as we were about to leave, a group of twenty or so guys in civilian clothes, reeking of coconut suntan lotion, approached the gate leading to the beach—all of them were from our Third Platoon. The man lighting up the grills turned, and we saw it was Captain Drake.

He and his favored platoon were getting ready for their first mission in Operation Enduring Freedom: an early-morning beach blow-out.

As we moved on to the next position the California Guard wanted to show us, the sergeant I was riding with just laughed. "Glad to know you guys are as fucked up as we've been. But it looks like you guys got it worse."

As we rode together, the sergeant from the California Guard pointed out another problem. Our company of about 120 men was replacing their unit, a battalion of nearly 500 men.

"How are you guys doing the math on this?" he asked.

The plan was to eliminate some of the duties that the California Guard had performed. For instance, we got rid of the foot patrols they had run round the clock through Camp America, freeing up some manpower. But what it really boiled down to was that we'd be working longer hours. The California Guard had done six-hour shifts, with weekends off. We would do twelve-hour and longer shifts, with only one or two days off a month.

I couldn't blame this on Drake. Some anonymous military genius in an office somewhere had decided it was possible to replace a battalion with a company. It probably looked good on paper to a bunch of officers who would never walk in our boots.

Late in the afternoon, the California Guardsmen took us down to the perimeter checkpoint dubbed ACP Roosevelt and showed us the SOPs for vehicle searches. Ninety-eight percent was what we'd already been trained to do: stop every car, check the ID of every occupant, and pick one out of every few vehicles for a more complete inspection. These cars would be directed to pull to the side. Every occupant had to get out while the guards looked inside, under the hood and trunk, and at the undercarriage. All this was standard.

They had a big blue canopy to work under, but I could see it was hot, and some senior officers gave the guards attitude because they didn't like having to show their IDs. Otherwise it looked like routine, if boring, security work. One of the guardsmen said, "The SOPs are that we do one hundred percent ID check, no exceptions—except for the Iceman and the paddy wagon."

I stopped him there. "What do you mean exceptions?"

"Well, the paddy wagon—sometimes we call it the pizza van—will be driven by a pair of navy guards and will be carrying detainees in the back," he explained. "Under no circumstances are you to look inside or search any part of that vehicle."

"What about the Iceman?" I asked.

"He'll be in a sedan with a tag that reads 'I.C.E.,'" said the guardsman.

"I.C.E.?"

The guardsman explained, "Interrogation Control Element. The Iceman is just one guy—a chief of interrogations. He looks sort of like Michael Douglas in the movie *Falling Down*. You know, white guy in his fifties, short-sleeve shirt. He comes through here most days, so you'll meet him soon enough. He's polite. Always says, 'Hi.' Just wave him through."

I couldn't believe what I was hearing. Going back to my first days as a marine attached to the National Security Agency—one of the most secretive intelligence organizations in the government—the one thing they drilled into me is that when we set up a security plan, there are zero exceptions.

We could have built the Great Wall of China around Camp America, but if a van or a white guy in a car was able to come and go without ever being searched, our security procedures were more theatrical than real. Exceptions to SOPs meant that the government was giving total discretion to a handful of individuals: the Iceman and the random navy guards driving the paddy wagon. These people could do whatever they wanted, carry anything in or out, and nobody would check on them. It was unsafe. I didn't mind the secrecy. I understood and completely accepted the idea that the US government had to keep secrets. But giving carte blanche to a handful of individuals was, according to my training, just plain sloppy. It made a mockery of the security plan we were there to carry out.

As the day wound down, the California Guardsmen took us into Camp Delta for the first time. Only then did I understand how prehistoric the camp's construction was. The entrance was a double row of chain-link fences topped with concertina wire. The first building, about fifteen feet from the entrance, was the medical clinic. It was the most modern building in all of Camp Delta—and it was made of plywood.

The clinic and every other building there sat on two-foot-high pylons because Camp Delta was situated in a flood zone. From the inside, the camp looked like an old firebase from Vietnam that I'd seen in pictures. I'd expected something much more high tech.

Inside Camp Delta were the detention areas called Camps 1 and 2/3. Each consisted of several open cell blocks—wire-fence walls under tin roofs. Clear Plexiglas covered some of the walls so that the cells weren't completely exposed to the elements, but I could see right away that the design combined the worst of two worlds: the cell blocks were partially open to the elements, and they were under tin roofs. In the hot sun, the cells baked the occupants like bread in an oven. I couldn't believe that a maximum-security prison wasn't temperature controlled. It was all very strange.

My first concerns weren't even for the detainees. I watched the navy guards who walked the halls between cell blocks and couldn't believe the heat they had to put up with. I never wanted to be in their shoes. On a "cool" spring day like that one, the temperature was 85 or 90 degrees outside, but it must have been at least ten to twenty degrees hotter under those tin roofs.

Camp 4 had nicer facilities. It housed detainees who'd been deemed "compliant," though we were never told exactly what that meant. We knew only that they had cooperated when interrogated. The cells in Camp 4 had the same open-air-under-a-tin-roof construction as the other camps, but many were large communal cells where up to ten men could live at the same time. There the detainees could at least move around and socialize, whereas in the other camps they were isolated. Even though their cell walls were transparent, they weren't permitted to communicate.

Camp 4 also had a basketball court and a small field where the detainees were permitted to play soccer. Camps 1 and 2/3 simply had a fenced-off twelve-by-twelve-foot "recreation area" where detainees who were on good behavior could come out for a half an hour at a time and play by themselves in the sunlight.

Watching over all the camps was Tower 1. That was the supervisor's tower. It held two men, the top guard on duty in Camp Delta and an assistant, called a "runner." Even though everyone had radios, the runner's job was to circulate to the seven other towers inside Delta, check on the guards, and pass word if the radios failed.

When I got to the top of Tower 1, what blew my mind was the noise. Talk between inmates on the cell block was forbidden, but that didn't stop them from trying. We heard navy guards yelling at the detainees to shut up and the prisoners screaming back at them, "Fuck you, America!" or "Send me home!" Some were standing or lying in their cells yelling at no one—or they were crying. I had never seen such chaos in a prison or jail. I thought the Baltimore jails I'd worked in could be bad, but Camp Delta was just bedlam. Complete chaos.

I looked down at the detainees and the navy guards screaming at one another, and it felt like I was staring into the pit of a man-made hell.

"It can't be like this all the time, can it?" I wondered. My confidence in the procedural standards of this surreal outpost had been shaken by the end of that first day, but I was willing to chalk up a lot of it to poor circumstances. We had surprised the California Guardsmen by starting our training early, we were unaccustomed to the heat and humidity, and most of us were running on very little sleep. "We've been here for only a little more than twenty-four hours," I thought. "Maybe I need to settle down."

After I descended the tower, I approached one of the California Guardsmen. "Is there something going on here today?" I asked.

He seemed confused by the question. "Going on?" he asked.

"You know . . . something unusual. Food riot? Hunger strike? It seems so . . . out of control."

"Nope," he said. "Just another day at the beach. Welcome to Camp Delta."

CHAPTER 4

Priorities

S EVERAL days after our arrival, Colonel Mike Bumgarner, forty-seven years old and the commander of all the guards at Gitmo, called the new arrivals into a meeting. Gitmo relied on about 1,100 guards in total, most of them from the navy. Our company had arrived along with several new navy squads, meaning that there were about two hundred new arrivals in attendance.

Colonel Bumgarner's aides ordered us into a large community room in the barracks. It was technically a housing area for "third country nationals"—Filipinos and Jamaicans who served as cooks and cleaners in Camp America—but the space had been cleared for the Colonel's address.

We waited for his arrival in chairs specially set up for the occasion. Unlike the higher-ups who'd briefed us the day we'd arrived, Colonel Bumgarner would have a more direct role in our lives. He ran day-to-day security operations from a command center inside Camp Delta. When I served as Sergeant of the Guard, or was working on the quick-reaction force doing cell extractions or dealing with other emergencies in the cell blocks, I would likely interact directly with him.

One of his aides shouted, "Attention!" as Bumgarner strode to the front of the room. He was a big man, about six foot two with a stocky build, and I could see right off that he ate up military customs and courtesies. He loved the power conferred by his authority. Most times in a formation, as soon as a commander called attention and everybody had stood, he or she would immediately say, "At ease," and let everybody stand at parade rest. But Colonel Bumgarner seemed to draw his inspiration from actor George C. Scott's portrayal of blustery World War II hero General George Patton in the movie *Patton*. As we stood at attention, he took several minutes to look up and down our ranks. It was a power thing that I'd seen certain officers do before. It meant, "If I say so, you'll stand like this all day."

When he finally told us to stand at ease, Colonel Bumgarner spoke to us in a booming Southern drawl that added to his commanding image. "Men," he said, "you have a very challenging year ahead of you. This assignment has put all of us under a microscope, and I expect a hundred and twenty percent from all of you." The colonel emphasized how dangerous the detainees were and how vigilant we all had to be. I felt better after listening to him. It was clear that Colonel Bumgarner took his job seriously. I was still troubled by the unusual security breaches built into the SOPs—allowing the pizza van and the Iceman to pass unchecked—and the general air of chaos in the overheated, shoddy cell blocks of Camp Delta, but Bumgarner's strict way of handling himself and us gave me confidence in his command. "This is a career military policeman," I thought, and I got the sense that he believed in all the protocols that went with that career: treating detainees humanely and following all the laws. Most soldiers liked having strong leaders—so long as that strength came with intelligence and integrity.

A few days later, my impression of the colonel changed. It was my first early morning on duty running the checkpoint into Camp Delta, when a navy guard ran up to me. He was frantic. "Make sure you call our office the second you see Colonel Bumgarner arrive at the checkpoint—and pass the word that whoever is on duty in the mornings here does the same."

"I will," I said. "But why?"

"The colonel likes to start his day by having us line up in formation when he steps into the office, while we play Beethoven's Fifth or 'Bad Boys' on a boom box."

I thought to myself, "Are you fucking kidding me? This is the stupidest thing I've ever heard," but the navy guard was an E7: a chief. He was the equivalent of a sergeant first class in the army—two ranks above me—so I just told him, "Roger that."

I may have thought that morning ritual was ridiculous, but to the men in Colonel Bumgarner's office, cueing up the colonel's theme music was practically a life-or-death matter. One morning a few days after I was given the order to notify the office of Bumgarner's arrival, we were overwhelmed at the checkpoint and failed to make the call. A few minutes later, the same navy chief came out to the checkpoint. He was perspiring heavily, obviously distressed from a very recent ass chewing. "Colonel Bumgarner is really upset he didn't get his greeting."

I pointed to the line of people still waiting to get through the checkpoint. "Chief, we're swamped here this morning."

"Making that call is your top priority," he said. "Everything else will have to wait. Don't ever forget again."

Despite my mistake, Colonel Bumgarner appeared to like me. He could see I ran a tight ship, and once I understood just how important customs and courtesies were to him, I followed every one to a T.

Like Colonel Bumgarner, Captain Drake's command also had some quirks. When the last of the California Guardsmen left at the end of our first week, Drake ordered that we not use the new towers inside Camp Delta. The new towers were enclosed metal-and-tinted-glass structures with air-conditioning and elevators to protect guards from the oppressive heat. The California Guard had been transitioning into the new towers when we arrived, but the captain wanted us in the old open-air wood towers because he couldn't see us behind the tinted windows of the new ones.

But the dumb stuff that our command rolled down on us were only minor irritations for me. Our guard duties consisted of doing the same things over and over again. I knew every day that we were going to wake up to a minimum twelve-hour shift repeating the same things we did the day before. We knew the day was going to be boring and that it would suck, but that was just part of the job. The real concern was the condition of the camps themselves. I couldn't understand why command didn't seem to notice.

One afternoon at the end of my first week on the job at Gitmo, I was sitting outside my barracks taking a break, when I saw General Hood approaching. As I jumped to my feet to salute, he said, "At ease, Sergeant. Mind if I sit?"

Before I knew it, the commander of the entire joint task force was sitting next to me talking about how he missed his family. "You know my biggest regret out here, Sergeant?" he asked. "That I've missed so many of my kids' soccer games. Be sure to stay in touch with your family while you're out here and take care of your men. Make sure they always get enough food, water, and sleep."

I'd never had a general talk to me like a regular Joe. He was leaving in a couple weeks, turning over his command to Admiral Harry Harris, and wanted to connect with the troops. However, as we talked, General Hood never said a word about the obvious disarray surrounding us. "Are the problems at Gitmo too big even for a general?" I wondered.

*   *   *

When I first began observing the detainees, I was mostly fascinated by how screwed up everything looked. I'd never seen such constant agitation in a detention facility. I didn't have strong feelings for or against the detainees as individuals. I was totally convinced that, as a group, all the detainees were absolutely guilty of being radicals who had attacked America or had been caught trying to. I believed they deserved to be there. But the conditions still seemed excessively punishing.

Aside from the specifics of the Geneva Conventions, our training had always specified that once we captured the enemy, we didn't abuse him. Any form of detention was unpleasant by its very nature, but the line between unpleasantness and abuse was not always clear—particularly at Gitmo.

The cells were small and primitive. Each six-by-eight-foot cage had a metal rack attached to the wall that served as a bed. Next to this stood a small toilet and sink. Each detainee was issued a sheet, a blanket, a washcloth, and two towels—all made of tear-resistant materials. They were permitted to have a single plastic water bottle, a small bar of soap, toothpaste, a small brush, and twenty-five sheets of toilet paper per day. Some compliant detainees had an extra blue blanket provided by the Red Cross.

They were not permitted to have any books or writing materials besides the Koran. Because the Koran was not allowed to touch the ground, someone had permitted each detainee to have a surgical mask that he tied to the mesh wall and used as a sling.

Camps 1 and 2/3 in Delta were considered maximum security, and Camp 4, with its communal meeting areas, was a notch lower. The detainees in Camp 4 were given tan clothing (as were some in Camp 1), and the most compliant detainees in Camp 4 could also wear *taqiyahs*, skullcaps worn during prayer. The rest wore orange and could not cover their heads.

The restrictions on space and belongings did not seem like unfair treatment to me, but some things did. One main difference between an American prison or jail and Camp Delta was the prohibition against exercise in the cells. Everything from push-ups to shadowboxing was prohibited. If detainees tried any form of exercise, navy guards would come to the door and shout at them to stop. The detainees almost always complied—at least in the short term—with the shouted commands, because the navy guards had four-man extreme reaction force (ERF) teams that could go in and restrain anyone disobeying the rules in flex cuffs. And if the ERF team couldn't handle it, they could call in our QRF.

Detainees were allowed only to lie on their cots or pace back and forth. Watching them was like looking at tigers in a zoo. When they prayed, washed, went to the bathroom, or masturbated, they did it all in front of us and the navy guards. There was no rest or privacy at night because lights inside the cell blocks blazed on.

The constant taunting between the navy guards and the detainees was also unusual. Insults and taunts are standard to any civilian jail I've worked in, but what made Gitmo different was the number of navy guards who would get into it with the detainees. They would scream insults right back.

In a professionally run detention facility, guards were not supposed to get into "your mama"–type insult matches with the prisoners. But in the cell blocks at Delta, it was always game on between the navy guards and detainees.

In part, I could understand the aggressiveness of the guards. The cell blocks had been designed so that the halls were even hotter than the cells. With no covered walkways, it was miserable. The navy guards were required to walk past every cell and visually check each detainee every five minutes. The guards were on camera, and their movements were carefully logged, so they were required to constantly walk in that heat.

Many of the navy guards were young: from eighteen to the mid-twenties. Most were trained as navy masters-at-arms—military police—but from talking to them at the chow hall, I learned that quite a few of them were just cooks or other sailors attached to the guard squadrons. This surprised me. Manning checkpoints and towers like we were doing was basic military work, but physically interacting with and controlling detainees was a specialized task. We had been told many times that all the detainees at Gitmo were not only dangerous but also individuals with high intelligence value. It made no sense to put them in the hands of twenty-year-old navy cooks.

Adding to the aggressiveness were the design and the rules of the detention facility. Detainees were not allowed to communicate with one another, but because the cell walls were open mesh, the detainees had a standing invitation to talk to their comrades in adjoining cells, which prompted the navy guards to threaten them. The same went for the rules barring them from running in place or doing push-ups in their cells.

It seemed to me that if one had intended to design a jail that would keep both inmates and guards in a state of constant agitation, those cell blocks in Gitmo could have served as the template. I couldn't fathom why this was allowed to happen.

Even if the navy guards weren't being taunted, they would find little ways to harass the detainees and rile them up. One day as a guard walked past an inmate's cell, I saw the guard lean in close, and the detainee—who'd been resting quietly on his bed—was suddenly on his feet screaming at the guard and practically frothing at the mouth. "What in the world?" I thought. When I finally got the right angle, I could see that the guard carried a Star of David. He would flash it as he walked past the cell blocks, and the detainees would just go nuts. I don't know if this guard was actually Jewish or if he just whipped out the Star of David to piss off the Muslims, but for a guard to taunt high-value detainees even once is roughly the same as a soldier accidentally firing his weapon. Flashing that Star of David at our Muslim charges was the equivalent of pulling the pin on a hand grenade just for kicks.

This type of behavior was petty and stupid, but it was only the tip of the iceberg. The California Guard warned us that we'd see a lot of late-night activity in the cells. The navy guards had developed a game they called the "Frequent Flier Program." At about midnight, guards would wake a detainee, flex-cuff him, and shackle his legs, and then run him from one cell block to the next. They'd put him in an empty cell, take off his cuffs, and then start the whole process over again. The guards would run the detainees in patterns, from cell block to cell block, until at the end, the hapless prisoner was returned to his original cell. It was a competition between the guards, and they timed themselves. They'd have different teams running different detainees, or they'd take turns with the same guy. Whichever guard, or team of guards, got the fastest time, would win free drinks at the Windjammer the following night.

I couldn't make sense of it at first. I was new and thought I was witnessing some kind of training drill. When I saw guards laughing and high-fiving each other at the end of the night, I realized it wasn't a drill. After I had seen a few late-night cell runs, I encountered one of the navy guards who'd been running one of the detainees. "That looked a little crazy last night," I said.

"Yeah," he said, a big, goofy grin plastered on his face. "We ran them hard but lost to the other guards by just a few seconds. Now we've got to buy their drinks. Those bastards have won the Frequent Flier Program three times now. Last night was the 'three-peat.' They're never going to shut up about it now."

I didn't see my first beating until my second week. I was in a tower by Camp 1. It was daytime, and I watched a navy guard bring a detainee from the recreation area into the cell block. This was routine when a detainee had been allowed exercise time. The guard had cuffed the detainee's hands behind his back and shackled his legs, as was the SOP. But for some reason, the guard started walking him fast, quicker than his leg irons would allow. The detainee kept tripping over himself, which angered the guard and caused him to push even harder. I was about sixty feet away in the tower and could see everything happen clearly as they entered the cell block. As soon as they reached the detainee's cell, the guard slammed the luckless inmate into the outer wall. An instant later, the guard punched him in the face. The detainee went down, and two other guards who were on duty in the cell block rushed in and started kicking him. After a good minute, there was blood all over the floor. The guards lifted the detainee, took off his leg shackles, and threw him onto his cot. All the detainees in the cell block started screaming. One detainee put his fingers through the mesh wall of his cell to shake it. A navy guard beat the detainee's fingers with his key ring so hard, a medic had to be brought in to treat him.

I guessed that when the navy guards reported on the incident, they'd spin it to say they were trying to put down detainees who were resisting or attempting to escape. This, I learned, was the unofficial SOP of the navy guards. They'd agitate the detainees, and when they resisted or lashed out, the guards would beat the snot out of them.

The detainees were hardly innocents in all of this. Just as we had been told they would back at Fort Lewis, some of them made a habit of tossing human waste at the navy guards. It was disgusting, but in corrections work, guards were supposed to take a higher road. Punching a cuffed detainee was a clear-cut case of excessive force, whether or not the guy had resisted an order.

That first beating I saw was tough for me to process mentally. When my shift ended, I told Staff Sergeant Hayes and Specialist Thompson what I'd seen. "Those navy guards beat the shit out of a guy today," I told Hayes.

"What do you mean, 'beat the shit out of a guy'?" he asked.

"I mean, they worked him over. Fucked him up."

"And your thoughts on this?" asked Hayes.

"Man, this is one fucked-up place," I said, and laughed.

I was flying blind, and still learning the ropes and culture of Gitmo. None of us was certain what we should report. Our command did not emphasize reporting abuse by guards. We had been given numerous lectures about the importance of operational secrecy, and we had been strictly warned about the protected status of the local iguanas, but there had been no specific instructions about what to do if we saw the abuse of a detainee. Colonel Bumgarner had never brought it up.

Our only guidance on the matter was informal: the casual attitude of the navy guards competing in the Frequent Flier Program and a popular T-shirt sold at the NEX printed with the words "What happens at Gitmo, stays at Gitmo."

So instead of reporting what I saw, I turned it into clumsy gallows humor and shared it only with Staff Sergeant Hayes and Thompson. I may have been new, but I was acutely aware that to report the incident would have aroused bad feelings among the navy guards and other soldiers. I'd have to be working with them for the rest of the year, and then, it seemed, it would be easier to just laugh it off. But it had already started to eat at me. For the first time in uniform, at the end of that day, I started to feel shame, both in myself and in my military.

CHAPTER 5

———◆———

Camp No

FOR a while, I attempted to lose myself in the day-to-day distractions of Gitmo. Before I was deployed, a lot of officers in my command told us that we would be living in the military equivalent of a tropical resort—and they did not lie about the beautiful beaches. The razor wire that coiled around nearly everything sort of ruined the illusion of paradise, though.

Outside of playing my guitar, which I was able to do only about once a month, it was my squad that sustained me. We had moved into better barracks after the California Guard left, and each of us got a four-man room with its own bathroom. Because of our long shifts, our sleep patterns were off, and despite the twelve- to fourteen-hour days, we continued to train. We ran a two-and-a-half-mile circuit from the barracks down to the beach and back every couple of days, and we lifted weights at the gym. I was feeling my age. I was twice as old as kids like Specialist Stewart, but because I wanted to show my leadership, I would run out front to set an example. After our workouts, I'd have to find an isolated spot where I could collapse like I had a sucking chest wound.

We were also constantly on the shooting range. There was one guy from another company who had memorized all the great speeches from the movie *Patton*, and between shots, you'd hear him in this ridiculous

36

George C. Scott voice imitating an insane general. It was little things like that—stuff that would be totally stupid in the civilian world—that, in the middle of the stress, the heat, and the isolation of a deployment, made military life fun and took my mind, however temporarily, off my problems and concerns.

During our downtime, while all of the younger guys in our company habitually played video games, my main interest was baseball—specifically the Baltimore Orioles. I bought a satellite radio, with a subscription service, so I could listen to the games. Camp America also had an outdoor theater near the barracks where they showed movies every night. *300* ran for more than a week, and our squad must have seen it four times. We would have gone every night if not for our schedule. I think every soldier in our company had the sex scene with Lena Headey etched in his brain by the time the movie's run ended.

Of course, one of the best ways to escape was in the simple pleasure of a decent meal. The military understood the importance of food. The main chow hall by Camp Buckley was a white, dome-shaped building that looked like a circus tent. It was festive inside, with big skylights, plants, and, best of all, air-conditioning that kept it near refrigerator temperature. There were TVs along the walls that were usually tuned to CNN or popular shows like *American Idol*, and the third-country nationals who manned the chow hall kept it stocked with unbelievable amounts and varieties of food.

But even with all that, sometimes I just wanted to get off base. One of my favorite things to do was to grab my squad and go to the Subway sandwich shop just outside Camp America. We didn't make it out there too often, but it was always the highlight of my week. Before we left the gates, we'd put on civilian clothes, and I felt like I was on vacation. The moment I shed my uniform, everything changed. Once I was in street clothes, I wasn't giving orders or taking them. The guys in the squad were just my friends. Subway was our low-budget Disneyland, the happiest place on earth. I know this sounds crazy to anyone who's actually been to a Subway, but in the military we were constantly getting told what to do, so the chance to walk up to a counter and take as much time as you want telling the employee on the other side how to make a sandwich made us feel like kings. All the guys in my squad would compete with each other to see who could come up with the weirdest sandwiches on earth. Meatballs and tuna salad on an Italian roll and garnished with bacon, avocado, and mayonnaise? That was bush-league stuff for us. Seriously, we lost our minds at Subway. It was the greatest place on Gitmo, and you could totally forget yourself while sitting at one of the Formica tables.

Near the Subway was the Windjammer bar. Occasionally US Navy ships with a high percentage of female sailors—sometimes as many as 30 percent—would put into port for three or four days, and the Windjammer would instantly become a happening spot. Still, I seldom went in. No matter what the male-to-female ratio was, the Windjammer was always packed with young guys, their testosterone raging, drinking as much as they could. Fights broke out constantly. When I was younger, it would have appealed to me, but I didn't drink at all at Gitmo, because I wanted—and needed—to stay sharp. I went only when the men from my squad wanted to blow off some steam. I'd accompany them to watch their backs.

The weirdest part of trying to have a social life at Gitmo was that, as a security precaution, all personnel were discouraged from sharing their names with members of other units. No one was supposed to discuss his duties, and maintaining anonymity outside our own unit was the operating rule. Consequently, even though most people lived two or four to a room, we never really got to know anyone. Camp America was like a fishbowl. We were seldom, if ever, alone. I saw the same faces every day, but nearly every one belonged to a stranger.

Living and working closely with all the men in my unit, I came to appreciate the small moments when I could be with a woman—even if I was just sharing a few words in the chow hall. While working the checkpoint at Camp Delta, I often noticed a navy medic passing through who worked at the clinic. Even in her fatigues, with her brown hair piled under her hat, she stood out. What caught my attention weren't her physical features but the sunny disposition she radiated even if she was just saying hello. Stuck in that grim place, with the sounds and smells and brutalities, she'd lift me out of the gloom for a moment simply by thanking me when I waved her through the gate. When I was younger, it was all about the hookup, but this woman was different. She had the power to change my whole day just by passing in front of me. The whole shift would go from sucking to tolerable if I saw her.

Once, when she arrived at the checkpoint, I said something trivial like, "You again," and she laughed. We started talking. Eventually she started calling me by my first name, and I used hers. Then I took the plunge. "Hey, would you like to get a meal the next time we're both off?" I asked.

"I'd love to," she answered. I was elated. I felt like a high school kid.

The best place to take a woman was, of course, the Subway. I told myself I wasn't taking Lisa on a date, but three weeks into my deployment, the prospect of spending an hour or two with a girl made me nervous with excitement. Despite the restrictions against sharing our last names, we got comfortable talking about our families back home and the things we liked to do in our nonmilitary lives. Lisa was in her twenties—many years younger than me—and had joined the navy to get experience and education money to become an RN when she got out. Life in Camp America and working at the clinic was a hardship for her, the same as my job was for me. But she had that optimism, because she was getting experience that would take her someplace better.

For me, guarding was just a tough, unpleasant, patriotic duty. It was also a pay cut from what I had earned in the civilian world before 9/11. Becoming friends with Lisa was a real bright spot in my time at Gitmo.

When we started having lunch together at the chow hall, I caught hell from the guys in my unit.

"Sergeant Hickman's a dirty old man!"

"Hickman, the army's got rules against stalking!"

"Hey, guys! Quit saying Joe's old enough to be her dad—he's old enough to be her grandfather!"

The jokes were funny enough, and the young guys like Stewart didn't quite get the concept of a purely platonic relationship. I'll admit that my attraction to Lisa created sexual tension, but it wasn't anything I chose to act upon. I had given up drinking at Gitmo to stay focused on my job. Likewise, having an affair in this place would have been crazy; a major distraction. From Lisa's perspective, I think she just liked having a guy she could relax around. In a way, I provided protection.

I understood this after we had one of our dates at the movie theater. She wanted to see *The Devil Wears Prada*. It was a chick flick and not something I'd normally watch, but for her sake I went. The Camp America movie theater was outdoors and consisted of rows of metal folding chairs in front of a screen. Being outside wasn't bad, but the theater—like the rest of the camp—was overrun with banana rats. They'd scurry under the seats, with their fat bellies and stubby legs, trying to grab whole popcorn bags and run away with them. They'd rub against your legs. Empty chairs would bang and rattle constantly from the scuttling rats. I never really noticed how bad it was until I sat next to Lisa watching *The Devil Wears Prada*. Seeing her horrified reactions made me more conscious of how lousy the rats were.

The rats weren't the only nastiness a woman had to endure at Gitmo. Within minutes of the movie starting, several navy guys behind us started to make insulting comments. I couldn't hear their exact words, but I caught the gist. Then one of them leaned between us and said to Lisa, "Why'd you go to the army for dick? You could've just stayed with us navy guys. We'd be happy to give you all the cock you want."

I jumped up and lunged toward the guy. Instead of fighting me, he fell over on his buddies. They were drunk. They probably wouldn't even remember their insults the next day. Lisa grabbed me. She was crying and insisted we leave.

We walked back to her barracks and sat outside on a picnic table. Because of her roommates, it was the only private place to talk. She said she was crying not because of what the guy had said, but because I'd almost gotten into a fight.

"Look," she explained, "I put up with that crap every day here. The sexual comments, the crude come-ons—it never ends."

"Why don't you just report it?" I asked.

"If you report it, you're labeled within your command as a male-hating bitch. You can't win by reporting it, so you just suck it up."

That was the first time I understood what it was like to be a woman in the military. I'd never been around women in uniform before, and I'd never realized how much it sucked to be female on a base with a bunch of guys. She was in the same situation as my black squad, trying to put up with the country boys who led the company. As if her job weren't hard enough, she had another layer of crap to deal with.

* * *

By my second month at Gitmo, I had something of an epiphany. I was on guard duty at the compliant camp, Camp 4, which was definitely the best camp to be on tower duty—and also the worst. It was the best because you didn't see abuse or the intense suffering brought on by isolation. But that was also what made it the worst camp to watch. Things were so relaxed at Camp 4, it was very easy to let down my guard, and that's the last thing I wanted to do while watching a bunch of suspected terrorists.

The soccer games that the detainees regularly competed in were the main distraction. Tower 5 was only about fifteen feet from where the prisoners played on a large exercise lot. Sometimes I'd become so engrossed in the games, I'd have to tell myself, "Stop. Look where you're supposed to look. Check to see if detainees on the sidelines are handing things off to one another, or getting too close to the fence or to the navy guards."

A big part of our job was to oversee the navy guards and make sure they weren't being attacked. As much as I'd come to dislike the people whom I'd seen abuse detainees, I took the job of protecting them very seriously.

During soccer games, I had a constant war going on in my head: do my job or enjoy a good game. I was in the middle of this conflict one day when a player's solid kick sent the ball arcing over the fence. It landed at the base of my tower.

I looked down and saw a detainee walk to the edge of the fence. The man had long, unkempt hair and a bushy, disheveled beard. He was covered in dirt and looked more like an animal than a man. "Holy fuck," I thought, suddenly nervous. "This guy looks dangerous." He looked up at me, smiled, and said—in perfect, British-accented English—"How's it goin' today, mate? Seems our bloody ball's gone over your fence. What do you say to a hand so we get it back on the pitch and finish our game?"

This was the first direct communication I'd ever had with a detainee.

I did a check from my perch to make sure all the guards were okay and that there were no disturbances. Everything was cool, and it was obvious that the errant ball wasn't some diversion tactic. I answered, "Sure. I'll get your ball for you."

I climbed down the tower, picked up the ball, and threw it over the fence. He smiled again and said, "Thanks, mate. Bloody decent of you. God bless!" He gave a little wave and trotted back to his game.

Before that day, all I'd ever heard from detainees was "Fuck you!" or some other tight-necked, spittle-flecked curses. It took me back a little bit. Obviously the guy was on his best behavior because he wanted his ball returned. I'm sure if the soccer player had been Osama bin Laden himself, he would have been just as polite. But I realized that up until that moment I had viewed the detainees as less than human.

With their long hair and wild beards, they'd looked dirty, disgusting, and mad. That little interaction changed my perception. I couldn't say I liked them. They were still the enemy. But I no longer saw detainees as subhuman. I saw them as bad people. It's not a huge difference, but it was definitely a change.

My experience with the soccer-playing detainee coincided with an unsettling discovery. By the end of April, Gitmo was really getting hot, regularly going over 100 degrees in the afternoons. On one of those scorching days, I was in charge of the Humvee mobile patrol. Private First Class Bradley, the fifty-one-year-old whose civilian job was working for the morgue, stood in our gun hatch and manned the .50 caliber machine gun, and Private First Class Vasquez sat up front beside me. Typically, in a military vehicle, the commander rides in the front passenger seat, but I liked to drive, so I was at the wheel.

When you're in a Humvee on a hot day, wearing your helmet with the chinstrap on as required, dressed in your ACUs, and also burdened with your load-bearing vest—a garment with loops and pockets for carrying up to twenty pounds of spare ammo magazines and other gear—you get a little toasty. Air that feels hot enough to pop corn billows out from the engine compartment and up your legs.

I hated Humvee patrols more than anything. There were only about two miles of paved road inside Camp America and a little less than that of dirt trails. Patrolling a few miles of road for six or twelve hours at a stretch could get tedious. It was also stressful with the constant worry that you might squish an iguana and derail your career.

The heat was so bad one particular day that we "patrolled" past the perimeter and went into the brush on the northeast side of Camp America to find a shady spot to rest. Our radio kept us in constant communication with our command post only a few minutes away. Allowing my men (and myself) a rest break was a complete violation of regulations, and a very serious one. But in my evaluation of the matter—self-serving as it was—I judged that the threat of an enemy attack from outside or an escape from within was low. If Al Qaeda decided to storm the base, we were just a radio call and minutes away to provide assistance with our rifles and Humvee machine gun. Besides, Captain Drake was still riding us hard, and my squad felt that it was being taken advantage of. I knew a little break in the shade would be good for morale.

I also knew the risk of getting caught was extremely low. The northeast perimeter of Camp America was so hilly and densely overgrown with brush that there wasn't even a fence. The narrow trail through the undergrowth was just wide enough for our Humvee to squeeze past.

To find a rest spot, I cut right—roughly north—into the brush and looked for a tree that would give us some shade. We went high up a steep angle, driving through scrub and chaparral, branches scraping the sides of the vehicle. I could see trees in the distance above us on the hill. But when we reached the tree-cloaked ridge, I decided to nose down the slope to see what was on the other side. As we busted through about another hundred yards of brush, it started to thin. I saw metal flashing in the distance—a row of buildings—and stopped the Humvee. We were now about 250 yards outside Camp America in a sloping depression about a mile and a half from the border with Cuba. Through the scrub growth ahead, I could make out what looked like concertina wire and possibly aluminum rooftops beyond. That was odd and unsettling.

There weren't supposed to be any buildings in that area. I knew because when we arrived at Gitmo, some of us were given a classified briefing about the location of every building on our side of the island. Our unit was tasked with defending the area and tracking down anyone who might be hiding. To that end, they briefed us on the locations and types of every structure in and around Camp America, all the way up to the guard towers at the border with Cuba.

The installation we saw was not on any map I had seen. It reminded me of the "pizza van"—another chink in our defensive procedures. I thought, "How are we supposed to guard the island or look for escapees if we don't even know where all the buildings are located?"

I stopped the Humvee about twenty yards from a chain-link fence topped with razor wire. "Bradley, stay with the vehicle and man the radio. Let us know if we get a call."

"Where are you going?" he asked.

"Just stay here. Vasquez, come with me."

We walked through the brush to the fence line. When we got up close, we saw that the facility was surrounded by two parallel fences, typical for detention installations, with brush growing between them. We walked around, looking for gaps in the brush, to see what was inside.

We could make out six trailer-type structures in two rows of three, with a larger building at the end, about the size of a double-wide trailer. The buildings were covered in aluminum cladding and resembled the newer structures that Halliburton had put inside Camp America. (Halliburton Company was the main contractor for most of the newer buildings in Camp America, including Camps 5 and 6, which were still under construction.) The buildings had small, shuttered windows. They appeared to be facilities for holding detainees, but there were no guard towers, and the small, dusty parking lot was empty. Private Vasquez and I crept along the fence, trying to figure out what this place could be. As we got a little closer to the eastern side, we could see an access trail that connected to the lane outside ACP Roosevelt. If we were at the checkpoint looking forward on Sherman Road, the lane that intersected it on the left would have led directly to this place.

I turned to Vasquez and said, "What the fuck do you think this is?"

"I think we just found our Auschwitz," he said.

Auschwitz? That was Private Vasquez being a smart aleck. But an apparent detention facility not on any official map—or ever referred to in secret briefings—made me wonder what my government was up to.

"Sergeant, this place is creeping me out," said Vasquez.

"Yeah. Me, too. Come on. Let's get back to the Humvee," I said.

Bradley, who was still on the .50 cal, waiting for us, asked, "What did you guys see?"

"Nothing much. Just some storage sheds," I said.

"Looks like they're going to build some new windmills," Vasquez added.

I'm not sure Bradley believed us. We were both drenched in sweat, sucking air from our climb back up through the brush, and I ordered us out of there.

"What about our rest break?" asked Bradley.

"Forget about it," I said.

He didn't ask any more questions.

One key to surviving military life, to making it as easy as possible, was to never ask questions or look where we shouldn't. People called it "staying in your lane." Neither Private Vasquez nor I was the type to fully adhere to that principle. We talked about our discovery in private a few more times after we got back. Later we would nickname the place Camp No—as in "No, it's not there" or "No, it does not exist." (In the fall of 2013, American news outlets revealed Camp No to be a secret CIA facility code-named "Penny Lane." Part of its purpose was to attempt to turn detainees into double agents.)

The place put the hook in me. After seeing Camp No for the first time, I took a deeper interest in the white "pizza van" used for transporting detainees. I even got the navy escorts who drove it to show me the metal lockbox in back used for holding detainees.

One day not long after discovering Camp No, I watched the pizza van as it left Camp America from ACP Roosevelt. I noticed for the first time that it made a left on the paved lane a hundred yards or so past Roosevelt. I could not follow the pizza van after it made that left, but I knew that Camp No was on the way.

It was possible that the pizza van had driven past the entrance to Camp No and proceeded to a T-intersection visible from OP Houston. At that intersection, one road looped back into Camp America, and another turned down to the beach by OP Houston. But when I was on post at Houston, I never saw the pizza van. To be fair, I was not on post all the time, so it's possible that the pizza van was simply picking up detainees, loading them into the metal box, and transporting them to the beach for a swim or a picnic. But, what seemed most likely, based on my observations, was that the pizza van was taking them to Camp No.

The only person I discussed this with was Private Vasquez. He, too, independently of me, had seen the pizza van turn left in the direction of Camp No after leaving Camp America via ACP Roosevelt. He also had never seen the pizza van driving to the T-intersection visible from OP Houston.

We both surmised that the van stopped before reaching the T-intersection and most likely went to Camp No.

We debated the nature of the facilities we'd seen. The six trailer-type buildings looked like detention facilities, in part because the windows were small and spaced far apart—as was typical of the detention buildings in Camp Iguana and Camps 5 and 6 (both under construction). Generally, in the civilian world, detention facilities had a similar design.

We wondered if the Camp No units could have been outlying administration buildings, but other such structures on the island weren't surrounded by fences and concertina wire. We speculated that the buildings were storage or secret technical facilities, but the doors on the buildings in Camp No were small. Buildings for storage or holding electronic gear usually had wide doors, and a greater number of them. We concluded that the most likely use for the buildings at Camp No was to hold detainees.

I returned to Camp No about a week after my first visit. I was leading a mobile patrol again, this time with a couple of other guys from my squad. I drove off into the brush where I'd gone before, stopped the Humvee far back from the fence, and told my guys to stay inside. I didn't want them to learn about the existence of a camp not marked on any of our maps. But I still had a burning curiosity about the site. I stepped out, lit a cigarette, and told them I just needed a break.

Had anyone questioned me for being there, I planned to say that I'd simply become lost while on a smoke break—something my guys could back me up on, since this is what they believed.

When I reached the fence surrounding Camp No, I walked east around it, all the way to the access road that led to the lane from ACP Roosevelt. I wanted a better look at it. The access road was unpaved and had a cable held in place by a lock, like you see at the entrance to a public park.

I saw a white van parked inside Camp No by the larger building. But it wasn't the pizza van. It was just a plain white van like you'd see military personnel driving outside Camp America.

The place was mostly silent. I could hear air conditioners humming, but not the sound of diesel generators. Diesel power generators, with their distinct growling, were a ubiquitous feature of military installations across the globe. But Gitmo had its windmills, and this place was close enough to the windmills that I guessed it was drawing power from them. Aside from the van and the air conditioners, I saw no other signs of life.

When I got back to my guys in the Humvee, I was drenched in sweat. One of the men, surprised by my appearance, asked sarcastically, "Did you have a nice smoke break, Sarge?"

To shut him up, I just said, "Yeah, it was fucking great."

Vasquez did not tell me at first, but he and Bradley had also returned to the secret facility. Private Bradley had become curious about what we'd seen that first day, so he pestered Vasquez until they both went back. On their visit, they'd seen a few cars in the lot, and two guys in black fatigues walking into one of the buildings.

Black fatigues were the unofficial uniform of CIA officers, as well as some private contractors who worked with the Central Intelligence Agency. I knew this because when we checked peoples' badges at the gates and checkpoints, their badges identified whichever entity they worked for. If they were CIA, the badges said so. It was the same if they worked for the FBI, or even if they were a food service company. We had all noticed that large numbers of the CIA guys wore black fatigues or sometimes arrived in vehicles with people—also in black fatigues—from other entities, such as CACI International, a private contracting firm headquartered in Arlington Virginia.

We dealt with the CIA guys and their affiliated buddies in black all the time because there was an interrogation building inside Camp Delta. As far as we had been briefed—as the world had been told—this was the only interrogation facility on Gitmo. It was there that we assumed the men in black congregated.

The fact that Privates Vasquez and Bradley saw the two black-clad men strongly suggested Camp No was used for interrogations. I worried that those two might try to return again and risk getting our squad in trouble, but both assured me that they would not.

I violated my command's orders, as well as those I gave my guys, by going back a third and fourth time. I was able to go alone because I went when I was serving as SOG. When I was on duty as Sergeant of the Guard, I got my own Humvee for roving around to all the positions. I used this opportunity to duck out, drive down the trail, and observe Camp No on foot. On my third visit, I saw nothing.

On my fourth, about five o'clock in the afternoon in late April, I saw several vehicles in the lot. I did not see any black-clad Americans or the pizza van. But as I hung out by the outer fence, I heard a voice.

It sounded like one man was screaming inside a trailer. He would hold it long, as if letting all his breath out, pause for a moment, and then start again. I couldn't say it sounded any different from the screaming I'd heard from detainees in Camp Delta who were having nightmares or mental breakdowns. But coming from this remote, secret facility, it felt surreal. The sound of a human screaming in a place that was not supposed to exist was chilling, especially because I couldn't say anything about it to my commanders.

What I saw at Camp No appeared to fly against all the US military history in which I had been steeped. There were no accounts I had ever heard of in which command set up secret detention and interrogation facilities. As much as I hated the enemy—the guys we held inside Camp Delta—I didn't see why they should be treated worse than the German or Japanese prisoners held under our charge during World War II. The detainees were no less human than any other enemy America had ever faced. They were still people. I was so disturbed by the screaming inside Camp No that I actually ran back to my Humvee.

To be clear, I did not see a detainee inside Camp No, and I did not see what was causing the person to scream.

After I told Private Vasquez what I'd heard, he tried to rationalize Camp No. He said, "Look, Sarge, for all we know, it could have been a guy working construction inside a trailer who hit his hand with a hammer." That was true—if the worker hit his hand repeatedly over the space of the three to five minutes that I stood by the fence.

My intent after that last visit to Camp No was to shut away the memory and not think about it again. There was too much pressure to do my job and take care of my guys without taking on outside problems. I needed to stay in my lane. The better I did my job, the fewer distractions I had, the smoother that deployment would go, and the faster I would get home. That's what I prioritized.

CHAPTER 6

By the Dawn's Early Light

GENERAL HOOD, the leader whom I'd so respected after we chatted one-on-one, was vilified throughout the world after he left Gitmo. We mostly got our news through CNN on the TVs inside Camp America, and we heard that after he left Cuba, the Department of Defense had posted him to Pakistan to serve as an American military representative. The action sparked global protest among human rights groups, both in the Western world and the Muslim one. People fixated on two accusations against the general: that he had ordered the forced feeding of hunger-striking detainees in 2005, and that under his command a female interrogator had put a Koran in a toilet to coerce a detainee into cooperating.

A hunger strike was defined in the SOPs at Gitmo as any detainee skipping nine consecutive meals, or three days, and such an action had two direct impacts on the camp. First, if a hunger-striking detainee had died, he would have been viewed as a martyr. Second, as soon as a detainee declined nine meals, he could no longer be interrogated, according to the medical SOPs at Gitmo.

The *New York Times* first reported on hunger strikes at Gitmo on February 9, 2006, about a month before my unit arrived. The story stated that the protest that began in the summer of 2005 peaked in

September, with 131 detainees denying food. The *Times* described how, under General Hood's orders, the strikers were strapped to chairs and had tubes inserted through their mouths or noses to force liquid nutrients into their stomachs to keep them alive.

Some humanitarians argued that force feeding was inhumane and violated a detainee's right to protest. The guys in my squad didn't spend much time following the news or debating politics and human rights issues. But when the issue came up, my personal opinion was that, by itself, forced feeding wasn't necessarily a bad thing. If a hunger strike was a form of attempted suicide, a guard's duty was to prevent it. In just about any prison in the world, guards took steps to minimize an inmate's ability to kill himself by taking away his belt and shoelaces.

Force-feeding reluctant strikers may have looked awful, but it kept them alive. People who said putting a tube down a person's throat was a severe human rights violation had obviously never been to a hospital. I didn't believe that General Hood gave the order to force-feed detainees because he sought to treat them inhumanely. I believe he simply didn't want detainees dying on his watch.

I also believed, based on the conditions I saw at Gitmo—the open cells, the oven-like temperatures, the rules against any exercise in the cells, the isolation, and the abuse by navy guards—that the detainees were making a basic and desperate protest against the appalling conditions in which they lived.

I continued to respect General Hood after he left, despite what we heard on the news. He had genuine concern for average soldiers like me. A commander like him created an environment where men and women were more likely to work hard, follow procedures, and take action when they saw wrongdoing. I believed that, had General Hood remained in command during my deployment at Gitmo, I would have spoken directly to him about my concerns over the treatment of detainees.

Whatever General Hood's flaws were in the eyes of the press and protesters, the man who succeeded his command, Rear Admiral Harry Harris, was worse. Ironically, Admiral Harris went on to become something of a hero during the Obama presidency after he commanded the

US Navy's Sixth Fleet during Operation Odyssey Dawn: the navy-led effort to back the Libyan rebels who overthrew Mu'ammar Qaddafi's regime in the spring and summer of 2011. In October 2011 President Obama approved Admiral Harris's nomination as assistant to the chairman of the Joint Chiefs of Staff.

My squad's first interaction with the admiral took place about a week after he officially took command in March 2006. Admiral Harris introduced himself to the troops by going around to the different posts. I was on checkpoint duty at Camp Delta when he walked up and called us to attention.

Admiral Harris was forty-seven years old at the time, with a trim build and dark hair. An unimposing man, he reminded me of an assistant baseball coach I'd had in eighth grade. Harris had started out in the military as a navy flyer assigned to P-3 Orion spy planes, and he had a snap to his step that made him seem confident. He praised the work we'd done but sounded like an officer just saying the right words.

He said that he expected us to perform our duties to the utmost and according to the regulations. Unlike General Hood, or even Colonel Bumgarner, he would seldom venture near our barracks. Whereas General Hood walked through Camp America in his last days shaking every man's and woman's hand, wishing each of us good luck, I never once had a personal interaction with Admiral Harris that was outside the bounds of business.

There was nothing wrong with that command style. We were glad to have any commander who ran a tight ship. Strict adherence to clearly defined regulations—which is what the admiral indicated he expected from us—could make a soldier's life easier. Unfortunately, our squad's first test at following the regulations brought us head-to-head with Admiral Harris.

We were working early one morning at ACP Roosevelt. I had my head under the hood of a car when, out of the corner of my eye, I saw a guy with skinny legs run past the control point in physical training shorts. For some reason, the running man reminded me of actor Don Knotts from *The Andy Griffith Show*. I heard Specialist Thompson shout, "Sir! You can't run!"

When the man turned, I realized he was Admiral Harris. Thompson stopped him on his morning jog because the admiral was not wearing his reflective belt—like the ones worn by school crossing guards. At every military base in the world I'd ever been to, joggers were required to wear reflective gear as a safety precaution. Somehow, Admiral Harris had never received that memo—or he had simply forgotten.

I turned my vehicle inspection over to another guy and walked over to Thompson and the admiral.

Specialist Thompson, who probably had at least eighty pounds on Harris, stood a few feet from him, saying, "Sir, you can't run through here because you don't have your reflective belt on."

Admiral Harris looked at him like he couldn't believe what he was hearing. He said, "Son, I'm the admiral of JTF-GTMO."

Specialist Thompson was not easily intimidated. "I'm aware that you are the admiral, sir, but you don't have your belt on, and that's the rule. You can't run through here without a belt."

I was sweating bullets as I walked up beside Thompson. Harris betrayed no anger, but he kept pushing Specialist Thompson verbally. "Are you giving me an order?" the admiral asked.

Specialist Thompson was too smart to fall into the trap. He simply repeated that he was obligated to enforce the rules. Before the admiral could badger him anymore with his rank, Thompson said, "Sir, I will get you a reflective belt, so you can continue your run."

Specialist Thompson turned his back on the admiral and stepped into the guard shack at ACP, where we kept extra reflective belts for just this type of problem. Thompson returned, handed the admiral a belt, and said, "Enjoy your run, sir."

As soon as the admiral was out of earshot, I turned to Thompson and said laughing, "What the fuck were you doing?"

Specialist Thompson said simply, "He told us to play by the rules. We're seeing who he really is now."

The next day, the admiral showed us. We were talking at our posts when Captain Drake walked up, smiling. Admiral Harris sent him an email informing him that our squad had done an excellent job while manning ACP Roosevelt the day before.

Of course, Drake informed us of the email, beaming as if he had been standing beside Specialist Thompson himself when he had enforced the rules, but we were gratified. The admiral wasn't a warm, back-slapping guy, but he had followed up an awkward incident with a generous email that reflected well on all of us. It was a touch we appreciated.

Unfortunately, Harris was not so deft in his handling of the detainees. Early on in his tenure, he made a seemingly trivial command decision that overturned the shaky balance between guards and detainees in the camps.

It all centered on the national anthem. Since I'd arrived, every morning at eight, "The Star-Spangled Banner" was played on the public address system throughout Camp America. When the first bars were heard, every soldier, on duty or off, would come to attention and salute the flag.

I loved the national anthem. When I heard it, I often got a lump in my throat. Since I was a young man in the Marine Corps, the anthem filled me with pride in my country and humility at serving it in uniform.

I never expected the detainees to feel the same way about our anthem and flag. To me, the beauty of America was that most of us came to her shores by choice, and those who didn't—like the ancestors of guys like Private Stewart and Specialist Thompson—grew to make it their own country, often by fighting for justice, with their own blood, sweat, and tears. I was sure that all of us in uniform saluting that flag felt a variety of emotions—all of them positive—as we listened to the national anthem every morning.

General Hood had wisely understood that the detainees probably did not have the same positive associations with our anthem and flag, and that blasting it from loudspeakers inside Camp Delta would likely rile them up. During his tenure, "The Star-Spangled Banner" did not play on the speakers inside Camp Delta. Detainees could still hear it from speakers outside the camp—just like we could hear the calls to prayer—but we weren't ramming it down their throats.

Admiral Harris changed that. Soon after taking over, he instituted the policy of playing the anthem loudly from the speakers inside Camp Delta. The first few days, this was especially chaotic because it cut into the broadcast of their call to prayer by about three minutes. Even after that conflict was straightened out, the anthem still agitated the cell blocks.

I was watching the compliant camp, Camp 4, when "The Star-Spangled Banner" started to play. Some of the young navy guards began to scream at the detainees, "Get up, haji!" "Show some respect!" When the detainees didn't comply and responded with their own insults, the guards shouted at them even more. The screaming escalated until all that could be heard was a cacophonous din.

Before the arrival of Admiral Harris, the camps had been relatively quiet in the mornings—in large part because of the prayers—but now the eruptions and anger started precisely at eight with the playing of the anthem. Had I ever been captured by the Russians and held as a POW, I wouldn't have wanted to stand and show my respect to their flag when they played their national anthem. I could understand why the detainees wouldn't want to do the same with ours.

Admiral Harris's order also marked the start of a behavioral slide among the detainees.

The first indicator that the prisoners were growing more restless— aside from the heightened noise of the cell blocks—was the increase in "snowballs" thrown at the navy guards.

"Snowball" was the term used by navy guards for a projectile made of feces or urine. The detainees would sometimes defecate in their hands and throw it at the navy guards, or they would urinate in their water bottles and spray this out through the mesh walls when the guards passed.

The incidents of harassment escalated on both sides with Admiral Harris's tenure. A few of us debated whether we should report the navy guards, but as Staff Sergeant Hayes and others pointed out, policing the guards wasn't part of our duty. We were there to support them, not to report them.

We also thought that reporting on the guards would be a waste of time. The cell blocks had cameras mounted throughout the corridors.

These cameras, we were told, captured everything the guards did and were monitored by their superiors. It was up to them to discipline the guards for things like flashing Jewish stars at the detainees or shouting at them to stand during the national anthem. As for the Frequent Flier game, there was no way their commanders didn't know. If the navy guards' own command structure wasn't disciplining them, we doubted reports we made would have much impact.

In March and April 2006, we started to see more signs of trouble. One day while the national anthem played, a detainee snapped and started beating his head against the wall. Even though it was made of only mesh and Plexiglas, his injuries grew so threatening that the navy guards had to extract him, flex-cuff him onto the back of a Gator ATV, and escort him to the medical clinic.

I had dinner with Lisa that night. "Have you noticed any change in the prisoners?" she asked.

"Things seem a lot more tense," I replied. "Why do you ask?"

"We're getting a lot more detainees brought into the clinic with injuries from being ERF-ed." That was Gitmo jargon referring to a detainee who had been subdued or extracted by a four-man navy emergency reaction force. She added, "The ERF teams are working a lot at night. That's when we're getting all these injured detainees."

Lisa didn't share any more details with me.

For the most part, the rising chaos inside the cell blocks had no effect on our work in the towers and checkpoints. The same was not true for our duty on the National Guard's QRF—quick-reaction force.

CHAPTER 7

"Disturbance in Camp 4!"

T HE QRF had been a big part of our training at Fort Lewis, where we practiced cell extractions of noncompliant detainees and dealing with other potential disturbances. The California Guardsmen we replaced had told us that during their year of deployment they had done only one cell extraction, and a very simple one at that. One detainee had refused to leave his cell. As soon as they rushed his cage, he gave up, and they pulled him out.

They described the QRF duty as "pretty mellow."

In our first weeks, we enjoyed QRF duty. Our squad was assigned to it about once every six days, and it was a nice break from the twelve-hour-day guard duties.

Behind Camp 4 stood the behavioral health building: the clinic where detainees were taken when they had mental breakdowns. Next to this was another medical building, where, during the big hunger strike of 2005, they would bring detainees to force-feed them. Since there was no hunger strike going on when we arrived in March 2006, this served as the QRF staging area.

The room was creepy. It was still filled with cases of Ensure, the protein drink given to detainees during forced feedings, and against one wall were piles of medical equipment, tubing, and straps used to

immobilize the hunger strikers. The place reminded me of Franken-
stein's lab from the old movies.

We kept our shields and batons along another wall and the other
tools of our trade—the pepper spray canisters, shotguns, M203 grenade launchers, and nonlethal munitions—in locked boxes.

On the days when we were assigned to the QRF, we'd inventory the
weapons to make sure that the previous squad had left them in good
order, and we would spend a couple hours outside practicing cell extractions and fighting techniques with batons and shields.

Most of our time, though, was spent inside the hut. It was air-
conditioned and had a TV and a DVD player. QRF duty was almost
like having a day off. We'd watch movies and help ourselves to the Ensure. We sat around like Maytag repairmen. But once the cell blocks
heated up with the introduction of the national anthem, I got the feeling our days of ease on QRF duty were numbered.

In late April we started training harder for cell extractions, and for a
new command structure within our squad's QRF. Normally, Staff Sergeant Hayes would command our QRF, but we found out that in mid-
May he was slated to leave Gitmo for about two weeks. Each of us was
allotted a two-week vacation during our deployment, but these were
staggered across the units. In his absence, the other team leader in our
squad, Sergeant Earl Pitman, would run the QRF. To augment our ten-
man squad—down to nine men in Staff Sergeant Hayes's absence—we
would borrow a guy from another squad.

My duty on the QRF did not change all that much. I was still in
charge of my five-man team. Because we had Specialist Thompson,
the biggest man in our squad and the designated doorman, our team
trained to go in right behind him. This never changed.

The day before Hayes was slated to leave Gitmo on May 18, Sergeant Pitman was injured. His loss meant that I would be the senior
NCO in charge of our squad, but we'd be down two men. It also happened to be our squad's day for QRF duty.

The morning of May 18, we showed up at six o'clock to begin our
duty on QRF. We had two guys from the platoon augmenting our
squad and spent about an hour going through drills outside our stag-

ing area. Whoever had been on QRF before us had misplaced a baton. Since Private José Vasquez had proven himself such a good fighter the day before on the basketball court, he was designated to go without a baton should we be called.

At about eleven, we were resting inside the staging area when the phone rang. I picked up and identified myself. Colonel Bumgarner was on the line. He said, "Hickman, get your men to Camp 1. There's a disturbance."

Everybody grabbed his shield and designated weapons and climbed into the Humvee truck assigned to the QRF. In the two or three minutes it took us to reach the entrance to Camp 1, a number of concerns played through my mind.

If detainees were injured or killed in a confrontation with my QRF, it would be a major international incident. That was the paradox of Gitmo. In some ways, it was a rear-echelon, backwater deployment, but it was the flashpoint for America's policies in the global war on terror. Even though we didn't follow politics much in my unit, we understood just how seriously the military wanted to avoid problems. Any interaction with a noncompliant prisoner offered the potential for some sort of problem, which I would be responsible for as senior NCO in charge of the QRF.

My biggest concern was the safety of the guys I was leading. They had all seen detainees go crazy, chucking snowballs at navy guards. Most of my guys were from tough neighborhoods in Baltimore, but I didn't know how they would react in an outright confrontation against a detainee with nothing to lose. In my corrections work, I'd seen how quickly caged men could flip in a confrontation and fight like animals. PFC Stewart, for all his mouth, was just a baby at eighteen years old. I didn't want any of my guys injured.

When we drove into Camp 1, we dismounted from the truck and lined up on the walkway leading to the cell block entrance. Even on a good day, the place sounded like bedlam, but the noise emanating from the cell block was much louder than usual. Also, more navy guards than usual were stationed outside—perhaps two dozen of them.

Colonel Bumgarner walked over to me and filled me in. "Two detainees tried to commit suicide by overdosing on drugs they'd hidden in their Korans," he said.

He didn't elaborate about what kind of drugs they'd taken. Detainees were sometimes given different pills in the medical clinic or in the behavioral health clinic that could be toxic if saved up to be taken in large doses. The two detainees who'd overdosed were in the health clinic and in no danger of dying, but Colonel Bumgarner feared that other detainees in Camp 1 might also be hoarding pills.

The navy guards had started to search their cells for hidden pills, but the detainees wouldn't allow the infidels to touch their Korans. One detainee had violently resisted, and those in the other cells went crazy, so they'd called us.

"I want your squad to go through the cell block, extract each detainee and restrain him, so the guards can search their cells," Colonel Bumgarner told me.

There were twenty-seven detainees in twenty-seven cells inside the cell block. I didn't like those odds. Even if each extraction went relatively smoothly, doing twenty-seven in a row almost guaranteed that someone was going to be injured. There had to be a safer way.

As the colonel and I were talking about his plan to extract the entire cell block, I had an idea. The military contracted out to a company called Titan Corporation, which provided civilian interpreters to help deal with detainees. Because 99 percent of US military contact with detainees involved basics such as sliding food into their cells and marching them to exercise areas, we seldom saw interpreters doing much. They were on hand mostly to help at the clinics when detainees showed up.

I seldom if ever spoke to the interpreters. I'd see them in the chow halls, and while I was pretty certain that most were Americans, I also believed they were Muslim. Standing there talking to Colonel Bumgarner, I said, "Sir, would the detainees calm down if we used a Muslim interpreter to inspect their Korans?"

"That's a really good idea," he said.

He walked over to the senior NCO of the navy guards and suggested using a Muslim interpreter. This guy thought it was a good idea, too.

I was surprised no one had thought of this yet, but the navy guards tended to be bullheaded in their approach to the detainees. Colonel Bumgarner had been called after the tensions had escalated and had probably been in reaction mode. Seeing the possibility of an uprising in the cell blocks, he'd jumped at the idea of using our QRF.

We stayed on hand as they brought in an interpreter. When the interpreter explained that he, a fellow Muslim, would inspect their Korans, the detainees calmed down. I felt it was the most successful resolution to a QRF mission there could be. We returned to our staging area without having to overpower a single detainee.

We would not be so lucky during our next call.

We barely had time to clean up and stow our gear when the phone rang again at the QRF staging area. It was about five thirty that same day. The caller, whose voice I didn't recognize, shouted, "Disturbance in Camp 4! Disturbance in Camp 4!" He sounded panicky.

For all my criticisms of Captain Drake, I will say that back at Fort Lewis, he was the only one smart enough to identify Camp 4 as the most dangerous place to put down a riot. We had been studying a chart showing the layout of Camp Delta, and some other officer had skipped over Camp 4, saying it was the compliant camp and therefore the safest, when Captain Drake interjected, "Camp 4 is the worst place because it has ten-man communal cells. It's the only place detainees can mass against us."

Once we arrived at Gitmo, we saw it was even worse. The communal rooms were each about the size of a two-car garage. The cell doors opened to the outside and had solid walls. Guards couldn't just walk around like they could in the open cell blocks in the rest of the camp to see what was going on. Even worse, when you opened the doors, the communal cells had rows of built-in cots that the prisoners could hide behind like bunkers.

Camp 4 was the last place I wanted to confront detainees. When we drove up, the scene that greeted us was unlike anything I'd witnessed before at Gitmo. There were nearly two hundred navy guards lined up in formation in the exercise yard. Their show of force was pitted against a wall of sound that rose from the inmates, who were pounding the walls and screaming from inside the cell blocks. When we stepped off the truck, it felt like the ground was vibrating.

As we walked forward with our riot gear, I saw Colonel Bumgarner standing with a navy chaplain. When I approached him, he shouted, "They're acting up in Whiskey block"—cell block W—"They won't come out."

I marched my guys in formation toward Whiskey block, a ten-man communal cell near the end of one building. There were about thirty navy guards standing outside the cell block—a solid-walled building with a single door. We'd drilled for months for this procedure. I would lead the squad to the door. They would line up, with Thompson in front, and me—or whoever was senior NCO—directly behind Thompson. Once in position, I was supposed to open the door just enough to assess the situation, to either enter in force, take a pause to negotiate, or pursue another tactic, such as throwing in a concussion grenade before entering.

But before my men got within reach of the door, a navy guard shouted, "There's a detainee in there hanging himself!"

The guard opened the door and jumped back. We had no chance to assess the situation. We were still a good ten to fifteen feet from the door, which was now wide open. Suddenly we were faced with the prospect of detainees rushing out the door. To prevent this from happening, I shouted at my men, "We're going in!"

I ran, with Specialist Thompson in front of me, to the door. As the senior NCO, I had no shield or baton, just my riot helmet with a Plexiglas visor, two cans of pepper spray secured to my vest, and a couple of flash-bang grenades that would be useless, or dangerous, to set off once we entered the cell. Thompson was my shield. I held his shoulder with one hand as we went through the door. The other eight guys from the squad followed and formed a line on either side of us.

The basic tactic was to move forward in a line, pressing the detainees with our shields. The more we squeezed them, the harder it would be for them to fight. Those who resisted would be beaten with batons. Those who ceased fighting would be pulled down our line to be flex-cuffed, one at a time, and then thrown out the door.

We had two guys with shotguns and a third guy with the M203, but because the room had a depth of only twenty feet, we weren't supposed to use them. At such close quarters, these so-called nonlethal rubber and plastic projectiles could inflict fatal injuries.

Like me, the guys with guns did not have shields. They were supposed to stay in the back and help flex-cuff detainees who surrendered—or, in the event of a lethal attack on one of my guys, use their weapons. This meant that only six of the ten guys would be in front with shields.

Each of the eight guys from my squad had trained so often that we knew the drill by heart. The guys who augmented our squad—one of whom carried the M203, and the other a baton and shield—had no problem keeping up as we entered.

But the moment Specialist Thompson and I set foot in the room, our situational awareness was severely diminished by a volley of piss, feces, and metal objects. The detainees had smashed apart a security camera in the room, the light fixtures, a fan, and an air conditioner and were using the shattered pieces as projectiles. There was no sign of a hanging or an attempted suicide. This was an ambush.

The detainees had prepared a small cache of feces and cups of urine to throw at us, and they'd covered the first five feet or so of the floor with soap. As we tried to form or line up, we skidded around like Keystone Kops, clutching at one another to keep from falling over.

Because Specialist Thompson was the biggest, he set the pace for our advance. We'd moved only about five or six feet forward when Thompson stopped. I shouted, "Keep going!"

I heard Thompson shouting over and over, "Motherfucker!"

I finally saw that one of the detainees was armed with a metal pole taken from a fan. It was maybe six feet long, and he'd targeted Specialist Thompson with it. He was just pounding and thrusting at his shield, trying to strike Specialist Thompson on his helmet or drive it into his face. But Thompson was able to duck the blows. He stood his ground but was unable to advance.

On our outlying flank, one of my men struggled with two detainees who attempted to take his baton. Both of them were pulling on the weapon, and now a second guy from my squad had joined in the melee to prevent the detainees from grabbing it.

Meanwhile, another two detainees were trying to rush past them to grab at our shotgun.

The detainees had either planned this or instinctually understood elemental tactics. They'd used their heaviest weapon—the pole—to stop our biggest guy, Specialist Thompson, and they'd probed our flanks for weakness and were now trying to push through the breach.

When we entered the fight, it was a shock. Being better armed and equipped was almost a disadvantage in the kind of close-quarters fight in which we had found ourselves. The shields made it tough to maneuver and, psychologically, created an instinct to hide. In the Marine Corps, they sometimes called this tendency "cocooning." When someone had a good fighting position or a secure-feeling vehicle, there was a natural instinct to cling to it for safety when attacked. We were cocooning behind the security of our shields.

The detainees seized the initiative. They were crazy from being caged up for all those years. They weren't intimidated by our shields or the handful of baton blows a couple of my guys landed. They didn't seem bothered by pain or worried about the guys in back carrying guns. Most of them were shouting in English, "Come on, motherfuckers! I'm going to kill you!" The navy guards had evidently taught them well.

My guys weren't angry enough. They were making polite shots toward the detainees' arms and torsos. We were starting to lose the fight.

My biggest fear was that the two detainees rushing our flank might grab a shotgun or the M203. I ran toward them. I grabbed the detainee closest to the shotgun by his shirt. As he turned, I got my right arm on him and pulled him into me. At the same time, I threw an overhand left and hit him right in the face. It was a very good connection. I threw him back, and he fell over, bleeding.

I threw several punches at another detainee who was grabbing for my guy's baton. I didn't connect with his face as well as with the first detainee's, but I landed two or three blows, forcing him to back away.

A third detainee tried bulling through our line and tackling me, but I came up with an elbow punch, starting my swing low from my stomach. I was able to put a lot of hip into it, and when I connected with his forehead, I busted his skin open. When you break skin, it makes a loud snapping sound. Suddenly there was a lot of blood mixed in with the rest of the filth on the floor.

I shouted, "OC!"—an abbreviation for pepper spray's active ingredient, oleoresin capsicum—at my men and fired a blast at one of the detainees closest to me. He went down. Then I tried squirting the guy with the pole, who was still beating on Specialist Thompson's shield. I used the entire can and never got him.

Before I could start on another can, four of the detainees raised their hands and came forward. Two of them were guys I'd beaten in the face. They were bleeding profusely, their long beards wet and red. The other two were coughing and wheezing from the pepper spray. It had panicked them. One was vomiting.

My guys were so disciplined that when these wretched detainees approached, nobody struck or kicked them. Privates Stewart and Vasquez made a space and grabbed each combatant one at a time. They handed them to me, and I turned them around and flex-cuffed them before I pushed them out the door.

From my jail transport experience, I could flex-cuff a person in about five seconds. We cleared out the four guys who didn't want to fight anymore in less than a minute. As I pushed the last one out the door, he looked at me and said in perfect English, "You fight like the devil."

Unfortunately, so did his friends. I had hoped the first four surrenders were the start of a trend. But as we pushed the last surrender out, the hail of hard objects increased. The remaining detainees had taken positions behind the built-in beds and were using them as cover as they aimed for head shots with hunks of metal. That son of a bitch with the pole was crouching low and still whacking Specialist Thompson.

Two of the detainees leapt up and rammed themselves into my guys' shields, trying to knock them over. This was their most ferocious assault yet. Anytime that we pepper-sprayed a roomful of people, those who didn't give in to hysteria from the shock of it tended to come back with great anger. On these types, using pepper spray was like kicking a hornet's nest.

From the corner of my eye, I saw Private Stewart's shield rising into the air, as if in slow motion. I thought, "What the fuck is he doing? Throwing his shield away?"

Stewart brought the shield over his head, exposing his body from the chest down. A detainee rushed him. As the detainee got close to tackle him, the private brought down the hard bottom edge of the shield, slamming the detainee on the head. It was like hitting him with a shovel. When the detainee tried to throw his arms around the bottom of Stewart's shield, the private brought it up again and slammed the guy once more. Defeated, the detainee crawled away. One of his buddies attempted to take his place, so Stewart raised his shield and clocked him. It was not any tactic we'd been trained in, but PFC Stewart was going nuts with it. I almost started laughing at the sight of this tall, skinny kid from Baltimore going crazy with his shield.

Stewart inspired all my other guys. Everybody started fighting like an animal. Private Vasquez was using his shield like a ram to try to knock over guys. Stewart's warrior spirit, as well as the pepper spray—which was burning us now as badly as it was burning the detainees—had riled up everybody. But these die-hard detainees didn't cave. My guys were now beating the snot out of them, but they kept coming back for more. Worse, we still had that one detainee with the pole hitting Specialist Thompson and anyone else who tried to maneuver toward him.

Two badly beaten detainees managed to knock down one of my guys. They piled on him to grab his shield and rip at his face and body with their hands. This had turned into a savage dogfight. One of the detainees was trying to bite my guy's arm and hand. As we were rushing to defend him, I saw a detainee crawl over the bunks holding a shank: a shard of metal about ten inches long made from a light fixture. The detainee was getting in position to stab whomever he could reach first.

Once I saw that blade, I made the decision to end the fight. If they didn't stab one of us, my men were reaching a point where we might beat one of the detainees to death. These prisoners would not surrender.

I grabbed the guard with the shotgun and pointed at the detainee with the shank. I shouted, "Fire!"

He hesitated. Shooting at such close range went against our training. I shouted, "Shoot him to death if you have to! Fire that fucking shotgun now!"

The gunner complied. The impact of the rubber buckshot lifted the detainee and threw him back five feet. The man was bleeding from the chest, but he was still holding the shank.

"Hit every one of them!" I shouted to both of my guys with shotguns. I wanted this fight over immediately. They let off four more rounds, making a total of five shotgun discharges. Every detainee but one was down, all of them howling in pain. Several were moaning, "Allah Akbar!" Some of their holy pleas were mixed in with navy cuss words, so it came out, "Allah Akbar! Motherfucker! Asshole! Allah Akbar!"

A couple of these detainees, curled up in fetal positions and rolling in pain, were still threatening, "I'm going to beat your ass!"

The fight appeared to be over, until the guy with the pole rose up and tried whacking us again. The detainee was like the Energizer Bunny of Islamic jail fighters.

I'd had it with him. I shouted to the man with the M203, "The guy with the pole! Hit him. Fire!" The M203 sounded almost like a cork popping from a champagne bottle when it was fired. The 40 millimeter "Evil Sponge Bob" round hit him in the chest from less than ten feet away. The shot lifted him two feet off the ground and carried him back six.

After we demonstrated what Evil Sponge Bob could do, even the detainee still clutching the shank let go of it. We heard it fall to the ground with a *clink*. Instead of taunting us, they started crying, "Help me! Please!"

The fight had gone out of them. We flex-cuffed the bleeding detainees one at a time. Some of the blood came from blows to the head delivered by my guys. Most of it came from the rubber shotgun buckshot. As I cuffed the detainees and saw them up close, it was obvious that "rubber" buckshot was a misnomer. The buckshot pellets are more of a hard plastic. It had ripped through their clothes and shredded or punctured their skin.

Thankfully, none of the detainees had lost an eye from the shotgun blasts. The man hit by Evil Sponge Bob was badly jacked up. My guess was that several of his ribs were broken, but he would recover.

My order to fire our weapons had been a gamble. But I still believe today that had we kept fighting with fists, clubs, and shields, we might have killed or permanently injured the detainees. Had one of them succeeded in shanking one of my guys, not only could one of them have been injured or killed, it would have been a lot tougher to rein in everybody else and prevent them from getting even more savage. It was dumb luck that none of the rounds had been lethal. I gave orders to use lethal force and stopped the fight, but nobody had died. Despite being covered in blood and filth from the detainees we'd fought, my guys were all up and walking. For me, that was the most important outcome.

I wanted my team out of that room as fast as possible. Our lungs and faces were burning from the pepper spray. But in rushing to leave, I committed a serious blunder: I failed to order a final sweep of the room. The room was filled with smoke from the gun blasts, and I hadn't ordered anyone to walk between the rows of built-in beds. I was sure that we had cuffed and sent out ten men, but as we were turning to leave, PFC Vasquez kept his head. He said, "We need to clear the room."

He walked into the rows and found a man we'd missed: a stocky detainee in his sixties. He was hiding under a pile of torn blankets, with his face pressed down in a puddle of urine and blood. I wondered, "Is he the reason the guys in the room wouldn't surrender?"

I couldn't be sure. All I knew was that Private Vasquez saved my ass from a serious screwup. Had we left that man alone in the room, God only knows what he might have done.

I checked my watch. The entire time we'd spent in that room was no more than twelve minutes. It felt like a lifetime.

CHAPTER 8

———◆———

Unacceptable Behavior

I WISH I could say that the fighting stopped after we'd subdued and flex-cuffed the detainees. But as soon as we stepped outside of the cell block, a strange scene greeted us. At least two of the detainees had been put on stretchers, including the guy who had been hit with Evil Sponge Bob. They were loaded onto the backs of the Gators to be taken to the medical clinic. The rest were having their legs restrained by the navy guards. Putting prisoners facedown in order to shackle them was an acceptable SOP. But when the guards hauled them to their feet, what happened next was beyond the bounds of any training or acceptable behavior.

The navy guards, in teams, clustered around the shackled prisoners and took turns punching and beating them. They'd knock the prisoners down and pull them up again. It looked like one of those old high school football drills called "the bullring," where one player was surrounded by his teammates and subjected to numerous hits. But this was no puppy play on a gridiron; this was closer to a series of Rodney King–style beatings by the Los Angeles Police Department.

The guards were careful not to kick out any teeth or eyes —or kill anyone. They were just beating the prisoners to get their jollies. It was semiorganized. Each group would spend a couple of minutes delivering its harsh punishment and then melt back into a loose formation to give another group a turn. I estimated that if there were two hundred navy guards present outside Camp 4, about a quarter participated in the beatings.

At first I couldn't believe that the senior NCOs standing among the navy guards were letting this happen. Then I wondered if they hadn't orchestrated the mass beating. Even more unbelievable to me, as the shackled and cuffed detainees were getting the crap kicked out of them, Colonel Bumgarner and Captain Drake were walking around as if they didn't see anything. I was astounded to see an army colonel allowing this mass violation of regulations—a possible war crime—take place right in front of him. I had never seen anything like this occur in my experience as a prison guard or in the United States armed forces.

I was shocked by the lack of discipline on display, but I was also angry with the navy guards. My feelings didn't necessarily come out of sympathy for the detainees. Instead, I felt that the guards hadn't earned the right to be angry or mete out extra punishment. I didn't believe in giving extra punishment to detainees, but if, for argument's sake, this extra punishment was permitted, it wasn't the navy guards' place to deliver it. They were the ones who'd lost control of the prisoners and made it necessary for our QRF to become involved. While we were inside the cell block doing their dirty work, the navy guards were outside standing in formation. It wasn't their place to punish these men further. However, I wasn't about to intervene, particularly with Drake and Bumgarner watching.

Despite my outrage, I focused on what I needed to do for my squad. I was completely drained and didn't have any fight left in me. My guys looked like they'd had it, too.

We dropped our gear by our truck, and my men formed up. "You guys all right?" I asked.

They all mumbled, "Yes, Sergeant."

I had seldom seen men look so exhausted. I didn't know what to say next, so I just looked at them a minute and said, "You know what? Piss really doesn't taste as bad as you think it would, does it?"

They all started laughing. Captain Drake had some men bring over a case of bottled water, and medics arrived to tell us we all had to go to the hospital outside Camp America for full checkups.

As we were throwing our gear in the truck, some navy guards walked a detainee—one whom we'd banged up in the cell and whom they'd tuned up even further—toward me as they were loading him onto a Gator. I approached the prisoner, and they pushed him closer, I suppose so I could give him a final punch or kick.

The guy was totally out of it, but he focused his eyes on me. "You're a fucking pussy," he said.

I suppose he said that because he was expecting me to punch him. But I just looked at him. I had no need to punch him. When he saw I wasn't going to hit him, he said, "You fight like a demon. You're Satan. You're a demon." It almost seemed like a compliment. Word spread among the detainees and the guard force, and for the next nine months at Gitmo, whenever I interacted with detainees or navy guards, they always called me Satan.

As much as I blamed the inmates for the riot, I respected how hard they'd fought. They were ready to fight nearly to death. If we had been running a good detention facility, I would have thought they were motivated by strong religious or political ideals. The sad truth was that they probably fought so hard because our poor facilities and shabby treatment had pushed them beyond normal human limits. Their motivation might not have been radical Islam at all but the simple fact that they had nothing to live for and nothing left to lose.

As we drove to the hospital, I sat by Specialist Thompson in the cab of the truck. We rode in silence for a couple minutes. We were all pissed off that we hadn't been given a chance to change out of our filthy ACUs and shower. Now we were all squeezed together, adding to the nauseating stench and feel. Thompson broke the quiet. "Yo, we got our asses kicked." The simple truth of that statement cracked up the men and released some of the tension.

By the time we reached the hospital, only a few minutes past ACP Roosevelt, my guys were all laughing. Mostly they talked about how crazy Private Stewart looked whacking guys with his shield. It was only a half hour after the riot, and already everybody had his own war story.

I loved those guys as much as anyone at that moment. I was so thankful that none of them had been hurt. I kept wondering if I could have done things differently to avoid the fight. Once the navy guards threw open the cell door, should I have tossed in a concussion grenade before entering? I didn't because I had been told there was a suicide in progress. Should I have given the order to fire our weapons within lethal range? I believed in my gut it had been the fastest way to end the fight; however, I wasn't so sure that my superiors would have such a favorable judgment.

The hospital had set up four examination rooms for us. We were told to go in four at a time—one man to each room—and to stand without touching the walls or furniture due to the fecal matter on our clothes and bodies.

The doctor who saw me put on gloves and ran them over my clothes to feel if I had any sore spots from broken bones or bruises. I had no pain or even bruises anywhere on my body. My main concern was whether I had been exposed to hepatitis C from contact with the detainees' bodily fluids.

The doctor told me that he could not reveal specifics of detainees' confidential medical records, but he could assure me and my men that there was no chance we had been exposed to hepatitis C.

It took a half hour for all of us to be examined. Aside from a few bruises, all of my men checked out. We were ordered to return immediately to Camp Delta. When we drove in, we could see that Colonel Bumgarner and a hundred or more navy guards stood by the flagpole just past the entrance. As we pulled up, everybody started to cheer.

It was quite a thing to receive such a welcome while covered in detainee filth. We lined up in formation. One of Bumgarner's men shouted, "At ease!"

The colonel, undeterred by our unsanitary condition, shook our hands. "Hickman, you did a helluva job," he said.

Then they handed out witness reports for my men to fill out. Colonel Bumgarner pulled me aside and asked, "Hickman, did you give the order to fire those rounds?"

"Yes, sir."

He told me I would have to go to the administration building near his office in Camp Delta and fill out a more complete statement. Before I left, he patted my shoulder and repeated that I had done a "helluva job."

Before I filled out my statement, I wanted to make sure that none of the detainees had taken a turn for the worse. I walked over to the medical clinic. I could see a couple of the detainees strapped to gurneys but with their clothes cut off where they'd been cleaned and bandaged. They looked sedated. One of them looked at me and gurgled, "Satan."

A male medic came up and said, "You were the NCOIC?"— meaning the NCO in charge of the quick-reaction force.

"Yes," I answered.

"You're the first person in the history of Gitmo ever to give orders to fire on detainees," he said, clearly in awe.

The sound of those words made me uneasy. I was starting to understand the gravity of what I'd just been involved in.

I turned to a female corpsman who was on duty and asked, "Do any of these detainees have serious injuries?"

She wasn't supposed to reveal much, but she said, "They're picking plastic buckshot out of some of them. There might be some broken bones. But they're all going to live and walk again and be back in their cells within weeks, if not days."

"Thank God," I sighed. I didn't want to go down in history as the first American to kill a detainee at Gitmo.

By about eight o'clock that night, I arrived at the administration building to fill out my report. I had taken a half hour to return to my barracks, strip off my ACUs, throw them in the garbage, and shower.

A couple of senior chiefs—navy NCOs—greeted me and ushered me into a small room. They gave me a pen and some sheets of ruled paper, and told me to write a true account of events from the moments before my QRF entered the cell until we'd cleared it.

I didn't recognize either of these senior chiefs. They were both about my age, or maybe a couple years older, and at least three ranks above a sergeant like me.

There were two important points I wanted to make in my report. The first was something I was very angry about: that we'd been told there was a suicide in progress and rushed in only to find an ambush.

The second point was that I had given orders to fire our shotguns and the M203 within lethal range. This was not an earth-shattering revelation. It was no secret that I was in charge when my men fired five rounds in a roughly twenty-by-twenty room. Even if my guys had stood with their backs to the wall and fired on a detainee pressed against the opposite wall, the weapons still would have been too close to discharge safely.

I wanted to state these facts clearly and take responsibility for them. I feared that my order to fire had the potential to damage my career, but I wanted to be up front. I wrote that I gave the orders because I had one man down, and I saw one detainee armed with an improvised bladed weapon and another armed with the spear-like pole taken from a fan.

When I finished the report, one of the senior chiefs took it from me and disappeared into another office. I didn't know whom he showed it to. We were near Bumgarner's office, but given my rapport with the Colonel, I believed he would have dealt with me directly were he reading the report. I have never found out to whom the senior chiefs reported.

After about ten minutes, the senior chief returned with my report. He held it up, crumpled it, and threw it in a wastepaper basket. He shook his head sadly. "Not good enough. You need to rewrite it," he said.

I wrote a new report, with the same facts. I tried to correct any grammatical errors or misspellings, and handed it back. The same chief read it—and crumpled it up again. "We can be here all night if you want," he said, a slight note of irritation creeping into his voice.

"What am I doing wrong?" I asked.

"This was a major incident. Donald Rumsfeld will be getting your report in the morning. This is going to be all over the news. Everyone will want to know what happened. You need to rewrite this."

I had the distinct sense there were bigger problems in my report than my grammar and spelling. I went over the statements about giving the order to shoot at lethal range. I took full responsibility. I didn't blame any of my men for shooting in error or without orders. There was no way to make this more clear, but I tried in my next report.

The same chief returned again. It was past midnight. I was sure that he and his partner and whoever was reading my reports wanted to finish duty and go home. His tone was increasingly frustrated, but he refused to dictate exactly what was wrong with my report.

"Help me out, so I can help you," I said.

"Why did you give that order to fire the weapons?" he asked.

"I had a man down."

"Didn't you want to protect the detainees, too?"

I looked at him.

"Weren't you acting out of concern for the report of the suicide attempt?" he said.

"There was no attempted suicide," I said.

Now he just looked at me. Then he added, "Are you positive the weapons were fired within lethal range?"

It finally came to me. They not only wanted me to lie to protect myself, they wanted me to lie to protect the entire command at Gitmo. I wasn't expected to give a correct account, I was supposed to deliver a politically correct narrative. While it's true I was concerned about the possibility of beating one or more prisoners to death if we didn't end the fight quickly, that had been a much lower priority than my desire to protect my own guys. But the sun was coming up, and it was clear I had no real choice. In the final version of the report, I emphasized my concern for the well-being of the detainees as if it were a higher priority than the safety of my men.

I also wrote that after I gave the orders to fire, it was possible that the shooters maneuvered to a distance of up to ten to twelve *meters* from the detainees before they fired. This was the distance that the navy chief suggested I include in the report, because ten to twelve meters was about the minimum nonlethal range of the weapons. Since the room was about twenty feet square, or seven meters, firing from a range of ten or more meters would have been possible only if my gunners had backed out the door three meters before discharging the weapons into the room. Clearly, that was a ridiculous idea, but possible. I never gave an order for my men to back all the way out of the room before firing their weapons, but the navy chief suggested that my report would "read better" if I included the possibility.

The final sticking point of the report was the attempted suicide. I could fudge other details in the report, but I couldn't bring myself to lie and state that I had observed a suicide attempt in progress. The navy chief and I went back and forth on this issue. I finally dealt with it by committing the sin of omission. I noted in my report that my QRF had been told that a suicide attempt was in progress inside the cell before we entered. I omitted the fact that no suicide appeared to be in progress inside the cell itself.

I spent roughly eleven hours in that room before they accepted my statement. It would be an overstatement to say that I felt like I'd been kept there as a prisoner. Instead, it felt vaguely like accounts I'd read of people being held in communist Chinese reeducation camps. I had spent eleven hours bending truths into untruths. For some reason, I was more ashamed about the BS in my report than I was about possibly having violated SOPs by firing the weapons at such close range.

When the chief finally came in, smiling, to tell me that my report was acceptable and I could leave, I said, "I hope Rumsfeld's happy now."

"You'll be his favorite sergeant when he reads this," he said.

I was going to be on the radar of the man who'd inspired me to reenlist after 9/11, but instead of earning renown for a heroic military deed, I had written a big fat lie for the history books.

As I walked out of the administration building and into Camp Delta that morning, I was struck by how quiet the cell blocks were. I'd never heard such a peaceful morning. No banging, no screams, no shouts at the navy guards. While walking to the chow hall in Delta, I saw a sergeant from another squad. "Why is it so quiet around here?" I asked him.

"The navy guards forced the detainees to take sedatives last night," he answered.

I was incredulous. "What?" Forcing sedatives on the general prison population was a violation of both international law as well as rules the United States pledged to abide by at Gitmo. In the drugged quiet of Camp Delta, my eyes were finally opened to the reality of my duty at Gitmo. I was serving a command that systematically engaged in violations of laws and codes of conduct that military and civilian leaders swore to the world we were upholding. For the first time in my military career, I was serving leaders whose command was based, at least in part, on lies and deception.

The big question for me now was, "What am I going to do about it?"

CHAPTER 9

All Spin Zone

Guantánamo Prisoners Battle Guards in Hour-Long Riot

Ten inmates at the U.S. Navy prison at Guantánamo Bay, Cuba, clashed with guards who intervened to prevent a "ruse" suicide attempt yesterday in the most violent uprising yet at the detention facility.

Prisoners used light fixtures, fan blades and pieces of metal to attack 10 guards who entered a medium-security communal living area to stop a detainee who appeared to be preparing to hang himself using bed sheets, Navy Rear Admiral Harry B. Harris told reporters on a conference call.

Prisoners spread feces, urine and soapy water on the cell-block floor in an attempt to trip the guards. Two guards were knocked to the ground after inmates jumped on them from beds. "We were losing the fight at that point," said Army Colonel Michael I. Bumgarner, who was also on the call.

Guards used pepper spray, shot the rioting inmates with five non-lethal shotgun blasts of pea-sized rubber pellets and fired a "sponge-type grenade," or blunt rubber bullet, in a fight that lasted about an hour, Bumgarner said. Fifteen guards worked in support of the ten-man rapid response team that subdued the inmates, he said.

Six detainees were treated for minor injuries.

—Jeff St. Onge, Bloomberg News, May 19, 2006

As soon as I awoke after finally getting some much-needed shut-eye after the riot, I found out that my fictional report wasn't just for Donald Rumsfeld. It was the story my leaders would tell to the world. The story was all over the news. I never realized how quickly history could be manufactured. Half the reporters covering the military should have just enlisted; they seemed even more eager to believe the things our commanders said than we did.

I watched the news and wondered if maybe the real purpose of it wasn't to report on events but to tell fairy tales that would make all of us feel better about what we were doing at Gitmo and around the world: the commanders, the guards, the political leaders, the viewers at home. Even the families of the detainees—if they watched CNN—could be heartened. Most of the reports said that the detainees involved had sustained only "minor injuries," but that hardly described the condition of the men I had flex-cuffed and pushed out of that cell during the riot—and that was before the navy guards "assisted" by beating the crap out of the prisoners once they got outside.

I started to get mad. I thought the worst of my anger had passed the night when I knuckled under and filled out my report as the navy chiefs wanted. I thought that when I left that office, my anger would be behind me. But once I saw the omissions and bent truths in my report being used to define everything that happened for the entire world, it reemerged.

Unfortunately, I couldn't wallow in my anger. I couldn't even let it out. "What are you going to do about it?" I had asked myself the night before. My answer was that I had to stuff it all deep inside. The safety and well-being of all the guys in my squad depended on it. It was a bitter tonic I had to drink.

It's not that the reporters wanted to get on TV and report utter non-sense. They were tightly controlled, not just the day after the riot but all through their time at Gitmo. The reporters understood that there were restrictions on where they could go and to whom they could talk, but I don't think any of them ever had a clue just how much they were manipulated, and how hard the military worked to deceive them. Fooling reporters was part of the job.

It was easy to do. The reporters stayed outside Camp Delta and usually waited to be called in for press conferences or briefings with the commanders. Occasionally the commanders would allow them to come into one of the camps. When that happened, we'd get word a few days in advance. We'd be told which routes the newsmen and -women would take and which cell blocks they would pass by. They would identify any detainees along the route who were loud or made trouble, so that the navy guards could shuffle the worst detainees out of cells adjacent to the routes and move in the most compliant ones. To make sure everything looked its best, the guards would walk the routes and inspect everything. They'd do two or three rehearsals before the reporters ever showed up. We used to watch as the reporters were led through the cell blocks. It was hilarious. The military escorts would put on a show and say things like, "Hey, let's go down this way," and take them toward a particular cell block, as if the tour were spontaneous, when, in fact, the whole thing was an act. Now, since filing my report on the riot, I realized that I was also part of the charade.

*   *   *

Everybody was still treating my team members like rock stars when we showed up for duty the day after the melee, less than eighteen hours after the riot ended. People were coming up and patting my back and high-fiving my squad because of the news.

Since filling out the report the night before, I'd had a question about Admiral Harris's statement claiming that a detainee had faked an attempted suicide. What about the cameras in the cell? During the riot, they'd attacked us with broken pieces of cameras, but I wasn't sure they'd gotten all the cameras in the cell or whether they'd pulled them down after we entered or before. Wouldn't those tapes have disproved my statement?

One of the guys who patted my back that day was a navy guard. He said he'd been there when we went in. I asked if he knew whether the detainees had gotten all the cameras and if anyone had seen the footage before they were ripped down. One of his navy guard buddies laughed and winked. "You know, those cameras don't always work when things go wrong," he said.

That was the first time I'd heard something like that, but it explained a lot. I didn't know if that meant cameras were switched off or if footage could be erased, but it was clear that I should never worry about things being caught on tape.

The navy guards also revealed an interesting detail about the events leading up to the riot. It was a mystery to me why that particular cell had rioted. It was even odder that the riot had taken place in Camp 4, the compliant camp. I'd seen that the rioters had all been protecting the last detainee we pulled out: a stocky, bearded holy man who used to strut around like Tony Soprano and whom all the detainees seemed to respect. It made sense that they had protected him during our fight, but if they revered this man, why had they started the riot in the first place? Wouldn't they want to keep their holy man away from a fight?

The navy guards told me that the riot started when the guards were inspecting the Korans. Of course, we'd first been called to Camp 1 hours before the riot, where the situation had been defused when Colonel Bumgarner ordered a Muslim interpreter to carry out the inspections.

The navy guards told us that after the interpreter inspected Camp 1, Admiral Harris found out and rejected the idea.

"I wonder why he did that," I said.

"Maybe he didn't want to use private contractors. They're outside the chain of command," one of the navy guards speculated.

"He was probably pissed off about the idea of negotiating with these assholes," offered the other guard.

However it came about, when the navy guards showed up at Camp 4 and tried to confiscate the Korans, the detainees started to resist.

Colonel Bumgarner or Admiral Harris—the guards telling us the story weren't sure—had the interpreter warn the detainees that if they didn't allow their Korans to be inspected, the guards would extract their beloved holy man and put him in isolation.

That version of events was only scuttlebutt, but it made sense and explained why the riot started in the holy man's cell. The detainees were rioting against an ill-conceived order.

In the days after the riot, guard duty in the camps was never easier. It was tense, to be sure. Camp 4 was emptied, and the detainees had been distributed into higher-security cell blocks. Everyone was tightly controlled in individual cells. We still manned the towers in Camp 4, but it was empty—no more soccer games. It would be many weeks before they put men back into Camp 4.

The navy guards were a lot more serious in their work, too. All the petty abuse, the verbal taunts, the Frequent Flier games stopped. It was a much more professional atmosphere. The guards' senior NCOs and officers were walking through camp a lot more, and I had never seen the detainees more obedient. The guards were doing cell shakedowns more often, but everyone was compliant. The detainees kept quiet. Even the sobbing we normally heard was tamped down.

I was sure that some of this calm came from the shock of the riot. The firm way we'd put it down definitely left an impression. Detainees seldom interacted with us, but twice in the days after the riot, I passed by prisoners who were being moved in the yard. They nodded to me and said, "Satan." They didn't say it like an accusation or insult, more like a title, but I wouldn't have cared if it were an insult. If that's the name they wanted to call me, fine. I was more interested in the fact that despite all their isolation, the detainees managed to communicate among themselves. Word of the riot and my new name had spread. Maybe they were all so quiet because they didn't want to get Evil-Sponge-Bobbed.

But my experience in corrections told me that most of the improved behavior wasn't because the detainees were intimidated or in shock. They were behaving better because the navy guards were treating them with professionalism. It was like a different camp. The guards treated them like humans, and so the detainees behaved like humans.

Unfortunately, there was an additional reason for the detainees' subdued behavior. Many of them had united together a few days after the riot in the most effective form of rebellion available to them: a hunger strike.

Since our arrival, the QRF had staged next to the behavioral health building behind Camp 4. The room where we stored our riot gear had also been filled with equipment and supplies for forced feedings. About three days after the riot, the Sergeant of the Guard informed us that the QRF's staging area had been moved temporarily to a different administrative office. "They're getting ready to start up the forced feeding again. A bunch of detainees have stopped eating, so we're prepping for a big strike," he said.

We had been instructed back at Fort Lewis on the SOPs regarding hunger strikes. They were a huge problem because the military obviously didn't want detainees dying en masse, but there were other problems as well.

Aside from whatever secret interrogations the government might have conducted at places like Camp No, inside Camp Delta there was the row of trailers used for the interrogations conducted more or less openly by the CIA personnel and black-garbed private contractors. Detainees who skipped nine meals in a row could not be interrogated at Camp Delta. The camp's SOPs prevented hunger-striking detainees from being transported there for interrogations. Hunger strikers were also not allowed to meet with their civilian attorneys at nearby Camp Echo. Even with their limited access, the media could pick up on the chaos that a hunger strike caused.

The forced-feeding program itself added to the burden of running the camp. Detainees being force-fed were taken one at a time from their cells, shackled, put on the back of a Gator, and driven to the facility behind Camp 4.

Three days of missing meals didn't alter a person's appearance much, and besides, at the end of three days, he started getting Ensure pumped down his throat. But by the end of May, I could tell that the strike was in full force by the numbers of detainees being transported

on Gators. Typically, I might see one or two detainees being transported every couple of days. By the height of the hunger strike, I was
counting twenty or more detainees being moved on Gators every shift.

In that first week of June, we were told that a media VIP was coming. Despite the hunger strike, the command had to keep up outward
appearances for the world. So amid all the extra transport duty for
forced feedings, they did the usual practice runs and role playing to
prepare for the famous journalist's arrival.

I walked into the chow hall one day after my shift and heard uproar-
ious laughter. Bill O'Reilly of Fox News was there. Of all the journalists who ever came, O'Reilly was the one who really seemed to enjoy
the troops. He was shaking hands, cracking jokes. He had people sit
and eat with him. When I went past, he reached over, shook my hand,
and thanked me. I couldn't believe how humble and open the guy was
with all of us.

But for all his on-air bluster about the "No Spin Zone," the Fox
journalist couldn't see that he was being spun. For all the days he was
at Gitmo, I don't think he ever picked up on the hunger strike that was
happening right under his nose, or at least I didn't see any mention of
it in his broadcasts. He told the world how brave we were for working
at Gitmo, and I appreciated that, but I didn't think Americans watching his show could learn anything of value about the prison we were
running. They learned only what the military wanted them to learn.
O'Reilly, like all the other journalists to visit Gitmo, gave a news report
about the made-up tour his handlers took him on. He missed, by only
a day or two, the biggest story to come out of Gitmo: the mysterious
deaths of three detainees in our custody.

———◆———

CHAPTER 10

June 9, 2006

MIDDAY on June 9, 2006, Staff Sergeant Hayes, who was supposed to be SOG that night and oversee all the positions in the camp, came down with a cluster headache. He'd suffered through several of these episodes since we'd arrived. The effects were alarming. One side of his face would swell up dramatically. He would look awful. The doctors he saw didn't know if it was a migraine or allergies, and I could tell he was in pain this day. "Staff Sergeant, you don't look too good," I told him.

"Another damned headache," he said. "I'm going over to see the doctor."

"Look, why don't I serve as SOG tonight?" I offered. "Shift starts at six. Happy to do it. You look like shit."

"Feel like it, too," said Hayes. "But I can handle it." He looked worn out.

"No need to play the hero," I said. "I insist."

"Not to put too fine a point on it, but the last time you filled in for me, there was a riot. Remember that?"

"Well, that was an unusual circumstance," I said. "You really look beat. Let me fill in for you."

"Okay, then, but know this: if there's another riot or some kind of serious incident, I will hold you personally responsible," he quipped.

In order to be alert for the night's shift, I went back to my bunk and took a long nap. At four, I showered, got ready for work, and checked on my guys to make sure they were preparing for the shift. I went over an hour early to talk to the SOG I was relieving. There were a total of thirty-five guys manning all the positions, with every tower and post reporting to me every thirty minutes. The SOG command post was in an administrative building across from our barracks. When I met with the SOG and asked if there was anything unusual I should look out for, he laughed. "No. It's the same old shit, same old day. We're still in the twilight zone, man."

Captain Drake came by to tell me to keep everything tight, because higher-ups might be coming by to visit some of the posts. This was nothing new since the riot and hunger strike. In the past couple of days, we'd all noticed that the number of detainees being shuttled around on Gators seemed to have dropped slightly. It seemed to me that the hunger strike was waning.

By 5:15, all thirty-five guys, mostly from my first platoon but also a couple of augmentees from the others in our company, showed up at the administration office. In the military, when they say your duty starts at 6:00, that's the time everybody needs to be in position. Getting ready always took at least forty-five minutes before the actual start time.

I called the thirty-five men into formation at 5:20, informed them that there were no new orders or alerts, and had them draw their weapons from the armory. I had everybody on his way to his post by 5:30.

I went to Sally Port 1 first, the main entrance to Camp Delta, because from about 5:30 to 6:30, everybody in camp would change shifts, and it was the busiest time of our shift. I had three guys working the checkpoint, and for about fifteen minutes while a line formed, I helped them out to speed things up.

I went up to Tower 1 a little after 6:30 when the call to prayers was starting. It had been getting warmer in recent days, and I wanted to make sure that the runner, who drove between the towers in a Gator, checking on guards and bringing water, was delivering enough to everyone.

Tower 1 was manned at that hour by Staff Sergeant Thomas Green and Specialist John Roberts. Green was from another squad, and I didn't know him well, but he seemed like an okay guy.

Staff Sergeant Green let me know that everything was fine, and it appeared to be so, until I saw the white van enter Delta and proceed to Alpha block. Unlike navy guards in the cell blocks, who used plastic flex cuffs to restrain detainees' wrists, the escorts from the white van used metal police-style cuffs. As I watched them take out the first detainee from Camp 1 Alpha block that evening and load him in the van, something about metal cuffs on a person being loaded into a windowless metal box bothered me. I watched the van leave, making a right out of Camp Delta and a left onto the road that went to ACP Roosevelt. It was leaving Camp America.

I had no doubt that it bothered the guys in the tower that I stayed up there with them. They didn't want the SOG hanging around breathing down their necks. But as I watched the van return some twenty minutes later and pick up the second detainee from Alpha block and repeat its route, I became curious. I knew that at this late hour on a Friday night, military commissions—tribunals for prosecuting the detainees—were not in session (and records that I later obtained indicated that there were no commissions held that day at all).

"Where could they be going?" I thought to myself. I had a suspicion. Twenty minutes later, when the van came to pick up a third detainee, before they left Camp Delta I went to ACP Roosevelt to see where the van was going. If the van went straight, it was heading toward the main base; but if it turned left, it was heading toward Camp No.

When I arrived at ACP Roosevelt, the men on duty were busy checking IDs and searching vehicles for bombs. I stood there pretending to watch them. When I saw the white van heading toward Roosevelt, I felt anxious. "If the van turns toward Camp No, what am I supposed to do? I am not supposed to know it exists," I thought. As the van passed Roosevelt, I watched it intently, and I felt my heart sink when it went about a hundred yards past Roosevelt and turned left, toward Camp No.

During the next few hours, I made rounds to a few other posts but decided to return to Tower 1. I told the guys I just wanted to have a good view of Delta that night. As SOG, I could roam or remain at any post I chose.

At eleven thirty, everything changed. Though I didn't know it at the time, my life in the military would be transformed completely. I was in Tower 1 when the van finally reappeared in Camp Delta. Instead of driving over to Alpha block, from where the three detainees had been removed, the van backed up to the medical clinic, with its rear doors facing the front doors of the clinic. The escorts inside turned off the engine and lights, and sat inside for a few minutes. From my vantage above them and about forty feet distant, I could see one escort, a male, on the passenger side sitting there turned to the other, as if talking. It was unusual for a vehicle to enter at this hour and just sit there with its lights off.

After several minutes passed, I saw the driver side door of the van open. I decided to climb down the tower to better see what was happening. By the time I reached the bottom of the ladder, the back doors of the van were open. I heard voices from the entrance to the medical clinic. It sounded like they were carrying in somebody, but I couldn't see, and I didn't feel comfortable walking up to the clinic and snooping. Instead, I walked to the Sally Port and waited there. I wanted to see the navy escorts when they drove out; look them in the eyes. It wasn't quite rational. But since I didn't have the authorization to search the van or question the escorts, I thought maybe I could discern something by looking in their eyes.

I didn't get that chance. The van remained by the clinic with its lights off. After fifteen minutes, I walked back to the clinic and got close enough to see that the escorts were not in the van anymore. Its back doors were closed, and there was no activity in the entrance area of the clinic. As I walked back to Tower 1, I saw one of the escorts exit the clinic and park the van about ten feet from the front entrance.

I climbed back into Tower 1 and asked Specialist Richard Foster and Staff Sergeant Sean Winslow, who had just come on duty to relieve Staff Sergeant Green, if they'd seen anything, or anyone, being unloaded from the van. While the tower did not offer a view of the back of the van or the entrance to the clinic, the front of the medical clinic and the walkway from Alpha block were visible. But they hadn't heard anything. Both guys were looking at me kind of funny. They knew the van's movements were not our business, but neither questioned me about my interest in it.

I returned to Tower 1. The van remained a quiet, dark mystery. I sent Specialist Foster down at about twelve fifteen to take his meal break. Fifteen minutes later, the whole camp lit up like a football field under stadium lights. I'd never seen it like this. It appeared that there was an emergency, but no alarms sounded, no messages came across my radio from the SOG command post. Just routine radio checks.

I climbed down the tower and saw Specialist Foster coming back toward the tower. I asked him, "What the hell is going on?"

Foster told me that when he'd climbed down the tower, a male navy chief ran out of the medical clinic and ordered him to find another navy chief at the mess hall. Specialist Foster explained to me, "I had to tell her there was a code red."

"What's a code red?" I asked.

"I don't know," he said. "All I know is when I found her and gave her the code red message, she left her food on the table and ran out."

By the time Foster told me about passing the mysterious code red message, I saw a half dozen or so navy guards jogging toward the clinic on the road from Alpha block. They weren't carrying anybody. There were no Gators with them. It was just navy cell block guards going toward the clinic. I followed after them.

When I got closer, I saw a face I recognized coming out of the clinic. While all the navy guards were heading in, Lisa was the only one walking away, almost like she didn't know what to do next.

As the SOG, I wasn't supposed to be hanging out away from a post or talking to a friend, but instead of walking toward the checkpoint, I cut over toward her and said her name. When she turned around, she looked really upset.

Because everybody was working long shifts at crazy hours, I was used to people looking bad. But I knew Lisa. Some three weeks earlier, I'd seen her working at the clinic during a hectic night when a dozen injured detainees, as well as navy guards, were brought in during the riot. I knew her expressions. Work didn't rattle her.

"What happened? What's going on with the lights?" I asked.

"Three detainees just killed themselves."

"What?"

"They had rags stuffed down their throats. And one of them was badly bruised."

"Who put rags down their throats?"

She couldn't answer. She told me that they had been brought into the clinic at about eleven thirty and she was told they had committed suicide. She and the other medics on duty had almost immediately discovered the rags stuffed deep in their throats. I knew that the three detainees had not come directly from the cell blocks. I, or one of my guys, would have seen them. They had to have been delivered from the back of the van. Though I had seen the black box in the back of the van only once, I figured it could probably hold three people, if breathing was not an issue.

I wanted to ask Lisa more questions about the dead detainees. Did she see the escorts from the van carry them in? Did they explain any further? But I could see she was emotional, and she wasn't supposed to talk to me about her work. That wasn't the time or place to press her with questions. I didn't think she'd seen dead people before, and I could see that she was having a hard time dealing with it. I told her to take care and walked to the checkpoint.

At that moment, several officers and an ambulance from the hospital outside Camp America were coming through. I watched the ambulance back up to the clinic. I couldn't understand what it was doing there if the detainees had already died.

I felt like my mind was playing tricks on me. I'd seen those three detainees picked up between six thirty and seven fifteen and loaded into the white van. It had to be the same men who were now dead. Between checkpoint 1 and Towers 1 and 4, I had five soldiers who'd been watching and logging every approach to the clinic. Between those five guards and me, we saw no detainees carried, dragged, walked, or hauled on a Gator or any other conveyance into the clinic. The only vehicle we saw that could have carried them was the white van when it backed up to the clinic. How could they have died in the custody of navy escorts, with bruises and with rags stuffed in their throats?

I asked my guys in Tower 1 if they'd seen anyone walking between the clinic and the cell block since I'd climbed down. They had not.

I walked down to Tower 4, which was closer to Alpha block and had an unobstructed view of the walkway connecting it to the medical clinic. I asked the soldier on duty in the tower, Specialist Anthony Williams, if he'd seen anyone on the walkway, but he hadn't. He told me that no one had come or gone on the walkway since our shift started. If so, it meant that the three detainees had not been taken to the hospital from their cells. "How could they have committed suicide if they weren't in their cells?" I wondered. A terrible thought entered my mind: "What if they died in Camp No?"

The detainees were the enemy. They were terrorists. They threw feces and urine at us. They were trying to starve themselves to death. They were the extremists; the bad guys. But our side didn't kill them in custody. As bad as navy guards could be—sadistic, juvenile, unprofessional, overworked, poorly trained—we didn't kill prisoners. That wasn't my military.

I had all these thoughts and questions racing through my head, and I was angry. I wanted to punch somebody. But I had my job to do. Even at this point, with lights on, guards and officers and ambulance at the clinic, there was no alert passed over our radios indicating a problem. For all intents and purposes, we were still doing business as usual. Whatever was happening was being kept secret.

A moment after the ambulance stopped at the clinic, I saw Colonel Bumgarner break away from a cluster of people now gathered by it and jog over to me at the checkpoint. "Hickman? You're the SOG tonight?"

"Yes, sir."

"There's going to be a briefing at oh-seven-hundred, and I want everybody who's been on guard to attend."

"Yes, sir."

I was eager to hear his explanation. But, I had thirty-five soldiers serving under me for the next five hours. I couldn't dwell on the questions turning in my mind. I did my radio checks and made sure that everyone was keeping his log and drinking water. Nobody reported anything unusual on the radios from the other posts. At Camp 1, where I stayed until the shift ended at six o'clock, everybody was talking about the lights coming on and the navy guards who'd appeared and stayed by the back of the clinic until about three, when the lights went off again and the van drove away. I didn't tell anyone what Lisa had said, but by dawn, some of my guards at the checkpoint told me that they'd heard about the rags. Word was spreading, but I kept my concerns to myself. I did my job.

I felt more than ever before that I needed my commanders to give me an explanation—one that made sense of what I'd seen in those hours. I needed my commanders to explain how I could feel good about myself again as an American. For the first time in my career, I felt dirty wearing my uniform.

CHAPTER 11

———

Lies

WHAT I didn't see was as important as what I did see. This is what the military taught me as a young rifleman in the Marine Corps, and it's the fundamental rule of guarding, too. What we all saw was the white van arrive at the medical clinic and a reaction at the clinic following its arrival.

None of my guards who had a close, unobstructed view of Camp 1 and the medical clinic saw any detainees taken from the cell blocks to the clinic. Neither I nor my guards saw any detainees removed from the back of the white van, because our view was blocked, but we did see and hear activity at the rear of the van as the doors were opened. Unless there was a secret tunnel, or a *Star Trek*–type transporter unit hidden somewhere on the base, the only way those three detainees could have arrived at the medical clinic was inside the white van.

I saw the van take two detainees out of cell block Alpha and drive them outside of Camp America. I then observed the van take a third detainee and personally watched as it drove him outside of Camp America and turned down the road that led to the beach and Camp No.

Following the departure of that third detainee, the van was absent from Camp 1 for the next few hours. My guards and I all noticed its absence. When the van appeared again at eleven thirty, it entered into Camp 1 via the Sally Port.

These were the basic facts of my observations and those of my men, whose job it was to make such observations. We were the guards for all the entry and exit points of Camp 1 and the rest of Camp America. There was no one else who had that duty but my men and me.

If, as Lisa reported to me, those men arrived dead at the clinic, then they expired somewhere outside of Camp 1. This is one fact about which I was an expert. It was my job that night to know that fact. The military paid me and the thirty-five soldiers I was overseeing to be absolutely certain of everything we observed—what we saw and didn't see. I was absolutely certain that those three detainees did not die in Camp 1. I was therefore eager to hear Colonel Bumgarner's briefing at seven that morning. I wanted to know how he would account for the facts I knew.

When our unit was relieved from duty at six, all the soldiers I had been overseeing turned in their logs to me at the SOG office. I inspected their reports before I turned them in to my platoon leader. Because of our standing order forbidding us to record the movements of the white van, there was no mention of it. I filed my master log with the expectation that my men and I would be questioned by our command and by investigators. We were the watchers on duty when, for the first time, three detainees died at Gitmo.

I shuddered recalling the twelve hours I'd spent being badgered by navy chiefs to fill out my report "for Donald Rumsfeld." I couldn't imagine how we were going to be put through the wringer for three deaths that occurred on our watch.

I hadn't resolved how I would handle any pressures they might place on me or on the men to bend the truth. It was one thing to twist the facts a little and come up with a fake story about observing a suicide attempt in a riot. I didn't know what would happen now that three men had died. The whole world would be watching. They couldn't just twist the facts again.

At just after seven, some seventy-five soldiers and sailors walked into the outdoor movie theater, where the guys from my unit had just a few weeks earlier spent our nights watching *300*, a story of epic heroism. Even the most cynical guys in my unit—like Specialist Stewart, who'd been working at a Baltimore McDonald's months before our deployment to Gitmo—felt inspired watching that movie. *300* was about democracy and how a brave band of soldiers insured its survival. Weren't we doing the same at Gitmo? All of us had talked about that for weeks. As much as things sucked or as stupid as things got, we were part of that tradition.

But as Colonel Bumgarner stepped up in front of the blank movie screen, I didn't imagine King Leonidas standing there or even General Patton, the man I believe our commander modeled himself after. When I looked at Bumgarner that morning, the image of Frank Burns, the pompous, weasely major on the TV show *M*A*S*H*, popped into my mind.

Colonel Bumgarner was stumbling and nervous that morning. He didn't do his usual routine of holding us at attention and then drilling into each one of us with his gaze. He didn't seem to want to look at us. He put us at ease and looked at his feet. He paced in front of us with his arms crossed, his face glazed with sweat.

I glanced at the men and women around me. Among them were navy guards, medics from the clinic, and my soldiers from the watch. I didn't recognize all their faces, but it was clear that we were a special group—those who'd been on duty inside Camp 1 or on general watch. I couldn't see any people from the other camps. It was just us. Most everyone had been awake for some twenty-four hours by now. Normally, people would be pissed about being called to a briefing at the end of a twelve-hour graveyard shift. But rumors had spread about the three deaths. The weary soldiers and sailors around me were ready to hang on our commander's every word. Someone had to make it right. I didn't know what other people saw, or if anyone knew the facts I knew, but the deaths in our camp were a failure for all of us.

The colonel finally collected his thoughts. "As you all know," he began, "three detainees died last night. Some of you might have heard how they died. They committed suicide by cutting up their bedsheets and stuffing them down their throats. You're going to hear something different in the media. They're going to talk about a different way that these detainees took their lives." Bumgarner then made eye contact for the first time. "This a direct order. You are not to talk about these deaths or anything you've seen or heard. It's a direct violation of my order if you talk to any reporter, any family member, or any military personnel on this base or anywhere else. I need not remind you all that your communications are being monitored by the NSA."

It might sound strange ordering us to not even discuss the matter with people in the military. But to us, secrecy was routine. There were guys detached from my company on Gitmo and assigned to duties that they were forbidden to talk about even with Captain Drake, their commander. It was called "op sec," or "operational security." But I'd never heard a commander use op sec as an order to cover up wrongdoing or a mistake. Op sec was supposed to be aimed at defeating the enemy, not at covering over failures or crimes inside a unit. Colonel Bumgarner wrapped up his briefing by telling us that the Naval Criminal Investigative Service (NCIS) would be investigating the deaths.

If Bumgarner was telling us that the media was going to report the deaths differently than the way we'd first heard, it was because he and Admiral Harris were going to tell the reporters a story that wasn't true. Those two, and whomever else they reported to, had a plan. Our briefing seemed to be part of the cover-up.

As we filed out of the theater, I recalled the most shocking words spoken by Colonel Bumgarner. They had been slipped in casually amid his more outlandish statements. He referred several times to the detainees having killed themselves "in their cells" in Alpha block.

As my commander walked ahead, I saw the back of his uniform soaked through with sweat and wondered, "Does he know he's lying? Is that possible? Is my commander an accessory to murder? And if so, has he just ordered us to participate in the same crime with him?"

At the edge of the theater, Colonel Bumgarner turned around and caught my eye. I had a sinking feeling. I thought, "Now comes the order for me to report to his office and fill out my statement of what happened. If they're getting all their ducks in a row, they're going to need my statement." I wondered if they'd make me report that my men saw the three detainees carried out of Alpha block. I couldn't imagine implicating my guys in a crime like that.

But instead of saying anything, the colonel simply nodded absently and walked past. I'd expected him to look different up close—I thought that lying in front of the people he led would change his appearance. But aside from the sweat, it was the same man I saw every day in the office. I wondered briefly if he had lied like this before.

As he passed by, I felt sick with shame.

I tried sleeping that morning, but I only tossed and turned. I was really starting to wonder what Gitmo was about. Colonel Bumgarner had warned us that the story would be reported differently from what we knew, but how could they twist the fact that three guys had died with rags stuffed so far down their throats that combat medics couldn't pull them out?

How could they turn that into a suicide? I knew the truth. My men knew the truth. It seemed impossible to me that lies of that magnitude could go out into the world and survive.

CHAPTER 12

Ten Days in the Real World

3 Prisoners Commit Suicide at Guantánamo

Three detainees being held at the United States military prison at Guantánamo Bay, Cuba, committed suicide early on Saturday, the first deaths of detainees to be reported at the military prison since it opened in early 2002, United States military officials said....

The three detainees were not identified, but United States officials said two were from Saudi Arabia and the third was from Yemen. Military officials said that the three hanged themselves in their cells with nooses made of sheets and clothing and died before they could be revived by medical personnel.

Rear Adm. Harry B. Harris Jr., the commander of the detention camp at Guantánamo, told reporters in a news conference that the deaths were discovered early on Saturday when a guard noticed something out of the ordinary in a cell and found that a prisoner had hanged himself. Admiral Harris said guards and a medical team rushed in to try to save the inmate's life but were unsuccessful. Then, guards found two other detainees in nearby cells had hanged themselves as well; all were pronounced dead by a physician.

Military officials on Saturday suggested that the three suicides were a form of a coordinated protest.

"They are smart, they are creative, they are committed," Admiral Harris said.

"They have no regard for life, neither ours nor their own. I believe this was not an act of desperation, but an act of asymmetrical warfare waged against us." . . .

He said the acts were tied to a "mystical" belief at Guantánamo that three detainees must die at the camp for all the detainees to be released.

—Excerpted from the article by James Risen and Tim Golden, *The New York Times,* June 11, 2006

I watched Admiral Harris's press conference live on CNN in the chow hall at about noon on June 10. The conference was being filmed less than three-quarters of a mile away from where I sat. But the admiral might as well have been speaking to us from the bottom of the sea. He didn't feel real.

Harris's story added layers of impossibility to what was now the official account. Had it happened, we would have seen the medical team he spoke of leaving the clinic to respond to the suicides. Had the detainees been carried back dead, we would have seen the medical team carrying empty stretchers into the cell blocks, and full ones out. But we saw no foot traffic in or out of cell blocks—just the navy guards who came after midnight.

I couldn't understand the fabrication that the prisoners believed three of them had to die at Gitmo in order for the rest to go free. I was reminded of reading *The Adventures of Huckleberry Finn* in high school. In one scene, Huck's slave buddy, Jim, tells a story about finding a magical hairball that enabled him to tell the future. I didn't like the book because that story annoyed me so much. I didn't think anybody could be so stupid that they would believe in such superstition. But when I saw Admiral Harris talking about the mystical beliefs of the detainees and how they were waging asymmetrical warfare despite the brave efforts of the guards, I was amazed.

The reporters mostly swallowed it. But what choice did they have? The admiral was their only source of information.

Over the next couple of days, I'd slink into the offices in Camp Delta expecting one of Colonel Bumgarner's chiefs to tap me on the shoulder and tell me it was time to give my statement, but they never did. In all my years in the military, I couldn't think of a single time when something went down and a supervisor who'd been on hand wasn't asked to make a statement. The military always covered its ass with paper. Whether we saw something or not, if we were on watch (or in my case, the SOG), covering an area where something happened, the military took a statement. But in this case, it seemed that the colonel and his chiefs already had their story down the way they wanted it.

I didn't talk to anybody in my unit about what we'd seen. A couple of the men who'd been on watch in Camp 1 asked me what I thought of the admiral's statement. These guys didn't even know about the white van or Camp No: they were just troubled that Admiral Harris described the suicides as having taken place in Alpha block, which they had seen was quiet up until the detainees were already at the clinic. They had listened to Colonel Bumgarner tell us that the detainees died with rags stuffed in their throats at the debriefing, but now he was saying they hanged themselves.

When my guys tried to bring this stuff up to me, I shut them down. I told them to focus on their jobs and their families at home.

Staff Sergeant Hayes had set the tone when I saw him the day after the deaths. I'd woken from my brief nap before the next shift. His cluster headache was better, and he was going back on duty that night.

He pulled me aside and laughed. "Man, I leave you alone for twelve hours, and look what happened," he joked.

I smiled. He squinted at me and asked, "But everything was okay, right? You guys were just on post, everybody doing their jobs, no drama?"

I looked at this man whom I admired so much and tried to imagine telling him the whole story: me chasing after the white van on its third trip out so I could beat it to ACP Roosevelt and see where it turned. How would I tell him about Camp No? My trips there were something I'd never shared with him.

Hayes was the kind of soldier I would follow into any battle. I trusted that he would lay down his life for any one of us. But I didn't want to be the one to lead him into a fight he didn't choose. I wasn't going to push this man into a battle with Colonel Bumgarner and Admiral Harris.

When he pressed me to make sure there had been no drama on our end while I was SOG, I told him, "Absolutely. Everybody was fine."

"I knew you'd do good on SOG duty. Thanks for taking care of things." When Hayes patted me on the shoulder, I felt like I was shrinking.

I'd just lied to the man I respected most on the whole island, and in doing so, I'd carried out Colonel Bumgarner's order.

One piece of information I had picked up within forty-eight hours of the deaths was that the three dead men had been the last hunger strikers. This fact, confirmed a couple years later by the military, had no significance to me at the time. Had I been working outside as a private investigator—or even doing a corrections job where every moment I was trying to keep my mind tuned to figuring out what plots the inmates might be up to—this information would have raised flags. The three men who died under suspicious circumstances also just happened to be the last holdouts? That was quite a coincidence. But when I heard this information, I just let it pass through my mind without paying any attention to it.

Thirty-six hours after the deaths, we were ordered to move all our QRF gear back to the old staging area behind Camp 4. Like before, one side of the room had the chairs with restraints on them, piles of surgical tubes, and cases of Ensure—all pushed together to make room for us and our gear. Some of the guys killed time by sitting in the forced-feeding chairs and sucking down Ensure when they got hungry. Days had passed since detainees had been strapped to the chairs with feeding tubes pushed down their throats via their nostrils, but I pictured them. I wondered if these terrorists used to sit around in their caves in Afghanistan cracking jokes like us.

I'd say that three-quarters of my guys, myself included, believed in God. We weren't religious like the detainees were, but if you locked us in cages and gave us nothing but Bibles, I'm sure we'd pray a lot more and look pretty fanatical to our guards, too.

In the days after the deaths, I started snapping at guys in my squad over little things like moving too slow at checkpoints. I stopped joking, or even talking much. One day I cursed out a young specialist in our platoon for making what I believed was a poor personal choice in his dating life.

Staff Sergeant Hayes pulled me aside that afternoon and asked if I was okay.

"Everything's good," I replied. "Why?"

"You seem quiet, is all."

"Nothing to worry about."

"You seem a little short-fused."

"I'm okay, really. I'd tell you if there was a problem."

My very defensiveness raised his suspicions. We were each given a ten-day leave during our year at Gitmo. Mine was slotted for later in the fall. But after talking to me, Staff Sergeant Hayes pulled some strings and ordered me to take a leave starting on July 6.

*   *   *

During my layover in Florida, I had phoned a friend of mine to stay at his house in Baltimore. As soon as I stepped out of the terminal at Baltimore-Washington International Airport to wait for my buddy Bill Meyers, I became extremely stressed. The heat felt just as bad as Gitmo's, and the civilian world looked like utter chaos to me: people were flying around in all directions, paying no heed to good order or common sense. What drove me crazy was everyone talking on cell phones. I'd been on the island for only four and a half months, but no one had cell phones on Gitmo.

I'd been friends with Bill since childhood. He'd put in his time on the same corners as me, and outside of my squad, there was no one I was closer to. I calmed down when he rolled up in his old blue Camaro. He wanted to show me a good time. Aside from being my friend, he was the patriotic kind of American who liked to show his appreciation to people who serve.

We drove straight to Gunning's Seafood Restaurant and laid out a feast of two dozen crabs, washed down with Natty Boh. Eventually he asked how things were at Gitmo. Mindful of my security rules, I told my friend as much as I could.

"Things are pretty screwed up there."

"Aren't they always in the military?"

"No. I mean they're bad. How the detainees are treated."

"What do you care? They're fucking terrorists. Let them all die."

His attitude was very similar to mine before I got there. I said, "If you lived there on the island, you'd understand. Even though they're terrorists. I'm worried."

He laughed and raised his beer. "Fuck you, man. I thank you for what you're doing there. Everybody does."

He offered the first of several toasts. Some of the waitresses and patrons in the restaurant came by and made a big fuss about my service, and I thanked them all for thanking me. I had a pretty good buzz on, but I felt awful.

When we drove home that night to my friend's house, I decided to research what was really going on at Gitmo. Nothing felt right. Not just the lies the colonel told about the three detainees, but the whole infrastructure of Gitmo: the racism, the brutality, the chaos. I had worked in some tough correctional facilities in the civilian world and knew that these things had no place as institutional SOPs. In the real world, a cool professionalism was the standard. Fairness and a strict adherence to rules and procedure kept a lid on potential problems. At Gitmo, there was none of that.

I wanted to find out what I'd gotten myself into. Instead of seeing other friends or old girlfriends, I spent the next eight days of my leave driving to the Enoch Pratt Free Library every morning. Until I started reading about Gitmo, I hadn't understood how divided the country was about it.

I saw that people on both sides—for and against Gitmo—took extreme positions. Many people writing about Gitmo, it seemed to me, fell victim to emotionalism or exaggeration. People on the far left portrayed Gitmo as part of a crusade against Islam, and people on the far right argued that every last person in there deserved anything we threw at them, from waterboarding to indefinite incarceration without trial.

As I sifted through the material, some facts jumped out. I found a study compiled using statistics released by the US government that said fewer than 5 percent of the men taken at Guantánamo had been captured by US troops. The other 95 percent had been handed over by Afghan warlords, bounty hunters, or foreign dictatorships in countries like Yemen. I had never imagined that the men I was guarding at Gitmo had been captured by anyone other than American troops or intelligence agencies using state-of-the-art methods and the utmost diligence. The fact that we had hundreds of people incarcerated based on the word of bounty hunters and warlords stunned me.

After reading about Gitmo, I had no doubt that some of the men I was guarding were guilty as hell and dangerous to America, but I no longer believed that all of them were criminals. One of the reasons I joined the military was because of my belief in the laws and principles of my country. I didn't believe people, or institutions, were infallible. If we stripped away all due process and rights for the individual, there was no way to correct if we locked up the wrong guy. How could we be sure all the people handed to us by bounty hunters and warlords were anti-American terrorists? As much as I hated terrorists, I didn't believe we should strip them of every right or treat them like animals.

As I turned over questions in my mind about Gitmo and my role as a guard, I started to miss the men in my squad. Strange as it must sound, by the end of my week in Baltimore, I couldn't wait to get back to Gitmo. When my friend Bill, whom I'd been staying with, dropped me off at the airport, he joked about how distant I'd been. "Good riddance," he said. "You're a waste of fine beer and cheap women. I hope you have more fun back at your prison with the terrorists."

CHAPTER 13

———◆———

Return to Gitmo

My whole squad commandeered a van and drove down to the ferry to pick me up when I came back. They were excited to tell me about all the changes that had happened since I'd left. It was as if I'd been gone a year. Colonel Bumgarner had been abruptly relieved of his command, though nobody in our command said why. His replacement, Colonel Wade Dennis, had made dramatic changes.

First, Colonel Dennis had reprimanded Captain Drake for numerous complaints from the inspector general related to bias and unfairness in our company. The Army Inspector General's Office investigates allegations of misconduct within the army. Interestingly, the majority of such complaints, more than thirty, had been filed by guys who weren't in my mostly black squad; other white and Hispanic soldiers had complained that Drake favored his cronies above others. Under pressure from Colonel Dennis, the captain completely restructured command of the company, firing his first sergeant, two platoon sergeants, and a platoon leader. This sweeping change seemed to vindicate complaints we'd had since Fort Lewis.

But one of the most significant changes came about as a direct result of the US Supreme Court ruling that shut down the military commissions at Gitmo. Captain Drake's favored platoon could no longer serve as guards at the commission hearings, a cushy job. Our new colonel ordered Drake to rotate these soldiers into our guard and QRF duties inside Camp America. The influx of these extra bodies dramatically changed our schedule. We could now work four days on, two days off. Guard duty inside the camps also became a lot easier, because in addition to getting two days off for every four we served, Colonel Dennis ordered Captain Drake to allow us to use the new air-conditioned metal towers instead of the old wooden ones. Being cool and comfortable actually made it easier to stay alert—not harder, as Drake had predicted. Everybody was really happy. Colonel Dennis had come in and fixed things in just a couple of days.

In the van, everybody was talking a mile a minute. I felt good, because I realized these guys missed me as much as I missed them. We went to Subway, and all they wanted to know was which girls I had hooked up with. I told them that every time I got laid, I shouted PFC Vasquez's name. They all cracked up.

I didn't want to ruin their fantasies with the truth that I'd spent the whole time in the library. Despite my changed perception of Gitmo, I felt calm. On the flight back, I had reached a conclusion: much of the big picture was above my pay grade. It wasn't my job to determine whether the things that happened at Gitmo were right or wrong. I would let the Supreme Court and media figure that out. My trip to Baltimore had shown me that no one seemed to question the story put out that the three detainees had died in their cells by suicide. My commanders had told their story to the world, and people seemed to believe it. What could I do?

The night I got back to Camp America, Staff Sergeant Hayes told me that NCIS investigators had come down and were looking into the detainee deaths. This gave me some confidence that the military cared about what really happened to those men. But as the days and weeks passed, no investigator with the NCIS or any other agency questioned me or the men in the towers. Our job that night had been to watch the very block where the detainees had hanged themselves. In any other investigation, we would have been witnesses. But in the deaths at Gitmo, which had the full attention of the government and world, some other standard seemed to apply.

Again, I pushed my concerns out of my mind. I had to move on. I wanted to be the best team leader I could be, for my men and for my squad leader, Staff Sergeant Hayes.

I was at ACP Roosevelt one evening my first week back when the white van appeared in the exit lane. I didn't recognize the navy escorts inside from the night of June 9, but as they pulled closer, I felt like a snake was uncoiling in my stomach. The van wasn't required to stop. I waved it through as it approached, but the driver halted next to me and rolled down his window. I looked at him, and he smiled. "How are you guys doing tonight?"

"Keeping cool," I said.

"We're coming back through in about half an hour. You or your men want us to pick up any coffee from McDonald's?"

I looked up at my guys and asked if they wanted any outside coffee. They said no, so I thanked the navy escorts and waved them through. The escorts acted like regular Joes. Who was I to accuse them of being involved in detainee deaths or a cover-up? Letting go of the past was as easy as waving them through.

* * *

In late August, after months of relative calm, I started to see an uptick in navy guards and detainees shouting at one another. The command had started pulling manpower away from our company and, I believed, from the navy guard units.

For weeks after the riot and then the three detainee deaths, senior NCOs and officers circulated through the camps all the time. Their focus seemed to shift to other matters, including a new secret camp that had been dubbed Strawberry Fields. The government had built a secret detention facility outside Camp America for a small group of high-value detainees that the CIA was sending to Gitmo. This group, which we were told numbered fourteen, included Khalid Sheikh Mohammed. The Sheikh, a high-ranking Al Qaeda member, had led the terror group's propaganda efforts from 1999 until 2001. He was a fiery

Islamic militant described as the "architect" of the September 11, 2001, terror attacks by the *9/11 Commission Report*, the official account of the events that led to the assault. He had been captured in a joint operation of the CIA and the Pakistani Inter-Services Intelligence Agency in Rawalpindi, Pakistan, in 2003 where he was held in CIA custody. However, by 2006, Mohammed was transferred to military detention and promptly sent to Gitmo. Under enhanced interrogation, he confessed to plotting not only the 9/11 attacks, but also carrying out the murder of *The Wall Street Journal*'s South Asia Bureau Chief, Daniel Pearl, masterminding Richard Reid's attempt to destroy an airliner using a "shoe bomb," and numerous other offenses reaching as far back as the 1993 World Trade Center bombing.

A special Marine Corps security team arrived to supervise this other facility, but many soldiers and sailors were pulled from Camp America to work there, too. The new facility, which we were told about in a top-secret briefing in case we had to respond to an incident there, was located in another part of the island, away from Camp No. The problem was that as soon as they cut manpower even a little and reduced the amount of supervision in the camps, the navy guards started acting up again.

I wasn't alone in observing increased tensions in the camps. I was on duty at ACP Roosevelt one day late in the summer when I heard via our radio that there was a disturbance involving some of my guys. Staff Sergeant Hayes was the NCO in charge of the towers that day, a step down from being the SOG. Hayes had passed an abuse complaint from a tower guard to a senior navy NCO in charge of the guards inside the cell blocks.

At the end of our shift, Staff Sergeant Hayes pulled our squad aside for a briefing. It turned out that Private Vasquez had reported an incident of abuse to him and that he'd reported it up the chain. As a result, several navy guards were threatening to jump Vasquez and the sergeant. In all my years in corrections, I had never seen anyone threatened for doing his job. Listening to this, I got the sense that we were now living under prison conditions, as if we guards were now like inmates. The way that Staff Sergeant Hayes laid it out, our squad was now in a sort of gang war with a group of navy guards.

The problem had started a couple of hours into Vasquez's shift on Tower 12. Tower 12 was one of the older, open towers from which occupants could hear goings-on inside the cell block clear as a bell. Vasquez heard a guard and a detainee shouting at each other.

Looking inside the cell block, he saw a navy guard we all knew, a huge sailor everyone called Monster. He was gigantic, with the acne-pitted skin and the thick, Cro-Magnon brow of a steroid freak. We'd never had any problems with Monster in the past. Some of my guys had eaten with him at the chow hall, and he was able to put sentences together and use cutlery without injuring himself. But on this day, according to PFC Vasquez, Monster was screwing around with a detainee. As Vasquez looked on, Monster stood outside the detainee's cell squirting him with water from a plastic water bottle and calling him "sand nigger." The detainee had been pounding on the wire barrier and shouting, "Fuck you!"

Vasquez did not know what had started this, but for a good half hour, Monster kept returning to the detainee's cell and taunting him. Finally, Monster opened the cell door, knocked down the detainee, and kicked him on the ground before letting himself back out of the cell.

Vasquez hadn't seen the detainee do anything to provoke Monster into entering his cell. It was always possible the detainee had spit at him or thrown urine or feces. But whatever the detainee had done, or not done, there was no excuse for a guard to taunt him or enter his cell and give him a beating. After six months of the island, the private had had enough. He logged the assault in his tower book and called it in to Hayes.

The sergeant followed the SOP and relayed his report to a senior navy NCO in charge of the cell block. While Vasquez watched, the NCO showed up, entered the cell block, and questioned Monster and the other guards on duty.

We later found out that the guards all swore nothing had happened and that Private Vasquez had made up his accusation. The NCO accepted their claims and violated the SOP by identifying Vasquez and Drake as the complainants.

A few hours later, navy guards ran out in the yard and threw rocks and full water bottles at Vasquez in the tower. Staff Sergeant Hayes came down into the yard from his tower, and they had a standoff during which navy guards accused him and Specialist Vasquez of being rats. They vowed that as soon as they could, they would jump my guys and beat the crap out of them.

Staff Sergeant Hayes had tried to use the proper SOPs to report a complaint, and it had backfired so dramatically that my squad decided to keep this problem in-house. We didn't want to involve command again. We all agreed to stick together and watch one another's backs. We always spent our time together anyway, but from now on, neither Hayes nor Vasquez would take a step anywhere in camp without the rest of us.

Staff Sergeant Hayes had always tried to deal with problems by having us focus on being the best we could be and avoiding confrontation. PFC Vasquez's decision to log an abuse complaint probably went against Hayes's personal philosophy, but he never second-guessed Vasquez. As the private's superior that day, he could have talked him out of it or dragged his feet passing it up the chain. But he was unhesitating in backing him up. Even now that it had blown up in our faces, he never once questioned Vasquez.

Of course, the rest of us gave José endless crap the next few weeks as we stayed on his ass. "Of all the guys to report, you had to pick Monster. What the hell's wrong with you?"

The incident resolved itself after Monster received a promotion. We reasoned that moving up in rank gave him more to lose if he jumped one of us and got caught committing an assault. His promotion also typified how things worked. Not only did Monster's supervisor discount Private Vasquez's report, but he also promoted the offending guard.

*   *   *

Soon Staff Sergeant Hayes was transferred to top-secret duty involving the high-value detainees kept outside the camp. In his absence, the other team leader, Sergeant Pitman, and I shared leadership of the squad. Technically speaking, Hayes remained the nominal squad leader, so Pitman and I took turns in the role of NCO in charge.

One such day in early February when I was the NCO, our squad was serving as the QRF. We were inside Camp 5, the special stand-alone camp outside Delta. Camp 5 was an enclosed, air-conditioned facility that held detainees with mental issues or physical disabilities. Since the riots, the QRF was ordered to spend its standby time circulating through the cell blocks. While walking through, we heard a fracas going on outside a cell. A couple of navy third class petty officers—the equivalent rank of army specialists—were shouting at a detainee on the other side of a door. They were trying to get him to slide his wrists out through the "bean hole" (the small opening in the cell door) so they could flex-cuff him, open the door, and extract him for a cell search. But the detainee inside was screaming, "Fuck you!" and throwing out bits of food or garbage or feces—you never knew which—through the mesh window.

As I walked closer, I could see that the detainee was of average height, in his late thirties, and balding. On the floor next to him was a prosthetic leg. The man was seated on his bed, crying, as he raged at the guards. When I came up beside the guards, he went silent for a moment and glared at me.

"What's going on?" I asked the two guards.

One of them said, "This detainee, he's an asshole. He always gives us a hard time when we search his cell." Then, he added, "Once we get him out, he's a lot of fun. We make him put on his prosthetic leg and shackle him, and we make him try to walk. It's fucking hilarious."

The other guard said, "We'll kick his leg out from under him, and he'll flop all over on the ground. All you do is tap it."

I looked at these guards, thinking, "No wonder the guy won't come out of his cell. You're the assholes, not him." I addressed the first guard who'd spoken to me. "How old are you?"

"Twenty-three."

"Been in the navy long?"

"About two years."

"How long have you been at Gitmo?"

"Maybe four months."

I turned to the other guard. "You think this is funny, too?"

He nodded.

"You know what I think?" I said. "I think you're a bunch of assholes."

My squad started to giggle, but I stopped them. The truth is, I'd demeaned myself by talking to the navy guards like that. My anger had gotten the better of me. I tried to ratchet it down a notch. I lowered my voice to the navy guards and said, "Would you want anyone in your family treated that way? We don't know what this man's crimes are. We have to be professional. If you guys keep riling him up, my QRF is going to have to extract him, and we don't want to do that."

"Okay, Sergeant," the guard said. His voice was respectful, but he and his buddies were pissed.

One of them said, "Maybe you can talk him into complying."

They backed away, waiting for me to fail. Now I'd really gotten myself into it. I walked over to the mesh window on the cell and leaned close. I tried to effect a neutral tone. I looked at the detainee and asked, "What's your name?"

The man stopped his crying. I asked for his name again, and in English he shouted his three-digit identity number given to all detainees.

"Okay. My name is Joe." Revealing my name was a violation of SOPs, but I reasoned it was less of a violation than taunting a detainee. What the hell. The detainee looked surprised. Once I had his attention, I said, "Sir, you're not a number, you're a person. Now, what's your name?"

He laughed angrily. "I am not human. You treat me like an animal."

"Sir, I just gave you my name. I haven't treated you poorly. Now, what's your name?"

"My name is al-Gazzar."

"Thank you. Mr. al-Gazzar, here's the situation: these guards want to search your cell, and if you don't let them, I'm going to have to come in with my men and make you let them. I don't want to do that, so why don't you let them in?"

"Because if I do, they will knock me down and make me do tricks for them like an animal."

Behind my back, one of the navy guards said, "He's lying. We don't do anything outside the SOPs."

I turned to the guards and said, "I'm glad to hear that." To the detainee, I said, "Mr. al-Gazzar, if you cooperate with them and let them flex-cuff you and escort you out, I will stand here and make sure it goes fast."

The detainee stared at me. I added, "Look, if you don't do this, I'll have to come in and pull you out. It's my job, but I don't want to have to do that. Mr. al-Gazzar, please put on your prosthetic leg, stand up, and put your arms through the bean hole."

The detainee put his leg on and stood up. I took flex cuffs from a navy guard and put them on him myself, and then escorted him out.

The guards finished their search in a few minutes, found nothing, and I escorted him back to his cell. "Thank you for your cooperation, Mr. al-Gazzar," I said, as I left him in there. The man looked at me with fear, like he was waiting for some worse trick or humiliation.

After we shut the door and I removed his flex cuffs, the guards looked at me like they wanted to kill me. "I'm not trying to show you up here," I said. "It's just easier this way."

After our shift ended, I was called into my company headquarters office. My platoon sergeant told me that the navy guards had complained about me interfering. I started to defend myself, and he cut me off. "Hickman, we're all in this cesspool together. Don't make waves. We've got three weeks to go, and we're off this stinking island."

Much as I felt I was right, he was probably more practical. What good would it do if I filed a complaint against the guards? The complaint wouldn't go anywhere, and if it did, it would probably just make them more frustrated and take out more aggression on the detainees.

One man wasn't going to change the system.

*   *   *

On March 10, 2007, my unit rode the ferry on our way out. Watching the rolling hills slide past, it was a pretty view, like it was when we came there.

We had already turned in our electronics to have them scanned for secret files by the NSA, but when we reached the airfield, the navy security patrol did another search. On the flight out, we boarded a big commercial jet. We made our way to Fort Dix in New Jersey for four days of processing and then took buses to our National Guard base in Frederick, Maryland.

It was kind of cool because the state police came alongside and escorted our buses in. The police cars had flags on them, and when we got into the base, it was like a celebration. Most of the younger guys had their moms or girlfriends and family members waiting for them. After fifteen months together, we didn't need to make big emotional good-byes. Most guys just ran off to their loved ones.

From my experience, I knew that having family come just slowed you down. Everybody would start introducing his loved ones to everyone else's, and it could go on for hours. I just wanted to get the heck out of there.

I had my buddy Bill Meyers pick me up. When I saw his beat-up blue Camaro, I just zipped away. I climbed in and said, "Let's get the fuck out of here."

It was over.

CHAPTER 14

Stress Dreams

WITHIN days of getting back, I put in my paperwork to remain on full-time active duty in the National Guard. Despite everything, I loved the military. Other guys were the same way. Specialist Stewart transferred into the army and went to Iraq for the 2007 surge, as did a couple of others from our squad.

I put in for a combat unit, but instead I was assigned to an Air Cavalry brigade in Annapolis, Maryland. The command promoted me to staff sergeant and made me a readiness NCO, responsible for training other guys going overseas.

I stayed with my friend Bill for a couple weeks after I got my new assignment with the Air Cavalry. Bill not only did mixed martial arts fighting but was also a pretty excellent guitar player. He'd gotten serious with a band, and one night I went out to a show they did at a bar in Pasadena, Maryland.

There were a bunch of kids there from Loyola University Maryland, and after my buddy's band played, he introduced me to some and told them I was in the military. Everybody asked if I'd been to Iraq or Afghanistan. When I told them I had just come from Gitmo, two kids got very upset. "Isn't that where they're torturing prisoners?" the girl asked.

"Well, I didn't torture anybody," I said.

A whole bunch of them gathered around. They didn't think they were being offensive, but one kid started talking about the "American gulag" at Gitmo, another was calling us "Nazis," and a bunch were quoting Noam Chomsky, the linguist/philosopher who has long been critical of US foreign policy, about our empire.

I got frustrated with these kids. I told them that people who said bad things about Gitmo might not be all wrong, but it wasn't as clear-cut as they made it out to be. One kid kept asking, "How clear does evil have to be for us to call it evil?"

I just said, "Really? That's a strong statement. How long did you serve in the military? Have you been to Gitmo?"

One of his friends said, "I didn't have to go to Abu Ghraib to know how fucked up that is."

I really wanted to flatten that kid's face, but that would have just proven their point that I was some kind of Neanderthal thug. The worst part was that these college kids were right. The news reporters didn't even see the tiniest fraction of how bad it was down there, and Americans like these college kids were outraged. What would they say if they'd known what I'd seen?

That encounter encouraged me to bury my unpleasant recollections of Gitmo. I reasoned that if the press ever heard about the so-called suicides and the abuse I witnessed, it would probably be misused.

*   *   *

I found an apartment in Baltimore and was settling in comfortably to my new post when I came home one night—nearly three months since my return from Gitmo—and turned on the news. There was a story about a new detainee suicide. His name was Abdul Rahman Ma'ath Thafir al Amri, a citizen of Saudi Arabia. The media reported his death the same way as it had the others. The newsman said that the detainee had hanged himself in his cell in Camp 5 and that guards discovered him and tried to revive him. The news reported that Camp 5 was for high-value detainees. Maybe it had changed since I was there a few months earlier, but in my time, Camp 5 was simply for disabled or mentally unstable detainees. But the reporters seemed to think the fact that al Amri had been a high-value bad guy better explained his suicide.

I never had any information about this detainee or the particulars of his death, but watching the news unfurl, I was struck by how the broadcasters made the alleged suicide sound like it could happen so easily. They didn't seem to question the story at all. I wondered, "How could this happen again in Gitmo?" Our ratio of guards to detainees was approximately three to one. In the Maryland jails I worked in—which were typical of those across America—our ratio was the opposite: approximately one guard per five or six inmates. Gitmo's guard-to-detainee ratio was public knowledge, but I didn't see any reporters saying, "That's strange. They reported three similar suicides less than a year earlier, and now it happened again. How could this go on with so many guards watching them?"

Maybe the problem with Gitmo was that it had become a litmus test of patriotism. I had seen what the issue meant to those college kids. To them, Gitmo was a sign that we were Nazis. To people who leaned more toward Fox News, it was like we were doing the Lord's work down there. No one could just look at the problem and study it on its own merits. Maybe the extreme opinions about Gitmo scared the mainstream media from digging deeper into the suicide reports.

The night I watched that news broadcast, I couldn't sleep. I went on my computer and started reading more about Gitmo. I didn't find anything new, but my mind was spinning. I showed up for work the next day without a wink of sleep.

For the next few weeks, I couldn't sleep. When I did finally shut my eyes, I began having nightmares. That summer I got high ratings on my job, but I really wasn't myself. I would work out like crazy in my free time to make myself tired, but it didn't work. On the job, I had a short fuse.

The anger that I'd felt right after the deaths at Gitmo came back. And the only way I could work it out was by training my guys for the

Air Cav. I was in charge of keeping the unfit guys in shape. Not all of them were physically unfit; they weren't malingerers. Some couldn't deploy because they had legal problems such as DUIs. One guy was waiting for surgery to donate his kidney to his brother. But I'd show up for work and smoke their asses in physical training drills.

If any of them ever looked at me sideways, it was on. I'd have them all get down in push-up position and hold that stance for twenty-five minutes. If any of them touched his knees to the ground, I ordered all of them to start over again and add more time. I was hoping that someone would try to take a swing at me, but no one did. Most of them had complete muscle failure at the end of my nastier sessions.

I had never been this martinet kind of drill instructor before, but suddenly I was running training like it was my own private Abu Ghraib camp. The funny part was that my superiors thought I was doing a great job keeping the men tough. I'm surprised none of them complained, but I probably seemed so psycho, they were afraid.

By the fall of 2007, I started calling some of the guys from my old squad. I needed someone to vent to, someone who understood and who had seen the same things that I had. I needed to know if I was right. José Vasquez was back in the civilian world working as a private investigator in South Carolina. When I reached him, he brought up Camp No and the white van. He also remembered Colonel Bumgarner's briefing telling us that we all knew the detainees died with cloths stuffed in their throats but that we would hear something different in the news. I spoke to Specialist Foster and five other men who were with me in the towers and at the checkpoint in Camp 1, to see if they remembered the white van's arrival at the medical clinic at ten thirty. Not all of them recalled the van's three trips out of the camp one hour earlier. But all of them were as certain as they had been the night of the deaths that no injured or dying detainees were brought from Camp 1 Alpha block to the clinic. On these points, at least, I had not lost my marbles.

I had grown up thinking that everyone in the media was like Woodward and Bernstein, taking on the most powerful men and institutions in America and challenging a president in their relentless search for the truth. As a lifelong conservative, I had the sneaking suspicion that the media was, if anything, overzealous in its challenges to the authority and credibility of our government. I was stunned at how uncritically the nation's toughest reporters and news outlets accepted the story put forth in the NCIS report. When I read the first accounts in the press, I finally understood that I was completely alone.

———◆———

CHAPTER 15

NCIS

Guard Lapses Cited in Gitmo Suicides

As the lights flickered off above them, more than two dozen detainees began to raise their voices in prayer and other songs, a din the guards dismissed as harmless. Three of the detainees furtively stuffed water bottles and toilet paper under their bedsheets to create the illusion of sleeping bodies, and they each strung up walls of blue blankets in their metal mesh cells, seeking cover from their captors' glances.

Then, with strips of white sheets, T-shirts and towels wound into nooses, the three detainees in Guantánamo Bay's Camp 1, Block Alpha, hid behind the blankets and hanged themselves, their toes dangling inches above the floor while their bodies became blue and rigid. For hours, the guards failed to notice the first deaths to occur at the controversial U.S. military detention facility. . . .

Contained in more than 3,000 pages of U.S. military investigative documents, medical records, autopsies and statements from guards and detainees is a rare view inside the detention center at Guantánamo Bay, Cuba, and one of the worst episodes of its six-year history. The documents from the NCIS investigation, which

will be released under the Freedom of Information Act, were obtained Friday by The *Washington Post*. . . .

Investigators found that guards had become lax on certain rules
because commanders wanted to reward the more compliant detainees, giving them extra T-shirts, blankets and towels. Detainees were
allowed to hang such items to dry, or to provide privacy while using
the toilet, but were not supposed to be able to obscure their cells
while sleeping.

Guards told officials that it was not unusual to see blankets hanging in the cells and that they did not think twice when they passed
several cells on the night of June 9, 2006, with blankets strung
through the wire mesh. Authorities believe the men probably
hanged themselves around 10 p.m., but they were not discovered
until shortly after midnight on June 10. . . .

—Excerpted from the article by Josh White, *The Washington Post*,
August 24, 2008

The media had been parroting the narrative put out by the military
since Admiral Harris's first press conference, but it wasn't until the
conclusions of the NCIS report were leaked in the late summer of 2008
that the government's story was laid out in its entirety. To accept that
the three men bound their ankles and wrists, gagged themselves, put
on face masks (a detail I'd never heard before but was reported later),
and then hanged themselves at exactly the same time and without
being detected for more than two hours required an almost complete
ignorance of the physical layout of the cell blocks, the SOPs followed
by guards, and events at Gitmo in the weeks before they died. The government story, as it was conveyed by the media, read like the plot of
a Hollywood prison movie, where inmates kept pets, operated secret
distilleries, and dug tunnels. It was the stuff of fantasy. I had spent years
working in corrections and never saw anything like that. Three simultaneous suicides could have easily occurred in those imaginary prisons,
but the image of Gitmo as presented in the NCIS narrative bore no
relationship to the place I knew.

Central to the NCIS's narrative was that the three men who died benefitted from a generally lax enforcement of rules and also received specific rewards as "compliant detainees." This was absurd. The riot at Gitmo, which took place fewer than three weeks before the deaths, had been widely reported, as was the closing of Camp 4, where compliant detainees had been held. All guards had redoubled their efforts to monitor detainees and force compliance with all the rules following the riot. As part of that effort, detainees formerly termed compliant were moved into areas of harsher control, such as Alpha block. Cells were searched every day, and privileges such as the use of an extra blanket or possession of a spare T-shirt were revoked.

What made the NCIS account even more nonsensical was the fact that the three men who died had been involved in the hunger strike. Even if there had been detainees receiving preferential treatment somewhere at Gitmo during those tense days in early June, hunger strikers would not have been among them. They were being removed from their cells at least once a day for forced feedings, and because a hunger strike was by definition a form of attempted suicide, they were put under strict watch for any signs that they might be trying to kill themselves by other means. No one engaging in a hunger strike was ever given extra blankets or towels with which to hang himself.

The NCIS said that the detainees constructed dummies, bindings, gags, face masks, and nooses from their clothes and bedding, with enough left over to cover the mesh walls of their cells and hide their activities from view. Few if any journalists asked how much bedding and other materials—including water bottles and toilet paper (for stuffing the dummies)—would have been required for the effort. Nor did they examine how much of these materials detainees would have had available to them.

The NCIS story also described the detainees hanging for nearly two hours with their feet inches above the floor. To prevent guards from noticing this would have necessitated blocking views into the cells from floor to ceiling—or at least the areas where each of the three men was hanging. The fact that, according to the NCIS, the men built dummies suggested that they would have left at least part of the cell walls uncovered. No one explained or diagrammed how in a six-by-eight-foot cell with walls made entirely of mesh a hanging body could be concealed from view without completely covering at least three of the walls.

To be fair, journalists may have been more credulous about the findings of the NCIS report because some of them did not understand the open design of the cells. Many who came to the island were shown Camp 4, with its soccer field and larger communal cells, where the suicides, as described in the NCIS report, would have been easier to pull off. At the time, Google Images and other search sites presented photos released by the Pentagon and by reporters that showed mostly enclosed cells from Camp 5, not the open cells in Alpha block.

Each Alpha cell block consisted of a single eight-foot-wide hallway walked by the guards. There were twenty such cells on one side and nineteen on the other. (The space where the twentieth cell would have been on one side was occupied by a bathroom for the guards.) Because the walls of the cells were made of mesh, and because the beds, sinks, and toilets were low to the ground, a guard standing in the hallway had clear, unobstructed views into the cells from both the front walls and from the side walls. In other words, you didn't have to stand directly in front of a cell to look inside. You could stand by a neighboring cell and look sideways two or three cell blocks in either direction. The open mesh walls were used to give guards clear views into the cells from multiple angles. This was especially true when an occupied cell was flanked by empty cells on either side.

As of June 9, Alpha block held just twenty-seven detainees, and, according to the NCIS report, each of the three men who died occupied a cell flanked by empty ones. We did this to increase the detainees' sense of isolation and to make it easier to watch them. Their enhanced isolation further belied the claims that these men were the beneficiaries of lax rules due to their compliance. The fact that the cells on either side were empty meant that to cover their walls and block guards from watching them as they hanged themselves, they would have had to cover the six feet of wall space facing the corridor, as well as their two eight-foot-long side walls. Had the adjacent cells been occupied, the NCIS might have been able to argue that their neighbors helped in the effort to cover their shared side walls, but this was not the case. To cover their hallway-facing wall and side walls enough to prevent navy guards from seeing anything in the cells would have required 176 square feet of material—equivalent to four standard-issue sheets or blankets or twenty-two towels.

But the NCIS also reported that the men fabricated dummies. This meant that they must have somehow left their cells partially open. In other words, they covered a portion of the cell from floor to ceiling to prevent guards from seeing them hanging, with their toes inches from the floor, but left views onto their beds open so that guards could be fooled by the dummies. No account I found actually diagrammed this to show how it might have been possible, but giving the NCIS the benefit of the doubt, perhaps detainees covered only 50 percent of their walls. This still would have required the use of two bedsheets or blankets, or eleven towels.

The NCIS report stated that the men tore their sheets, their T-shirts, and their towels into strips to fabricate their nooses and bindings. It also stated that the dummies they made had been placed under their bedsheets. The dummies themselves, according to the NCIS, had been stuffed full of toilet paper and water bottles to give them volume. The quantities of the materials required for all this was problematic. According to the written SOPs, each detainee was issued only one set of clothes, one towel, one bedsheet, and one blanket. In addition, they were permitted only one water bottle in their cells at a time and twenty-five sheets of toilet paper per day. Water bottles were tightly controlled because they were used as weapons—filled with urine, or with dirt, or with pebbles—to assault guards. During the more relaxed period in the camp prior to the May riot, compliant detainees were occasionally given one extra towel and an extra blanket. According to our SOPs, compliant detainees were theoretically permitted one small stretching mat—similar to a roll-up yoga mat—but I never saw these in the possession of any detainees except in Camp 4, which was, of course, closed at the time.

Some media accounts of the NCIS report suggested that the detainees had hoarded extra clothing or sheets. That might have been possible prior to the riot and hunger strike, but since the closing of Camp 4, most cells were being "tossed"—emptied out and searched—on a daily basis. As hunger strikers, the three men who died were extracted from their cells at least once a day for their forced feedings, during which time their cells would have been searched. I knew from my own experience inside Alpha block that even a quick visual search of a cell would have likely revealed a bundle of extra, hoarded clothing or fabrics.

Yet another factor made the notion of hoarding extremely unlikely: the three men who died had been moved into Alpha block seventy-two hours before their deaths. The cells had been clean and empty. They would have had almost no opportunities to hoard, to observe patterns of the guards' behavior, or to communicate and coordinate their simultaneous suicides.

Furthermore, journalists noted that detainees were permitted to hang towels and blankets on the cell walls in order to dry them or obtain a measure of privacy when using the toilet, but the SOPs regarding this were straightforward. Items could not be hung on the upper half of the cell walls, and they could be put up only for less than three hours. Even if the detainees had managed to accumulate enough fabric to cover their walls and beds, and to create nooses and dummies, it would have been very difficult to rip the sheets into "strips" the way the NCIS claimed they did. The detainees at Gitmo were all issued "correctional sheets," which met federal standards for tear resistance, meaning that they were very difficult to cut up. Even cutting correctional sheets with a sharp knife is a struggle. To claim, as the NCIS report apparently did, that three detainees in three separate cells tore their sheets into strips without using blades or other sharp objects was amazing. Not impossible, but tearing one sheet into strips by hand would have been a time-consuming endeavor. The NCIS timeline did not address this issue.

According to the NCIS, the guards in Alpha block made half-hourly reports that detainees were accounted for throughout the night, but with their views obscured by the materials on their walls and fooled by the dummies, they did not see the men hang themselves at about 10:00 that night, or notice the first of the three corpses until about 12:20. Five guards were on duty in the cell block, according to the NCIS. Five guards assigned to a single 120-foot-long hallway in order to watch twenty-seven men was a large number. The guards were required to check on each detainee every three minutes in addition to their half-hourly reports. By day, SOPs required the guards to ensure that none of the detainees was communicating between cells, practicing martial arts, or engaging in any other proscribed activity. At night, guards were required to make visual contact with each sleeping detainee and observe two things: motion indicating regular breathing; and skin—a hand, a foot, or the face uncovered by a blanket. If a guard could not verify that a detainee was breathing and see his skin, he was required to make a noise sufficient to awaken the detainee. These SOPs were designed specifically to prevent detainees from using dummies to fake their presence in their cells.

The narrative provided by the NCIS was not an impossible one—*if* each of the three men had been veritable Al Qaeda Houdinis able to (1) hoard materials; (2) fabricate them under the noses of guards into dummies and ropes; (3) partially cover their cells in ways that would make their hangings invisible to guards; (4) make dummies that presented the illusion of skin and breathing movements; and (5) like acrobats, climb onto their sinks or cots, shove rags deep into their throats, bind their feet, affix their necks to their nooses, tie masks over their faces, bind their hands, and then jump or fall from their perches—but silently so as not to attract the guards' attention. The odds against one detainee pulling this off seemed slim. The chances of three simultaneously achieving this goal without detection were exponentially more remote.

The NCIS's narrative might also have been possible if the guards on duty in Alpha block had permitted the three detainees to carry out numerous violations of the rules, from hoarding materials to covering their walls. The guards would have had to ignore their SOPs by not properly observing the detainees and submitting false half-hourly reports to their superior officers claiming that they had.

Part of my team's job was, of course, to monitor the navy guards. We saw nothing irregular in their behavior the night of the deaths, and during my entire time at Gitmo, our complaints about navy guards were never for laxness or dereliction but always for overzealous enforcement of rules, or monitoring detainees excessively as a means of stirring them up. One of the most stunning paradoxes of the NCIS report was that it was premised on navy guards' permitting numerous violations of the rules, yet did not specifically accuse any of the guards of dereliction. In fact, according to the report, none of the guards or any of his direct superiors was punished for any infraction whatsoever.

Admiral Harris, the top navy officer at Gitmo, not only kept his position but was promoted soon after, becoming commander of the navy's Sixth Fleet and leading the military operation to oust Qaddafi in Libya, then becoming assistant to the chairman of the Joint Chiefs of Staff. The lack of punishment or any type of censure was remarkable. The military had what was called a "zero-tolerance" policy for errors. When a ship ran aground, the captain was typically removed, even if the accident was attributed to faulty navigation charts or an act of nature. The deaths of the three detainees were a global event, described in Admiral Harris's statements and then in the NCIS report as arising from a string of preventable errors and SOP violations. Yet no one was held accountable.

According to the NCIS, no video evidence existed of the detainees' actions in their cells. It was true, so far as I knew, that video cameras inside the cell blocks were not aimed directly into the cells. But they did offer complete views of the hallways and captured the actions of the guards. Such videos would have shown definitively whether guards were stopping by the detainees' cells every three minutes for their visual inspections. Such videos would have also shown guards responding to the detainees after the hangings were discovered. But such videos were never mentioned in the NCIS report.

In addition, there were no photographs of the dummies and of the cells following the detainees' deaths. After Admiral Harris declared the deaths "acts of asymmetrical warfare," I expected that the detainees' cells and the props and tools they used to carry out their deeds would have been photographed, diagrammed, and studied like elements of a crime scene. But no such photos were mentioned, either.

Most telling was the fact that NCIS investigators never interviewed me or my men on duty in the towers in Camp Delta even though we were tasked with observing the walkway between Alpha block and the medical clinic—the only route to the clinic. But to reporters unaware of the command structure at Gitmo, the layout of the camps, and the duties of the tower guards, the omissions of our eyewitness statements were not easily noticed.

Reporters who analyzed the NCIS's findings and judged them comprehensive and satisfactory did so on the basis of summaries of the report. The actual NCIS report, more than three thousand pages of documents, had not yet been released. Back then, I hadn't read the whole report and could not prove that the narrative was impossible, but I knew that it was certainly incredible. Yet no accounts I came across in the mainstream media questioned the government's account for its numerous inconsistencies and the improbable circumstances it required. None paid attention to its omissions, from absence of evidence, to lack of punishment for those responsible for the gross derelictions necessary for the narrative to have worked. Some journalists on the left assailed the NCIS for supporting the government line, but their attacks were as baseless as the mainstream media's support. It was as if all reporters, confronted by the complexities of Gitmo and the opacity of procedures there, just threw their hands up and allowed the government to dictate the stories they wrote.

One couldn't completely blame the media for accepting the government's narrative. The story of the Gitmo suicides seemed very similar to the 9/11 attacks in which Arab men used suicide as an element in their inventive and well-coordinated attack. Admiral Harris's assertions that the June 9 deaths at Gitmo were committed as acts of "asymmetrical warfare" did not come out of thin air. As improbable as the details were in the government's version of the suicides, the general idea that several detainees would kill themselves to undermine American interests made sense.

It was possible that the full NCIS report, when it came out in its entirety, would fill in the gaps and smooth over the inconsistencies that I had found. The tenor of media reports indicated that journalists overwhelmingly accepted the leaked summaries of the NCIS's finding. The three-thousand–page report itself would just be a sort of afterthought. But by the late fall of 2008, the issue of the detainees' deaths was moving into the nation's rearview mirror. President Obama had won election in part on his promise to shut down Gitmo within a year. This dark, confusing chapter in our history was to be closed forever. The public and our political classes were moving on.

But I wasn't. I had been freed—mostly—from the nightmares and anxiety I'd suffered. What remained was a simple desire to reconcile what I'd witnessed at Gitmo the night of the deaths with the government's story. I had enormous advantages compared to reporters. I had lived in Camp America for a year, I had been inside the cell block, and, a few weeks after the deaths, inside the cells where the men were alleged to have died. I was intimately familiar with the SOPs at Gitmo and had more than a decade of military experience outside of the camps. I had handled detainees and spent countless hours watching them in their cells. I'd fought them. I had touched the bedding they were alleged to have torn and fabricated into ropes. I, of course, could not see directly into the cells at the time of the alleged suicides, but I was fewer than two hundred feet away, a witness to the alarms raised, the reactions of the personnel on the ground, and the fact that the three men were not carried from Alpha block to the medical clinic after midnight (or at any time that evening), as was claimed in the NCIS report. Most important of all, I was witness to three men being taken out of Alpha block hours before the suicides were reported. Were these the same men who died? If so, how did they die and why? Ultimately, I wanted to know if my government was involved in a cover-up. I knew I needed help. I needed to take my story to a professional. I found him at Seton Hall University Law School.

CHAPTER 16

―――◆―――

Seton Hall

My assignment with the Air Cavalry concluded shortly before Barack Obama's election in November 2008. I had received stellar performance evaluations and was chosen to become an army recruiter in Green Bay, Wisconsin. Recruiting was a plum job in the military because the hours were good and it wasn't physically demanding. It was also one of the most rewarding assignments. As a recruiter, I was able to help young people find options in the military that would change their lives for the better.

Yes, I still believed that the military was a life-changing, positive experience, and yes, I was leading a sort of double life. I still believed in the principles of the military that I had signed up for as a young man: protecting the country, defending the Constitution, duty, and honor. I believed that the young people I was helping to recruit were being offered the greatest reward there was: to serve one's country. But I had lost faith in the command. My initial reading of the NCIS report suggested that the agency itself—one of the most venerated investigative services of the federal government and the home of hard-nosed, honest investigators ready to kick ass in the name of truth, justice, and the American Way—had been deceived or co-opted into perpetuating a cover-up.

At the same time, I felt it was my duty to pursue my own investigation into the NCIS report. To challenge the Naval Criminal Investigative Service was tantamount to heresy. Contradicting senior military commanders like Admiral Harris and possibly top civilian leaders perhaps as high up as Secretary of Defense Donald Rumsfeld could destroy my career. Inadvertently disclosing secrets could subject me to prison. I would also be going against the media and running the risk of public ridicule. I didn't take any of this lightly, but I saw no other way. As a young marine, I was trained to charge into enemy machine-gun fire if necessary. I felt that pursuing the truth no matter the obstacles was just as important as defending my country. It was a matter of honor.

I was still open to the possibility that I was wrong about what had happened at Gitmo, and that somehow I was missing key information or perspectives that would prove the NCIS report was right. I just wanted to know the truth.

As far back as that ten-day leave in July 2006 when I first began researching Gitmo, I wondered to whom I might tell my story. At the time, I still believed that military investigators would interview me about what I had seen the night the deaths occurred, but given my experience after the May riot, I was not entirely optimistic about how they would respond. And I was not sure that I could go to a reporter without more evidence.

I had come across the work of law professor Mark Denbeaux, the director of Seton Hall University Law School's Center for Policy and Research. In February 2006 the Center for Policy and Research issued its *Report on Guantanamo Detainees: A Profile of 517 Detainees Through Analysis of Department of Defense Data*. That study was the first to determine that only 5 percent of the detainees at Gitmo had been captured by US forces and only 8 percent were Al Qaeda fighters. What was more interesting than the report's findings was its underlying methodology. As the title of the center's paper suggested, Denbeaux's researchers had relied entirely on reports and other data compiled and released by the military. Unlike reporters, they weren't mixing in opinion, anonymous sources, or information that the government disputed. They took the government's own data at face value and used it as the basis of their investigation. The results were surprising. Until the Seton Hall Center for Policy and Research released its study, few had asked where the detainees at Gitmo had come from. In our training at Fort Lewis, our commanders, like our political leaders and members of the press, spoke of the detainees with the assumption that we had somehow caught them in the act of being terrorists. Denbeaux's report demolished those assumptions.

By the fall of 2008, the Seton Hall Center had produced a half dozen more reports. The paper that interested me most was released on August 21, 2006, titled *June 10th Suicides at Guantánamo: Government Words and Deeds Compared.* The report contained nothing that questioned the suicides themselves, but it pointed out broader contradictions of logic, as well as lies made by Pentagon spokesmen, including Admiral Harris. After the deaths, Pentagon spokesmen had told the media, as well as members of Congress, that none of the men who died had lawyers. The implication was that the men who died were among a group of die-hard resisters who refused to participate in the commission's process. But the Seton Hall researchers, working under Denbeaux's direction, found numerous government reports and federal court filings that contradicted this. Not only did the detainees accept legal representation, but also their lawyers had registered with the government numerous complaints that the military had, in fact, denied them access. The Seton Hall report flatly contradicted Admiral Harris's statements that at the time of their deaths the three men were "dedicated jihadists" and "violent terrorists." Authorities at Gitmo had never categorized them as such, and one of them was scheduled to be released at the time of his death.

The paper also revealed more about the backgrounds of the men who died. Ali Abdullah Ahmed was a Yemeni, twenty-six years old when he died, having spent four years in captivity. Mani al-Utaybi, twenty-five at the time of his death, and Yasser al-Zahrani, twenty-two, were both Saudis.

Al-Zahrani was sixteen—or seventeen, depending on conflicting dates of birth—when he was captured by Afghan bounty hunters and turned over to US forces for a cash payment of an unspecified sum just weeks after the US invasion of Afghanistan began in late 2001. Al-Zahrani had fled his home in Saudi Arabia in July or August 2001 to join the Taliban. After his transfer to American forces in late 2001, he had openly admitted his allegiance to the Taliban, but he said he was unable to join the front-line fighters. Given his short time in Afghanistan and young age, his claims seemed credible. The authorities at Gitmo never obtained evidence that he'd fought US troops or even put up a fight when the Afghans captured him.

Al-Utaybi, the other Saudi, had been captured in Pakistan with three other men whom Pakistani authorities turned over to the United States on suspicion that they had been to a terrorist training camp. But authorities at Gitmo found only evidence that one of the four might have been to a terrorist camp and released two of them. Al-Utaybi had also been cleared and was on a list awaiting release, which was slated to take place a month before his death. US government spokesmen then stated that al-Utaybi had confessed to belonging to a terrorist organization, but as Denbeaux's Seton Hall report pointed out, the group he was affiliated with was a Muslim charity, Jama'at al Tablighi, a politically neutral organization that sought to preach to other Muslims the importance of enjoining good and rejecting evil. While many Muslim charities rightly fell under suspicion after the 9/11 attacks as fostering terrorist aims, the one al-Utaybi claimed to work with did not have such nefarious ties—which is probably why he had been cleared for release.

Of the three detainees, the US government claimed Ahmed, the Yemeni, was the most dangerous. He had been arrested by Pakistani authorities in a 2002 raid they'd launched on a college guest house—a sort of dormitory—suspected of being inhabited by students who were Al Qaeda sympathizers. After his death, US authorities described Ahmed to the media as a "mid- to high-level Al Qaeda operative" and stated that throughout his entire four years at Gitmo, he had been "noncompliant and hostile." The problem was, as the Seton Hall paper revealed, that during Ahmed's captivity, the government never presented any evidence to substantiate its claims that he had any Al Qaeda ties what-soever, let alone that he might have been a senior- or high-level opera-tive. In fact, in 2008, government sources admitted to the *Washington Post* that "there is no credible information to suggest Ahmed received terrorist-related training or is a member of the Al Qaeda network." Denbeaux's researchers pointed out that suspected mid- or high-level Al Qaeda members were never kept in Alpha block, or in Camps 1 or 2/3, where Ahmed had been held. If Ahmed was an Al Qaeda operative, he would have been kept in Camp 5 or in the unacknowledged facility where Khalid Sheikh Mohammed was held.

Another question struck me as I read the Seton Hall report. If Ahmed was an Al Qaeda member—one who, according to a govern-ment spokesman, had been "noncompliant and hostile" throughout his stay at Gitmo—why would he, as the NCIS report claimed, have been receiving lax oversight by guards and extra blankets as comfort items?

The Seton Hall report on the alleged suicides affected me in an-other way. I had already seen the names of the three men who died, but I'd never seen them with such question marks beside them. I began to wonder, "Who were they really? Bad guys dedicated to the destruction of America? Or knuckleheads in the wrong place at the wrong time?" They had not been picked up by US forces, so we were relying en-tirely on foreign services or operatives to define them as bad guys. Yet as *June 10th Suicides at Guantánamo* pointed out, not even the foreign allies who handed them over could provide any hard evidence that the men were up to no good. Al-Zahrani admitted after his capture that he had signed up to fight with the Taliban, but he did so at age sixteen, in July 2001, before the Taliban was openly at war with the United States. The other two appear to have been caught up in broad sweeps conducted by Pakistani intelligence services. I wondered if maybe they were just handed over after 9/11 to placate the Bush administration. Pakistan's government and intelligence services were well known for being highly unreliable—a notion supported by the fact that America had cleared al-Utaybi for release. It all seemed haphazard, as if the US authorities running the system didn't care whether the men received even the barest amount of justice, or even whether they were terrorists.

As I thought about the three dead men, I wondered if they were the same men I'd seen taken from Alpha block on the night of June 9. I'm not sure I could have even picked them out from a police lineup. I didn't have distinct memories of them. They were three Arab detainees in their midtwenties glimpsed from a hundred feet away. Yet I did think of their families. I wondered if the men's families had missed them and if they had believed the government's story.

It disturbed me that I had been caught up in a system that didn't seem to follow any rules and appeared to cover its actions with misinformation and lies. But why did the system work this way? Was there a method to its apparent madness?

As I went through the website for Seton Hall's Center for Policy and Research in the fall of 2008, I wondered if it would be tackling the complete, three-thousand-page NCIS report. I also wondered if Professor Denbeaux was someone I could trust to take my story to. Would he even be interested? According to the Seton Hall website, the Center for Policy and Research had been founded in 2006 to investigate government policies related to national security and intelligence matters. It also served to train law students, who worked as research fellows developing skills in what the law school called "pattern recognition, factual evaluation, and data analysis." As I understood it, the researchers at the center treated document statements like crime scenes, digging into them to find contradictions and hidden meanings. Denbeaux himself was billed as a national expert in "forensic testimony": the analysis of statements and documents. He had served as an expert in trials ranging from those of former Black Panthers to Sydney Biddle Barrows, the New York escort service owner known as the "Mayflower Madam." Denbeaux had also testified before Congress in 2008 regarding his center's research on Gitmo.

I wasn't sure if a story from a lone guy like me would fit with his center's work, based as it was on analyzing documents. And certain facts that I read about Denbeaux worried me. Though the work put out by his center at Seton Hall seemed objective, what I read about Denbeaux made him seem like some kind of left-leaning wingnut from the 1960s. Before becoming a professor at Seton Hall in 1972, he'd been a political activist who represented draft dodgers for the Vietnam War and Black Panthers. More recently, he'd served as an attorney who, starting in 2004, came regularly to Gitmo to represent detainees. The funny thing was, the fact that he helped detainees prejudiced me *against* him.

Despite all of my questions about what I'd seen at Gitmo, my outrage at the brutal conditions, and my strong conviction that even suspected enemies of America deserved US justice, I still worried that a lawyer drawn to represent them might be too far left for me. Despite the help I'd received dealing with my sleeplessness and anxiety, I was still afraid. My fear was rational: taking my story to someone outside the military was a big step. It was life changing and potentially ruinous.

It took three months, until January 2009, before I was ready to call Denbeaux. With Obama coming into office on the promise to close Gitmo, I figured that the environment had changed enough that I could bring my story out safely. Despite my misgivings regarding Denbeaux's political leanings, the work done by his Seton Hall Center was top notch, better informed and more objective than any work being done by reporters. Denbeaux had also been inside Camp America. He knew the ground I'd been on. He knew at least a little bit how it sounded there, how it smelled. Denbeaux's work at Seton Hall also showed some backbone. The guy was not afraid to put his name on reports that took on the government. And, most importantly to me, Denbeaux's Seton Hall reports made mincemeat out of what the government said about Gitmo—and yet the Defense Department had never attacked them as wrong.

*   *   *

Friday, January 23, 2009, was an icy but blue-sky day in Green Bay. The recruiting center I worked at was in a suburban National Guard armory on Military Avenue. Traffic had been minimal all morning. Maybe in the wake of Obama's inauguration, people figured he'd be dismantling the military and there was no reason to sign up. Whatever it was, I finished some paperwork on pending recruits and had nothing left to do. On busy days, I worked through my lunch breaks, but that day I wandered out to a Starbucks, ordered coffee, and pulled a slip of paper out of my wallet. On it was the number for Seton Hall University. After months of deliberation, I dialed and asked for the office of Professor Mark Denbeaux. A woman answered and told me he was off campus. I said, "I was supposed to reach him today. Can you get me his cell number? I've misplaced it." Technically, there was no lie in anything I said, but I did fool the woman into giving me his cell phone.

I hadn't been nervous when I made the first call, but faced with the cell phone number of the man whose work I'd been following for a couple of years now, I became anxious. I had to go back to my office. I wasn't ready to call him.

I wasn't shy about telling my story. My fear was that this would be another dead end. Starting with the failures of my command to talk to us honestly about what we'd seen the night of the deaths, through the obfuscations—or perhaps outright lies of the NCIS report—through the dereliction of the media, I wasn't sure I could handle it if a person like Denbeaux refused to hear me out. I was ready to fight—to be called a liar, or a kook, or even unpatriotic—by making my story public, but I wasn't sure if I could take being alone anymore with my story. I had so much fear that I almost didn't call Denbeaux's cell phone at all.

Later that afternoon, there was absolutely nothing for me to do at the office. I'd made every work call, filed every paper, and straightened the contents of my desk countless times. I stepped out of the office and pulled out Denbeaux's cell phone number.

PART II

DISCOVERY

——◆——

CHAPTER 17

Meet the Denbeauxs

I STOOD on the street and watched a few late-afternoon stragglers shuffle along drinking Starbucks coffee against the winter chill and chatting idly. Could they even comprehend what I knew or what I was about to do? I felt like a man holding a gun to his own head with one sweaty finger resting on the trigger. I took a deep breath and pulled. I punched in Professor Denbeaux's cell phone number.

There's always that odd, frozen moment when one makes a phone call. The slight hesitation before the ring and then, as you wait for the person on the other end to pick up, that seasick feeling of not knowing exactly what you're going to say or how the conversation will go. I had built up this conversation in my mind for so long that a dose of Dramamine might have helped. I almost hung up. But just as I was about to, I heard a voice.

"Hello?"

I could hear noise in the background. It sounded as if he was in a large hall. "Is this the professor Denbeaux who did the report on the suicides at Gitmo?" I asked.

"Yes," came the response. "But I'm about—"

I was so in the moment, I didn't let him finish. "I don't think they were suicides. What they said happened there isn't true, and I can prove that."

"Well, that's very interesting, but I'm about to go onstage and give a lecture. I'll give you a call back sometime at this number." A man doing his type of work probably attracted more than his share of nuts, and the way he dragged out his words made me suspect right away that he thought I was some kind of crank. I had to grab his attention and let him know I wasn't part of the tinfoil-hat brigade.

"I was a soldier at Gitmo," I said. "I was involved in the riot that happened three weeks before the deaths. I'm the only soldier to date to give an order to fire on detainees. I was on duty the night of those so-called suicides on June 9—and I'm still in the military and taking a great risk talking to you."

There was silence on the line for a moment. "Where are you calling from?" Denbeaux asked.

"Wisconsin," I said.

"I can fly out to see you tomorrow," he said.

I had definitely gotten his attention.

After he finished his lecture, Denbeaux called me back. I told him more about my background but held back a lot of the details. I wasn't sure I could trust him yet. I didn't tell him about the white van, Camp No, or that neither I nor my men had seen the detainees who'd allegedly killed themselves taken from Alpha block to the medical clinic. I said simply, "What I have to say casts doubt as to whether these men really killed themselves."

Denbeaux said, "I have never before doubted that the men committed suicide. What you say requires a real leap."

I was impressed with his skepticism, but I told him, "If you hear me out, you'll see that it's a bigger leap to accept the government's story. I can't prove that the men did not kill themselves, and I can't say exactly how they died. But I think I can make it clear they did not die in their cells."

Denbeaux explained to me that his son, Josh, practiced defense law in Westwood, New Jersey, and, given the complexities of my being in the military while coming forward with my story, he suggested that his son represent me through his firm Denbeaux and Denbeaux. "Is that a father-son practice?" I asked.

Denbeaux laughed. It wasn't his firm. His son practiced law with his wife, Marcia, so it was a mother-son firm. Mark proposed that his son, thirty-nine at the time, represent me to ensure I didn't run afoul of any laws regarding secrecy or my employment with the military. We agreed that instead of him coming to see me, I would fly out to meet him at Seton Hall University in New Jersey on Sunday.

I arrived late in the afternoon, and the winter sun was already sinking in the icy sky. A security guard checked me in at the entrance. Mark didn't look the way I had expected. He was tall, clean-cut, and had a commanding way of talking; not loud, but direct and serious. He struck me as the kind of man people listened to. His son, Josh, was looser and had a pronounced Jersey accent that made him seem more easygoing. Both seemed eager to talk to me.

The Denbeauxs led me through a maze of angled walkways to an upper-floor conference room that Mark referred to as "the Guantánamo Room."

"This is where we do our work, Joe. Usually there are ten or fifteen student fellows here neck deep in government papers. Sunday evening's one of the rare times it's quiet in here," he said. I noticed stacks of documents along one wall, and empty pizza boxes piled next to a trash can. These were the people—students—to whom I was entrusting my life. The three of us sat at the conference table. Mark and I were directly across from each other, and Josh sat slightly to the side. Both of them took out legal pads, and I told them my story.

I started by describing the unchecked comings and goings of the "pizza van," and then the events of June 9. I was careful to explain that I could not prove the men had been taken to Camp No, or even that the three men I saw removed in the van were the same ones who died. But I sketched the layout of Alpha block, the locations of our towers fewer than two hundred feet away, and the road to the medical clinic—the only pathway from Alpha to the clinic—and explained that neither I nor my men saw any detainees moved from the cell block to the clinic. Nor did we see medics go from the clinic to the cell block, as the NCIS report described. I explained that there were four guards assigned to the two towers watching the road, in addition to me. It would have been impossible for us to not see the detainees' movements or hear the medics' voices. I told them with complete assurance that no detainees were moved from Alpha block to the clinic at any time that night. I also told them about Colonel Bumgarner's briefing in which he told us that the men died as a result of rags stuffed in their throats, but that we would hear something different in the media.

When I finished, Josh said he believed me, but Mark Denbeaux sat at the table without saying a word. "You don't believe me?" I asked.

"Joe, I don't know what to think. I cannot believe that the authorities at Gitmo would fake a single suicide, let alone three. I don't believe in conspiracies." Then, as if thinking out loud, he turned to Josh and asked, "How many people would it take to cover up something like this—and then involve the NCIS?"

He turned back to me and said, "Joe, I think you're sincere, but I find this story hard to believe in its entirety."

Mark then left the room and returned shortly followed by a woman. "Joe, I'd like you to meet my wife, Marcia. She's a lawyer as well." She struck me as a gentle person but very firm. She and Mark spent a few minutes telling me about their backgrounds. His father had been a chaplain in Patton's army during World War II and had been present at the liberation of two concentration camps. What his father had seen and experienced had shaped Mark's life. As a young man, he marched in Selma, Alabama, with Dr. Martin Luther King Jr. and then got involved in representing draft resisters. He explained to me that pursuing civil rights and challenging the unchecked power of the government were part of his father's legacy. Denbeaux's wife had been raised a Quaker. While I'm not sure if she was still religious, as a Catholic I could understand her commitment to pacifist beliefs.

She advised me to reconsider coming forward with it. "It's not easy going against the government," she said. "You could get hurt." Her concern struck me. Not only was she willing to believe me, but also she wanted to keep me safe. But I knew the truth was more important.

Mark asked me what I wanted. I told him two things: I didn't want to go to jail, and I wanted to tell my story. Josh agreed to represent me and to tell my story through proper legal channels.

Mark still hadn't committed the resources of the Center for Policy and Research to investigate my claims. Before dropping me off at my hotel, he asked if I would mind returning the next day so that one of his students could interview me. I was happy to do anything they required and told him that if he researched my story and determined my worst suspicions were unfounded, I would consider that a win. I wanted, more than anything, to believe in the military again. If his research could explain the things I had and hadn't seen, I would have been over-joyed—relieved, even. It would have saved me from going public.

But whatever the outcome, telling my story to the Denbeauxs felt like someone had taken a huge boulder out of a rucksack that I'd been lugging for too long. When I stepped into the hotel that night, I conked out on top of the bed in my clothes and slept for ten hours straight. I don't think I slept through the night like that since before I deployed to Fort Lewis and Gitmo more than three years earlier.

The next morning, Mark met me at the center's front door and led me straight to the Guantánamo Room. When I walked in, a student was sitting at the table drinking a cup of coffee. "Joe, this is Paul Tay-lor," he said. "Paul's a research fellow with the center and a second-year law student. He's also an army veteran who served with the Eighty-Second Airborne." I knew right away what Mark was doing. He was seeing if my story held up with another veteran.

I was happy to talk to Paul and handed him my complete military record out of my computer bag. I had brought it with me on the trip because I thought they might want to see what kind of soldier I was. Paul went through the document, and I told him what I'd told the Denbeauxs the night before. I was at ease talking to him and I felt that he understood my story and issues better than Mark and Josh did sim-ply because he grasped how the military worked. He understood the importance of SOPs, of hierarchy, and of secrecy. When I was done with my story, he left the room for about fifteen minutes and came back with Mark.

"Joe, I'll get the center to look at the NCIS investigation," Mark said. I was relieved. He told me that his students' inquiry into the NCIS report would have nothing to do with me. "The way things work at the

Center for Policy and Research," he continued, "is that I'll turn a document or set of documents over to my students and ask them, 'What does this really say?'" He explained that he ran each research project as a Socratic exercise. His students were to read the data, question them, look for contradictions, and pull a logical narrative from it.

The timing of my arrival was perfect. A new semester was just beginning, and Mark was able to obtain the three-thousand-page NCIS report, which had been placed on a Pentagon server in response to a media Freedom of Information Act request. His student fellows would tackle the report, but without any input from me. Besides Paul Taylor, who was allowed to work on an isolated portion of the NCIS report on the condition of his silence, none of the students would know about my story or even my existence. This was to ensure that they didn't embark on the project with any bias. In fact, they wouldn't even be told what they were looking for. Their discoveries, good or bad, would be based entirely on what they found in the report. As I left the school, I felt like I had allies for the first time in two years.

As the plane took off from Newark, I had mixed impressions. I particularly liked Josh Denbeaux. He was closer to my age, easy for me to read, and he had a simple plan. He would present my statement to the inspector general, and he and his father would contact people they knew in the US Attorney General's office to initiate an FBI investigation. This plan not only seemed workable but also didn't expose me to any legal risk. I was taking my complaint, as it were, through the proper channels. I was less sure about Mark Denbeaux using his students to dissect the NCIS report. I would have preferred to speak directly to them, but Mark wanted his students to approach the NCIS report with open minds. He said they would probably take months. As frustrated as I was with having to wait, Mark had impressed me as a serious man interested in finding the truth.

Marcia Denbeaux had taken me aside before I left for the airport. She seemed concerned, but her eyes held mine in a steady gaze. "Joe, are you absolutely sure you're willing to file a complaint with the inspector general?" she asked.

"As sure as I've ever been of anything, ma'am," I told her.

CHAPTER 18

———◇———

Discoveries

THE anxiety I'd felt keeping my story bottled up inside had been intense, but it was rivaled by the stress I felt knowing that Denbeaux's students were sifting through the NCIS report while I waited. To follow, in some measure, what was going on at Seton Hall, after I arrived back in Wisconsin, I downloaded the more than three thousand pages of PDF documents that composed the NCIS report.

The government had done an interesting job putting together the report. Names and lines of information were redacted, as I had expected. But whoever loaded the report into the server had dumped the pages in haphazardly. They were out of order, sometimes upside down, and many pages were numbered incorrectly or not numbered at all. I went to the local copy center and printed it out. It took me more than a week just to get the pages in order. I put them in binders that filled almost an entire file box.

I called Mark Denbeaux a week or so after he had handed the report to his class and asked him how his students were progressing. I may have been forbidden from talking to them, but Mark had no problem relaying their findings to me. He told me that after ten days of working on the report, the fourteen student research fellows were frustrated and discouraged. He had given them no directions or clues, and they still hadn't been able to piece together what the NCIS was claiming had happened.

They had found one interesting fact, though.

"This was kind of weird," said Mark. "Do you remember Paul Taylor, the army guy that talked with you when you visited?"

"Of course," I said.

"He found that, according to the NCIS file, the necks of those three detainees had been removed during the autopsies—and these had not been returned to their families with the rest of their remains. There were also no autopsy photos of the necks of the deceased."

"So what does that mean?" I asked.

"Well, think about it," said Denbeaux. "If they died by hanging, their necks would show distinctive patterns of bruising. If they died by asphyxiation from rags blocking their airways—"

"There'd be no bruising," I interrupted. "What do the students think of that?"

Denbeaux laughed. "I've instructed Paul to keep that to himself. I want to see what the other students—who don't know about you—find on their own."

Denbeaux reminded me that the Center for Policy and Research's methodology was to have his students "ask questions of the documents" and sift for facts and patterns that revealed the "real policies or principles" of the bureaucracies that produced them.

I said, "So, in other words, a week in, and they haven't found a thing."

Denbeaux corrected me. "No, no. It's not as cut-and-dried as that. The students have already reached one conclusion: Every single page in that document has been very carefully vetted. Just about all of them have redaction marks."

"And?" I asked, not sure where he was going.

"In order for those pages to have been vetted, they had to have been read in order. Yet what was released is a huge, mixed-up, jumbled mess. The students haven't been able to decipher the NCIS's narrative. But just based on the presentation, whoever compiled it for release was either careless to the point of incompetence—or they intentionally made it difficult to read."

I didn't have the heart to tell Denbeaux that the assistant manager at the copy shop had said pretty much the same thing when I had printed out the NCIS report.

However, ten days into his students' efforts, I got a call from Mark. "We found our first anomaly, Joe," he said.

"What did you learn?" I asked.

"Well, based on statements made by guards and other officials at Camp Delta—most of whose names were redacted, as you know—the detainees died at about ten at night and arrived at the clinic two and a half hours later in full rigor mortis. *Full* rigor. Make a note of that. In fact, an unnamed medic from the Camp Delta clinic described the rigor mortis as so advanced that one of the dead detainees had to have a metal bar inserted into his mouth in order to pry it open. The poor guy's jaw was so tightly clenched, they broke his teeth inserting the bar."

"Jeez," I said and exhaled.

"Now, several of my students are familiar with police and medical reports from some of the other projects they've worked on, and they know that rigor mortis takes at least three or four hours to set in."

"Are there other conditions that speed that process up?" I asked.

"Sure," said Denbeaux. "Temperature, humidity, and other conditions can affect the speed at which rigor mortis sets in, but according to my students' research, there were no circumstances under which the three detainees could have reached that level of rigor mortis in anything under three hours."

"So what are you saying?" I asked.

"My students don't trust the NCIS's timeline. I'll call you back if we find anything else," he said and hung up.

I was impressed that they had found an error among the avalanche of material in the report, but it hardly suggested that the men didn't die in their cells. In fact, given that the NCIS's account was premised on the guards having been completely fooled by the detainees, it would not be out of line if they had gotten the times of their hangings wrong.

I began to despair that Denbeaux's students would not find much else wrong with the report, but a few days later, Denbeaux called me in a state of excitement. "We found the Rosetta stone!" he said.

"What?" I asked. I had no idea what he was talking about.

"Two of my students, Kelli Stout and Meghan Chrisner, just pulled off an amazing feat! Okay, you know how the erratic page numbering and the fact that few witnesses or investigators are identified by name make it almost impossible to follow who was talking?"

"Absolutely," I said, remembering what a jumbled mess I'd printed out earlier.

"They fixed that problem using old-fashioned elbow grease. These two girls got together and spread all of the witness statements out on the floor and assigned numbers to each one. They then cross-referenced the statements and identified individual witnesses whose statements had been broken apart in the report. It took them some time, but they did it. We can follow the report now," he said.

"That's great," I said, but Denbeaux continued.

"They also determined that in a lot of instances, individual witnesses had been double or triple counted by NCIS investigators. So where the report claims more than sixty witnesses had been interviewed, the real number's closer to twenty-six," he said.

After I got off the phone with Mark, I wondered if he and his students would just chalk up this sloppiness to government inefficiency, or if they would start to see a more suspicious pattern.

I didn't have long to wait. Once the Seton Hall researchers had organized the statements according to their "Rosetta stone," they began to ferret out contradictions and missing details at a furious rate.

For instance, the students noticed that two medics described all three of the detainees as arriving at the Camp Delta medical clinic in states of rigor mortis, but two other medics present at the same time stated that they had performed life-saving measures, such as CPR, on all three of the detainees. In addition, the NCIS report stated that one of the detainees had been taken by ambulance to the navy hospital, still alive, only to die at one thirty in the morning. The law students couldn't understand how some of the medics could provide such drastically conflicting accounts of the detainees' states of rigor mortis, and wondered why trained medics would have performed life-saving measures on all three of them, when one or all arrived in a state of rigor mortis. Even the most dedicated medic wouldn't attempt to resuscitate a corpse.

Additionally, none of the medics mentioned entering Alpha block to save, cut down, or help transport the detainees to the clinic, despite statements by other personnel claiming that medics had come into the clinic from the cell blocks.

Denbeaux noted that his students were having their biggest problem with the cell block guards' statements. The NCIS report contended that the guards had been ordered to write out sworn statements hours after the deaths but were then ordered to stop writing their statements and turn them in. Afterward, the NCIS account grew slightly surreal. It said that each guard was charged with writing a false statement and read his Miranda rights. Though the charges were later dropped, whatever the guards had written was unknown. Those original statements weren't in the report. Instead, the report contained summaries of *subsequent* statements from the guards.

"My students are very bothered by these summary statements," Denbeaux said.

"Why?"

"They think they're absurd. None of the summaries identify which guard or guards first discovered the suicides. And according to the summaries, all of the guards assigned to the cell block carried out the first dead detainee they found on a stretcher. My students keep asking, 'How could they have all left the cell block unattended?'"

This was the same question I had asked when I read the original media accounts of the NCIS report. Every guard leaving a cell block to transport a dead prisoner was like a platoon of soldiers walking off the battlefield in the midst of combat to carry off a dead comrade. It was ridiculous. No reporter had noticed this, but the Seton Hall students had. My confidence in them was starting to grow.

Several of the students had also latched on to Colonel Bumgarner's written statement. His name, but not his rank, was redacted, and it was clear that he was the most senior officer to arrive the night of the deaths. Bumgarner's statement said that early on the morning of June 10, he had called the five cell block guards into his office and asked them what happened. This made sense to Denbeaux's students, but the rest of the Colonel's statement did not. He stated that he "could not recall" what the guards had told him they'd seen in the cell block. Nor did he take any notes during this early-morning interview. In addition, Bumgarner stated that he could not remember any of the guards' names, but might be able to "identify their faces" if he saw them again.

"My students are livid," said Denbeaux. "How could the commanding officer not remember what the guards, who were key witnesses, told him the night of the biggest event that had happened during his command? No notes? *No names?*"

But the students' discoveries didn't end there. The navy platoon leader who had been in direct command of the cell block guards that night had a very peculiar set of interview summaries as well. The NCIS had titled his report, "Re-interrogation Summary." The military was very precise in its language: an "interview" was performed with a cooperative witness; an "interrogation" was done with someone in captivity or under arrest.

In his re-interrogation summary, the platoon leader claimed that he "could not recall" if he had been in Alpha block the evening of the deaths—either before or after them—but he added, "If other witnesses say that I was there, I will not contradict them." This was hardly the clear-minded, forceful recollection one would expect from a US military officer during a time of crisis, but the NCIS accepted it.

This narrative astonished the students. They wondered why his statement was so evasive and vague. I hadn't told Denbeaux or his students about my own experience writing statements for the navy chiefs after the May riots. But they still guessed that the platoon leader provided his statement reluctantly and under duress because it concealed some other truth.

"They smell a rat," Denbeaux said. "They've gone through every period and comma in those reports. My students keep asking how come the US government can't identify which guards went into the cells or describe what each one was doing before, during, or after the deaths? You know what one of my students asked the other day?" he said.

I was impatient because my lunch break was nearly over, and I had a mountain of paperwork at the recruiting office. "You'll have to tell me what your student said, because my mind-reading skills are a little weak today."

Mark laughed. "She said, 'I'm starting to doubt that those three detainees were in the cells, or even in Alpha block, when they died.'"

He explained that Kelli Stout, who'd first helped organize the NCIS report, had greeted him the previous day with a series of pointed questions. Denbeaux said she asked, "Is it possible they died somewhere else, that the guards had nothing to do with taking them to the clinic, and that the platoon leader didn't remember entering the cell block because nothing happened there that night? Is it possible the guards aren't identified with any specificity because they saw nothing at all out of the ordinary and had nothing to report?"

When Denbeaux described her questions, which he said were vigorously seconded by other students working on the project, I felt an intense connection to his class, people whom, with the exception of Paul Taylor, I'd never met. They were starting to see the same things I'd seen that night. They'd entered Gitmo not through the physical gate at ACP Roosevelt but through a series of dry, heavily redacted, deliberately garbled NCIS reports. They hadn't heard of Camp No, the white van, or spoken with my guards in towers who had seen no detainees carried from the cell block to the clinic. I did not exist to these students. Yet they were nearing the same conclusion that I had: the *three prisoners* did not die in their cells.

I was no longer a lone guy with a wild theory. A group of bright, young legal researchers, starting on a separate track, were converging on my story. I was dying to meet them. I asked Denbeaux, "Why not let me talk to them now? They've already cut the NCIS report to pieces."

Denbeaux told me to be patient. "You can't interfere with the research process, Joe."

* * *

That process yielded more results by May 2009, when the term at Seton Hall was nearing its end. By then, a team of Denbeaux's students had calculated how much fabric would be required to pull off the suicides and construction of dummies, and they concluded it would have required an amount of bedding and clothing far in excess of what the detainees had been issued. The students also studied the effort required for the detainees to climb their sinks, stuff cloths down their throats, bind their ankles, place nooses around their necks, tie masks over their faces, bind their hands, and hang themselves. They attempted to reenact this scenario and concluded that while it was not impossible to pull off this feat, the notion that three detainees did so at the same time and in the same way was unbelievable.

The students had also picked up on something I hadn't. The report included a statement that early on the evening of June 9, one of the detainees who later died had "walked through the hallway of Alpha block shouting, 'God is great. Tonight we will strike back at the Americans.'" Not only did the quote seem over the top, the students' now understood the guards' SOPs well enough to question how a detainee had been permitted to walk the hall shouting threats. The students knew that detainees were not allowed to communicate with one another. They wondered why, if a detainee violated this policy, guards would later permit him to cover his walls with bedding. Even if the guards had not understood Arabic, wouldn't they have watched a shouting, recalcitrant detainee more closely?

Denbeaux's students summarized a list of key omissions in both the NCIS's story and in the report itself, including the lack of punishment for any cell block guards, despite having allegedly permitted numerous violations of SOPs. The students understood by then that the military invariably punished personnel, either through its nonjudicial system or through the courts-martial, when there had been a colossal failure such as the suicides of three detainees. The report also lacked a sworn statement, or even a detailed summary, from the senior medical officer. The students discovered that in addition to the medics' sworn statements, the NCIS referred in several places to a senior medical officer who examined all three of the detainees and pronounced them dead.

However, the investigators had apparently failed to take a statement from him. Finally, there was the lack of any video or photographic evidence. Denbeaux's students discovered, as I already knew, that the cell blocks had cameras both inside and out. But a note in the report stated, "No video evidence is available." Denbeaux's students were flabbergasted that the military provided no footage of the guards' movements before, during, or after the suicides, nothing from the clinic, and no crime scene photos.

As the students wrapped up their analysis, Denbeaux emphasized to me that their job wasn't to come up with alternate theories or even to disprove that the men had died in their cells. The conclusion his students reached was simply that the NCIS report did not support—and in many cases contradicted—its own narrative. With their research done, Denbeaux finally gave the okay for me to meet his students.

CHAPTER 19

Feds

THROUGH the first months of 2009, I had not spoken to anyone about the detainees' deaths. I remembered Colonel Bumgarner's orders to not disclose any details of what I—or anyone else on duty—had witnessed on that night. However, speaking to the Denbeauxs and to Paul Taylor, who was serving as their investigative intern, fell under protected legal privilege. The military allowed members to air grievances and expose wrongdoing to others, but only after first pursuing proper channels through the inspector general's office. Within days after meeting the Denbeauxs, Josh prepared to contact the inspector general on my behalf and also to notify the FBI.

Josh wrote a summary of my statement along with a list of significant witnesses and sent this to the office of the inspector general in Washington. A few days later, someone from that office called Josh and asked, "What am I supposed to do with this statement?"

"Why don't you investigate it the way you're supposed to?" was his curt reply.

In early February Mark and Josh traveled to Washington to present the outlines of my story to the relevant officials. They met with the general counsel of the US Senate Armed Services Committee and then with a special investigator for the House Judiciary Committee. Mark told them that he was representing me, and I was coming forth with allegations that challenged the prevailing accounts of how the detainees at Gitmo died. The law required only that I take my story to the inspector general's office, but Mark and I thought it best to cover every base.

Our most significant contacts were with Justice Department officials. Eric Holder hadn't been confirmed as US attorney general yet, but an assistant US attorney based there, Theresa McHenry, agreed to meet with us at Seton Hall.

Josh and Mark Denbeaux, Theresa McHenry, the FBI, and I met in the Guantánamo Room in mid-February. The several thousand pages of printouts that Mark's students were analyzing were stacked along one wall. Mark never referred to the papers during the interview, and neither McHenry nor the federal agents ever asked about them. We sat at a scuffed-up conference table that Josh told me had been cleared of pizza boxes and take-out cartons just minutes before the arrival of the feds. There were a few stray crumbs that had been missed in the hurried cleanup. Mark, Josh, and I sat on one side of the table, and McHenry, one of her associates from the Justice Department, and the two FBI agents sat on the other. Josh made a preamble to Theresa about my willingness to speak freely because I was not disclosing that I had committed a crime, and then gave the floor to me. Once again I told my story, focusing on the white van, Camp No, events of June 9, and Colonel Bumgarner's speech telling us that the men died as a result of rags stuffed in their throats but that we would hear a different story in the media.

As I told my story, one of the FBI agents, who appeared to be in his late forties and slightly older than the other, took the lead. He stopped me frequently and asked questions, clarifying details about other witnesses, locations of our towers, and where I'd been on the ground outside the medical clinic. The other agent and McHenry made frequent notes while I spoke. When I finished, the lead agent asked, "If the three detainees didn't commit suicide in their cells, what do you think happened to them?"

"I honestly don't know," I answered. "That's why I'm here talking to you. You're the investigators. My story doesn't fit with the NCIS report, and if you speak to the other members of my unit, they'll tell you the same things I have. You have the power to reinterview witnesses mentioned by the NCIS, like the navy guards. They could shed more light on this than anyone."

McHenry interrupted. "Josh, would it be possible for us to speak with Sergeant Hickman alone about some classified matters?"

I shot Josh and Mark a look. Was it a good idea for me to speak without counsel present? Josh leaned over and said, "You're not the target of a criminal investigation. It's cool." Then he and Mark left the room, and I was alone. The FBI had me sketch out the location of Camp No with respect to the other secret facilities. They wanted to be clear that when I described Camp No, I wasn't referring by accident to another facility. My sketches seemed to satisfy them, and Josh and Mark were called back into the room.

McHenry, as if noticing for the first time the papers stacked against the wall in foot-high piles, turned to Mark and Josh and asked, "Are you doing an independent investigation on this?"

Josh explained that his father's work at Seton Hall was independent of my story, and that his research fellows were examining the NCIS report on its own merits without my input. He also told them, "My client has offered his full cooperation with you. Joe will not interfere with you. We contacted a couple of witnesses early on when we met Joe, but the rest are yours. We don't want to step into your process. This is all your job." I told McHenry what I had said to Mark Denbeaux when we first met: if all of my suspicions could be proven wrong, I would be relieved.

McHenry stood up and thanked me. The lead FBI agent walked up and shook my hand. "We really thank you for coming forward," he said.

The meeting had lasted nearly five hours.

On her way out, McHenry turned and said, "Joe, we really appreciate you not going to the press with this."

It was a strange comment. They all knew I was active-duty military. The last thing in the world I wanted was to be in the center of what was sure to be a media circus. I believed the FBI was the best agency on the planet to handle my case. If they did their job right, spoke to the guys in my unit, and reinterviewed the navy guards, the medics and everyone else who dealt with the detainees that night, I'd be one of the least important witnesses. At least that's what I hoped would happen.

About a week after my meeting with Theresa McHenry and the FBI, Josh Denbeaux called to say he'd received a letter from the inspector general's office.

"Joe, they're not going to investigate," he said.

"What? Why not?" I asked, puzzled.

"Well, let me read you a quote from the letter," he said. "'There's no corroboration for the claims made by Sergeant Hickman.'"

We would later discover that the inspector general's office hadn't contacted a single witness we'd provided—and they hadn't spoken to anyone from my unit. They apparently just blew it off.

I think Josh was more upset by the inspector general's reaction than I was.

I was still confident in the Justice Department and the FBI. President Obama was running into roadblocks closing Gitmo, but he remained adamantly opposed to the place and the extrajudicial measures—such as renditions, and the apprehension and transfer of suspected terrorists from one jurisdiction to another—associated with it. Surely his Justice Department was a natural ally in my search for the truth.

In April Mark received a surprising phone call from the Justice Department. An assistant from Theresa McHenry's office wanted to know the names of the witnesses I'd provided in my interview weeks earlier. Mark was stunned. He said to the assistant, "I saw Theresa McHenry and the FBI take notes. Did they lose them?"

Days later, a member of my unit, José Vasquez, was contacted by an FBI agent. He asked Vasquez if he would accompany a team of FBI investigators to Guantánamo. Vasquez was not a witness to the events in Camp Delta on the night of the deaths, but he was aware of the existence of Camp No, and this was apparently of interest to the FBI. Unfortunately, several weeks passed, and the FBI never followed up with Vasquez.

Later in the spring of 2009, Mark received another phone call from McHenry. She expressed her concern that I might talk to the media.

Mark reminded her that I had obtained legal representation with Josh for the express purpose of taking everything through proper channels, and I had made this clear in my previous interview with her and the FBI.

Mark said, "Joe and I have every reason to believe the investigation is under way. Is it?"

"I think we're pretty close to wrapping it up," she said.

Mark asked, "Which of the witnesses we provided have you spoken to?"

"I'll get back to you on that," she said.

McHenry called the next day. She said that they spoke to some witnesses, but the investigation was about over. Mark asked, "Did you find that Joe was wrong about anything? Or that he said anything false? If you've found something, I'd like to know. It would help me."

She said, "We found that the gist of his allegation is not confirmed."

"'Gist?'" said Mark. "That's not a legal term. What part of his allegation could you not confirm?"

"I don't know how to answer that question," she said. "Why don't you tell me his allegations, and I'll tell you if they're wrong."

"We gave you five hours with Joe Hickman and a list of witnesses," Mark said, incredulous. "Can you identify a specific thing he told you that you have found to be inaccurate or untrue?"

"Let me put it this way," she said abruptly. "Our investigation is over."

I was not surprised when Mark Denbeaux informed me about his interaction with McHenry. Vasquez had told me weeks earlier that the FBI never got back to him about its trip to Gitmo. In fact, the agency hadn't contacted any of the other witnesses, either. It seemed to me that when McHenry told Denbeaux the investigation was "over," she had misspoken. There didn't appear to have ever been even a rudimentary investigation. As we neared the three-year mark of the deaths, federal investigators still had not spoken to the four men on duty in Towers 1 and 4 in Camp Delta. However the Justice Department or the FBI may have assessed my credibility, they made no effort to find out what these other witnesses had to say.

I wasn't bothered that the government didn't believe my claims, but it disturbed me that there was no effort made to prove or disprove them. I had come forward, with the help of Seton Hall, and was well aware that I might be attacked or discredited. Being ignored was something else.

Josh Denbeaux told me that because the inspector general's office and the FBI had declined to investigate, I was nearly free to take my story to the media. Only one more step remained. To speak out, I would need to resign from active duty. After that, there was no turning back. Since joining the military in 1983, I had reenlisted twice. Military life was comfortable, familiar. Outside of my deployment at Gitmo, I had enjoyed my other assignments. I was made for military life. I had even racked up a string of commendations during my deployment to Gitmo. Recently, I'd been promoted to staff sergeant. That promotion and my record meant that if I stayed in for just four more years, I would qualify for generous retirement benefits, as well as lifetime medical coverage.

But I remembered the oath I took at age eighteen when I became a marine, and again with each of my other enlistments: I had sworn to defend and uphold the Constitution of the United States. My oath said nothing about looking the other way when I saw a crime committed in order to secure retirement benefits.

A part of me wished I'd never taken those oaths. There were many mornings I woke up thinking, "What if Staff Sergeant Hayes hadn't had that migraine on June 9 and asked me to fill in for him as SOG? I'd probably be facing none of this." The mysteries of the white van and Camp No by themselves wouldn't have been enough to motivate me to speak out. It was what I saw and heard the night of those deaths. It was the contradictions—lies—of my senior commanders. I had no choice.

I put in the paperwork to take myself off active duty in the National Guard and to go on part-time duty for one weekend a month and two weeks in the summer. A week later, my request was approved. I still had no clue whom I might talk to in the media or how my story would be received. I felt like I had climbed to the top of a high diving board, shut my eyes, and was walking to the end of the board, not knowing when I would take the fall—or if the pool below even had water in it.

CHAPTER 20

Going to the Media

T HE first time I told my story publicly was for Denbeaux's class of research fellows. Before I spoke to them, he warned me, "The students' research is closed, Joe. They've outlined their findings and are set to write them soon."

"And that means what?" I asked.

"It means any new information you offer can't go into their report," he explained.

I was a little disappointed by that. I had read the NCIS report, and I'd begun to think there were a few contradictions his students hadn't found yet. I had hoped to bring some of these to their attention, but Denbeaux asked me to stick to telling my original story.

I flew to Newark in late May and went to the law school straight from my hotel early the next morning. It was a sticky morning that felt like it would grow into a hot summer day, and I was sweating when I sat down before the students. I was surprised by how young most of them looked.

I had this flash of fear that these students might turn on me. From what little Denbeaux had told me about the students as individuals, I gathered that most were typical liberal college kids. I worried that they'd accuse me of being a pawn in an immoral war or having engaged in something nefarious. But as soon as I began speaking, I could see that something had transcended the usual political divide. They were just interested in discovering the truth, as I was. I suddenly felt safe in that room.

I described generally what my job had been, and then, at Denbeaux's prompting, I told them what I had seen that night. I told them about the "pizza van" and the existence of Camp No. My words rippled through the room. I could see in their faces a sort of disbelief, not at what I was saying, but the fact that I was actually there. They'd been living the night of the detainees' deaths for months now, and there, suddenly, was the face of someone who had been there. But despite the surprise they felt at having a living, breathing Gitmo guard in front of them, they recovered fast.

They began correlating my story with the NCIS report immediately. They peppered me with questions.

"How come there are no interviews with you or the other guards on duty in the report?" one of them wanted to know. I told them I didn't know why, either.

"At exactly what time did the navy chief order Foster to transmit the so-called code red?"

"Foster's break had been before midnight. He received that order at approximately eleven forty-five," I said.

"But the report states that the guards in the cell block didn't discover the first suicide until twelve twenty-three a.m. Why would they issue a code red before the discovery that something was wrong?" the student asked.

I explained that I couldn't definitively say what a code red meant— since it wasn't a part of our SOPs—but that it did seem to be related to a crisis in Camp Delta, given that all the lights came on shortly after Foster transmitted it.

The students questioned me over the next two days. I went very quickly from feeling like a minor celebrity to feeling like a witness being grilled by an aggressive Congressional committee. Denbeaux's students were relentless.

When I first entered the Guantánamo Room at Seton Hall, the students already knew that the NCIS report was a lie. My story at least made some sense of it. If the men did not die in their cells, someone removed them, and they were taken to some other location where they met their violent ends—either by their own hands or at the hands of someone else.

After our sessions ended, the students took me out to a bar in Newark. I had a great time getting to know the people to whom I'd entrusted my story. They were the first people who really understood what I had been through at Gitmo.

*   *   *

I still believed that the right reporter would be able to tell my story, and that his or her efforts, more than anything, would force the truth from the government. I had left the military only a few months earlier in order to speak to the press and was now under enormous financial pressure. I was living off my savings, and my future felt uncertain. But after it became clear that neither the inspector general nor the Justice Department was pursuing serious investigations, I thought the gamble would be worth it. I was naive. I believed that if I did the right thing, everything would turn out right.

With Mark's and Josh Denbeaux's guidance, I reached out to several news organizations in the summer of 2009. I spoke to Jim Miklaszewski at NBC, producers with *60 Minutes*, and Brian Ross's investigations unit at ABC. Ross's show sent cameramen to Seton Hall and video-taped interviews with me, Mark Denbeaux, and some of his students.

Unfortunately, Mark and his students were still in the process of writing their report on the NCIS investigation. Not all of their findings were ready to be released yet, so the interviews were limited.

In addition, Josh had legal concerns about my discussing certain matters on camera. Even though the buildings that composed Camp No had been published recently on Google Maps—partially visible as a sort of herringbone pattern of white rooftops in the scrub—it was unclear if I would be violating military laws by identifying its location. Josh also advised me to limit some of my descriptions of the movements of the detainees and the operations of the guards.

ABC producers contacted three members of my unit: Richard Foster, José Vasquez, and Anthony Williams, who had been in Tower 4 the night of the deaths. Both Foster and Vasquez were out of the military and therefore able to speak on camera. Williams, who was still in uniform, was able to corroborate key elements of my story—particularly that none of the detainees had been brought to the clinic from Alpha block the night of their deaths—but he couldn't do so on camera.

Early in the fall of 2009, Brian Ross phoned Mark and said, "We are about to run the story, but we want to go to the Pentagon and give them Joe's name so they have a chance to comment."

Josh had grave concerns that if they floated my name past the Pentagon but didn't run the story, I would be left dangling. Ross, or one of his producers, said they couldn't make any guarantees. Josh phoned me and asked what I thought. I said, "Go ahead. They can use my name. They can tell my story to the Pentagon, if that's what they need to run their report."

In the midst of dealing with ABC, Mark received a call from Theresa McHenry in the Justice Department. She had gotten wind of our discussions with the media and asked Mark, "Why is Sergeant Hickman talking to reporters?"

"Well, because you've done nothing, Ms. McHenry," Mark said.

"That's not accurate," she said. "There was nothing for us to find."

Mark pointed out that federal investigators had spoken to only one of the four guards whose names we provided.

The very next morning at eight thirty, four federal agents showed up at the South Baltimore house where Richard Foster lived. They took him to a nearby Denny's restaurant, asked him a few questions, and brought him back home. According to Foster, they asked only basic questions, such as how long he'd served and how long he knew me, and nothing about the night of the deaths.

The following Monday, McHenry called Mark back and said, "After our extensive investigation, we cannot confirm the facts that Joe Hickman presented."

"So does this mean your investigation is now closed?" he asked.

"I can't confirm that," was her terse reply.

Throughout this period, we were all expecting the Brian Ross story to appear on ABC, but it never did. In November Mark left messages with Ross's office that all went unreturned. Finally, near the end of the month, one of the show's producers called Mark back. "We've run into some problems with the story," she said.

"What problems?" Mark asked.

"Other news events have pushed the story back," she said.

"So when will the story run? Do you have a tentative date?" Mark pressed.

"Look," she said. "Joe's a good guy. But we can't do that story, at least not in the foreseeable future, and I don't want him sitting there with his legs crossed."

ABC had passed on my name to the Pentagon, and possibly those of the other former military personnel it had interviewed, shared the substance of what they had to say, and then not run the story. It had exposed us to the maximum risk but given us none of the protection that would have come with running the story.

Mark and I were furious and frustrated. But I still had hope that another reporter would pick up the story. Particularly because I had found new information that corroborated some of my worst fears about the night of the deaths.

By the time I talked to ABC News late in the summer of 2009, I was also working full-time researching Gitmo independently from Denbeaux and his Seton Hall group. I'd started contacting other people involved in detainee issues—lawyers and former military and intelligence people, mainly—and one of these sources shared legal documents related to a detainee named Shaker Aamer.

The man had an unusual background. He was married to a British citizen and was awaiting British naturalization at the time of his capture. As a result, his legal status was somewhat different from the other detainees. The United States provided British authorities some details about his captivity, and Aamer claimed that British intelligence officials were present during his interrogations, which explained why his alleged beating may have been less severe than those that may have been meted out to the detainees who died. Since his capture by Afghan units in late 2001 and his transference to American forces a few months later, the US government had accused Aamer of being an Al Qaeda member but admitted the evidence against him wasn't very strong.

For all I knew, he could have been a top bad guy, but what interested me was his history at Guantánamo. Like the three men who died, Aamer had been a stubborn hunger striker. The documents I received included an affidavit from his attorney, Zachary Katznelson, based on an interview he conducted with Aamer on August 8, 2006, a few weeks after the three detainee deaths. At that time, the media was widely and uncritically reporting Admiral Harris's story that the men committed suicide in their cells. Neither I nor anyone else I'm aware of had come forward to question that story. But on September 19, 2006, Katznelson filed a declaration with the Department of Defense recounting his interview with his client Aamer. According to Katznelson's declaration, Aamer claimed that on June 9, the same day as the deaths, he was taken from his cell to an unspecified location and subjected to what could only be described as a torture session. Katznelson's declaration read in part:

> [Aamer] was beaten for two and a half hours straight. Seven naval military police participated in his beating. Mr. Aamer stated he had refused to provide a retina scan and fingerprints. He reported to me that he was strapped to a chair, fully restrained at the head, arms and legs. The MPs inflicted so much pain, Mr. Aamer said he thought he was going to die. The MPs pressed on pressure points all over his body: his temples, just under his jawline, in the hollow beneath his ears. They choked him. They bent his nose repeatedly so hard to the side he thought it would break. They pinched his thighs and feet constantly. They gouged his eyes. They held his eyes open and shined a mag-lite in them for minutes on end, generating intense heat. They bent his fingers until he screamed. When he screamed, they cut off his airway, then put a mask on him so he could not cry out.

Aamer's claims were just claims. However, taken with the violent deaths of the other three men that same day, they warranted further examination. His alleged ordeal did not completely mimic what happened to the other three men, but it seemed relevant. It was particularly significant that he described having been choked and having his face obstructed with a mask, as was the case with the other detainees.

Fortunately, I soon found another journalist who felt the same way. Even before ABC News had told us that it was not airing its interview with me, Mark Denbeaux put me in touch with Scott Horton.

Like Denbeaux, Horton was another liberal activist I never would have imagined having anything in common with. He was a lawyer, a lecturer at Columbia University, and a contributor to *Harper's* magazine. We first met at his office in Manhattan in November. He was a preppy-looking guy with glasses who seemed slightly too young to be a university lecturer. But he was a careful listener who took a lot of notes, and by the end of our first interview, I could tell he was a kindred spirit: he cared about the truth. We met several times, and Horton compiled an article for *Harper's* that largely told my story, along with corroborating interviews from Foster, Vasquez, and Williams.

Although Denbeaux and I talked to Horton about Seton Hall's work on the NCIS report, that was not the focus of the article. What Horton did instead was take my story and then use his own sources to obtain more information on Aamer's alleged June 9 beating. Horton studied Aamer's statement and then zeroed in on the detail that had first caught Denbeaux's and my attention shortly after we met: that the US government failed to return the necks of the three dead men. Horton noted that while the NCIS report asserted that the men died by "hanging," it did not identify the American officials responsible for the autopsies. When the family members of two of the dead men received the remains from the US government, they hired their own pathologists, a Swiss doctor for al-Utaybi and a Saudi for al-Zahrani. Both pathologists noted that the refusal of the US government to turn over their necks made it impossible to verify that the men had died as a result of hanging. The pathologist who examined al-Zahrani also detailed wounds on his head and other parts of his body that suggested he'd been beaten or tortured near the time of his death.

Al-Zahrani's father, a former high-ranking Saudi police official—who had subsequently sent videotaped appeals to President Obama requesting that his son's death be reinvestigated by the US government—agreed to speak with Horton for the article. In describing the conditions of his son's corpse, he said, "There was a major blow to the head on the right side. There was evidence of torture on the upper torso, and on the palms of his hand. There were needle marks on his right arm and on his left arm."

Horton's article, "The Guantánamo 'Suicides': A Camp Delta Sergeant Blows the Whistle," was published in the March 2010 issue of *Harper's*, which hit newsstands in early January. Seton Hall's Center for Policy and Research had published an analysis of the NCIS report just days earlier. The students' 136-page report, *Death in Camp Delta*, functioned as a companion piece to Horton's article. Their work shredded the government narrative, and Horton's article presented a new one in its place. But, as I had done in my interviews with him, Horton's article refrained from stating definitively that the detainees had died at Camp No and from describing the exact circumstances of their deaths. Neither I nor his other sources could explain for certain what happened to them. As I understood it, his intent in writing the article was the same as mine when I contacted Denbeaux: we hoped to spur the government into undertaking a more complete and transparent investigation of what happened at Gitmo.

A week later, Keith Olbermann covered the *Harper's* story on his MSNBC show *Countdown*. Prior to its airing, one of his producers contacted Colonel Bumgarner—who'd retired from the army in 2009—for his reaction to the article. His statement, which Olbermann read on-air, was, "This blatant misrepresentation of the truth infuriates me. I don't know who Sergeant Hickman is, but he is only trying to be a spotlight ranger. He knows nothing about what transpired in Camp 1 or our medical facility. I do. I was there."

According to Olbermann, Bumgarner declined to specify which of my many quotes and allegations in the *Harper's* piece he believed were false. But what I found most shocking was that in making his blanket attack, the colonel had blatantly lied.

During the more than three months that I served under his command, Colonel Bumgarner appeared to know me by name. In fact, following the May riot, he held a ceremony in his headquarters in front of at least twelve soldiers where he cited my "courage and meritorious conduct" while serving as the NCO of the QRF. Bumgarner pinned an Army Commendation Medal on my chest and handed me a commendation letter addressed to me by name and signed by him in which he wrote in part: "Sergeant Hickman's leadership on the quick-reaction force secured a detainee uprising in Camp Delta. His actions were performed in close quarters without regard to his own safety, thus securing peace in the camp."

His comment that I knew nothing about what transpired at Camp 1 or the medical clinic that night was contradicted, of course, by the fact that I was SOG that night. As SOG, I was therefore, per written orders and SOPs, "responsible for all movement" inside Camp Delta. Witnesses and logbooks could confirm that I spent the bulk of my shift in or near Tower 1 and Tower 4. Both of those towers were located within 150 feet of Camp 1.

Colonel Bumgarner's most baffling assertion was that he knew what transpired that night in Camp 1 because, as he told Olbermann's producer, "I was there."

In his sworn statement to the NCIS, the colonel said, "On the night of 09 June 06, I was not in the camp." That night, according to additional statements that Bumgarner made, he was at Admiral Harris's house outside of Camp America. It was true that Bumgarner entered Camp Delta just past one in the morning on June 10, but his statement to Olbermann's producers was not only misleading but also gave him the unfortunate appearance of being a liar—especially because Olbermann read the excerpt from Bumgarner's NCIS statement on-air.

Several days later, Olbermann aired a rebuttal from the Justice Department in which an unnamed official called Horton's reporting "sloppy and lopsided." It went on to say, in comments apparently aimed at me, "The Justice Department took this matter very seriously. A number of experienced department attorneys and agents extensively and thoroughly reviewed the allegations and found no evidence of wrongdoing."

My feelings weren't particularly hurt by this. In the best case, my statements accused the government of lying and incompetence and in the worst of covering up serious war crimes. I'd never been shot at in combat, but I'd been in more live fire drills than I could remember and quite a few fights. I understood how defensive the Justice Department might have been feeling. But I'd had detainees throw urine and feces at me; statements from Justice Department officials or officers didn't feel that bad.

As far as I could see, any reporter worth his or her salt could find out that the officials were stretching the truth. It would be easy to determine, for example, that despite claims by the Justice Department that my allegations had been "extensively and thoroughly reviewed," their officials spoke to only two of the four witnesses we provided.

More importantly, Horton's article was clearly well researched. It included numerous other witnesses and facts, even Google photographs of Camp No—the existence of which officials in the Obama White House would neither confirm nor deny. The truth was, even if I had been removed from the Horton article, the autopsies and the allegations made by the other guards and the fourth detainee should have prompted inquiries. On top of that, there was the Seton Hall report that gutted the NCIS's findings without any help from me or other guards.

On January 20 the *St. Louis Post-Dispatch* ran an editorial in response to Horton's article and the Seton Hall report. It called for Obama to appoint a special prosecutor to "dig further" into allegations of detainee abuse and cover-ups at Gitmo. I expected a drumbeat of similar calls to follow.

But outside the left-leaning side of the blogosphere, the national media largely ignored the work of Horton and Seton Hall. John MacArthur, the publisher of *Harper's*, wrote a letter published in the

New York Times complaining that "the mainstream media is ignoring [the Scott Horton article] to death." In May 2011 Scott Horton won a National Magazine Award for his reporting of the story, but nothing seemed to get better.

A short while later, on May 23, 2011, Alex Koppelman wrote a story in *Adweek* about Horton's reporting. This article, two pages long, constituted one of the most lengthy analyses of Horton's reporting to date. The title summed up Koppelman's argument fairly effectively: "The National Magazine Award and Guantánamo: A Tall Tale Gets the Prize."

Most of the article was an attack on my credibility and that of the other guards working under me that night. Koppelman described us as "perimeter guards," leaving out the fact that we were positioned inside Camp Delta under orders to watch the cell blocks and the walkways to the medical clinic. He quoted Colonel Bumgarner, who told him that when it came to what was happening inside the camps, men in my unit "didn't really know what's going on in that world."

Koppelman also wrote that I had "shopped" my story to numerous sources, with the implication that I had sought personal gain or the gratification of being in the spotlight. Koppelman never spoke to me or examined my military records, which showed that I voluntarily separated from the Guard after receiving a promotion and a series of commendations. I knew that personal attacks might come from telling my story, but it bothered me that his article lumped the other guards who spoke to Horton in the same category. Not only did they have nothing to gain from speaking to Horton, but unlike Foster and Vasquez, who were friends of mine, Williams and Winslow were men whom I barely knew. Koppelman, so far as I knew, never interviewed any of those guards, either.

Aside from Colonel Bumgarner, Koppelman's most significant interviews appeared to be with other reporters. He quoted one unnamed journalist who told him that I and the other guards were prone to "flights of fancy." He quoted NBC correspondent Jim Miklaszewski, with whom I'd spoken only briefly, as saying, "Ultimately I just didn't find the story credible, quite frankly."

Another reporter, Rowan Scarborough, writing in *Human Events*, described the *Harper's* article as a "left-wing conspiracy story" and "a preposterous tale of murder and torture." Mr. Scarborough quoted a Pentagon spokesman who said that the "speculative and unfounded accusations" leveled by me and others in the *Harper's* piece "do a serious disservice to the honorable men and women who serve at Guantánamo Bay and in the U.S. military."

Despite the blows I was taking, I still had legs for the fight. Working on my own and with a group of Denbeaux's Seton Hall students, we continued to dig into the NCIS report. Flaws previously missed or not understood quickly emerged, and the narrative spun by the NCIS unraveled further. Soon I would discover I was not alone in my dissent. But first Denbeaux's students and I had our work cut out for us.

CHAPTER 21

"All Accounted For"

I VISITED the campus several times throughout 2010 and 2011, following the publication of Seton Hall's seventy-eight page *Death in Camp Delta* report, and traded calls and emails with a core group of students to further explore unanswered questions about the NCIS report.

Their work ethic astonished me. All of them were nearing graduation, and most were preparing for the bar exam. Top law firms in New York had already interviewed some of the students. But despite all they had going on in their lives, they kept digging into the NCIS report. From our first meeting, they drilled me about my allegations.

Kelli Stout, who along with Meghan Chrisner had first assembled the jumbled NCIS pages into a coherent order, never let go of her faith that the people in our government were the guys in the white hats. She was from Kansas and, like me, had been raised with a bedrock belief in the goodness of our armed forces and their top commanders. She fought hard to defend the NCIS's story, and that made our findings even sharper. Meghan struck me, in some ways, as Kelli's opposite. She fit my concept of a "Jersey girl." Tough, cynical, and street smart, she provided the yin to Kelli's yang, and that's what made them such a formidable pair. Rounding out our team were Sean Camoni and

Brian Beroth, both whip-smart bulldogs who would bombard me with question after question if our investigation hit a snag. Beroth would eventually lead efforts with Mark Denbeaux to publish new Seton Hall reports that sprang directly from our work together.

What we initially focused on were small yet significant statements buried in the NCIS report that had gone unnoticed in their first pass. Among these was an interview summary on page 2319 with an identified navy guard. He was among a group of guards interviewed by Criminal Intelligence Division (CID) agents, who acted as a sort of FBI for the army. The Seton Hall students had paid less attention to the interviews with these guards because they hadn't been on duty at the time of the prisoners' deaths. But buried among these statements was a single paragraph from one navy guard who had been on duty until six o'clock on the evening of June 9. He told the CID investigator under oath that he "entered every cell in Alpha block" between two and four on the afternoon of June 9 and searched each one, finding "no contraband, including extra bedding, towels, or implements in violation of SOPs." He stated that he "did not find any violations in any cells in Alpha block." It was a stunning paragraph. Media reports often speculated that the three men carried off their "suicides" by hoarding materials in their cells with cooperation from others on the cell block. But there *in the official report* was a statement from a guard that there had been no extra bedding in their cells or in any of the other cells on the block.

The next discovery we made was even more subtle. On page 1721 was a statement from a CID officer regarding the Alpha block "detainee management logbook." This was a written notebook in which guards were required to record the times that any detainee left or returned to the cell block—whether for medical checkups, forced feedings, interrogations, or transfers. "The logbook is usually the most important record in any cell block," I told the students.

"Explain why," said Sean Camoni.

"Knowing the whereabouts of all detainees at all times is one of the most important responsibilities of any detention-facility guard," I answered.

Meghan joined in: "Here on page 1721, there's a weird statement by some unidentified CID officer."

Kelli read the passage aloud, having caught it herself. "'The page or pages from 09 June 2006 [detainee management] log were not available for me to examine. The page or pages pertaining to 09 June 2006 are missing from the logbook.' Oh my God."

This two-line statement was a bit of a bombshell. Even if there hadn't been any deaths on June 9, a missing or destroyed page from a detainee management logbook would have been a grave matter. That this page was missing for the night of the deaths was an absolute shocker.

"Joe, had the three men been taken from the cell block on June 9, their removals would have been noted in the logbook, right?" asked Camoni. I assured him that we noted everything in the logbook.

"Even if they were in the white van?" asked Kelli.

"Even then. We couldn't track the white van's movements, but we sure had to note the movements of the prisoners," I explained.

The NCIS spokesmen hadn't mentioned the missing logbook page, and, apparently, no reporters had noticed it. Like so much of import in the NCIS report, the bombshell was contained in a couple of terse sentences buried amid thousands of pages.

Brian Beroth spoke up. "Joe, doesn't that seem to be refuted by the DIMS log?"

The NCIS had included a copy of a DIMS report, short for Detainee Information Management System, in its investigation. The DIMS report was like an electronic version of the logbook, but in the DIMS system, cell block guards would use a computer to log half-hourly reports on the conditions in the cell block. For some reason, the NCIS included only a single entry from the DIMS report for the entire day of June 9. It was made at 11:43 that night by an unidentified guard who stated that the detainees assigned to the cell block were "all accounted for." If anyone from the media had bothered to read page 2239 of the NCIS report, he or she probably thought the guard was reporting that all the detainees were *in* the cell block at 11:43 p.m. on June 9. Denbeaux's students had believed that. In fact, when I had first described to them watching three men leave the cell block that night in the white van, one of the students had cited the DIMS report to contradict me. I hadn't noticed it the first time, but once Beroth brought it up, I had to laugh.

"Brian, you have to take into account the language used by the military. It's very precise in its meaning."

"I'm not following you. It says right there, 'all accounted for.'"

"It doesn't get much clearer than that," Camoni agreed.

"No, no. Look," I said. "The military has a time-honored convention for reporting on the whereabouts and well-being of personnel—soldiers or prisoners—under watch by a supervisor or guard. If they are all in their assigned places, a proper report should state, 'All *present and* accounted for.' A report that simply states, 'All accounted for,' indicates personnel or prisoners are *not* in their assigned locations, but just that their whereabouts are properly accounted for. By writing only that detainees were 'accounted for' but not present, the guard indicated that one or more were not in their cells at eleven forty-three."

"The NCIS report doesn't address this discrepancy at all," said Kelli.

Each of these three discoveries on its own might have been evidence of a mistake—or a lie—by an individual source. Maybe the guard who reported searching the cells hadn't really done his job and was covering up his dereliction of duty. Possibly the page from the detainee management logbook had been accidentally torn out or destroyed through mishandling. Perhaps the guard who made the 11:43 DIMS entry had been too lazy to type in "all *present and* accounted for." In the military, like any other big organization, lots of screwups happen. But these reports, individually and taken together, stood as powerful contradictions to the NCIS's overall narrative. Even though the NCIS included the three records in its report, it did not acknowledge them or draw attention to them in any way. The NCIS had hidden the information deep within the report, where journalists wouldn't find it. No media reports mentioned any of those discrepancies. But, of course, Denbeaux's students hadn't, either, in their first Seton Hall paper.

I was glad at least that we were still making new discoveries.

Whether or not they would make an impact, I was filled with a stronger sense of vindication for having come forward. But as our attention turned to the suicide notes the NCIS claimed had been left by the dead men, my mood darkened. It was a feeling that lingered like a low-grade cold. It didn't stem from any new sympathy I'd grown for the detainees. My focus wasn't on them but on the actions of my government, and it was this part of it that bothered me.

CHAPTER 22

Admiral's Memo

As June 2010 approached, it had been nearly a year since I left the military to tell my story. I hadn't expected that this much time would pass without a significant new investigation being launched. Neither had I planned on spending so many months sifting through the same documents and staying in constant communication with a group of graduate students. I definitely hadn't contemplated being unemployed. I began looking at offers to do personal protection—bodyguard work—for a corporate security agency. I'd done similar work in the 1990s and had maintained my PI license and contacts in that world. The work paid decently and offered flexible hours that would permit me to continue my research into the three deaths at Gitmo.

My phone rang one morning with a blocked number. I was expecting a call from a buddy of mine at a corporate security firm, so I picked up. A voice at the other end said, "Joe Hickman? I'm calling about the detainee deaths at Gitmo."

Since the *Harper's* article had appeared, I had occasionally been contacted by nut jobs—the kind of people who wanted to discuss things like radio transmitters they believed CIA officials had implanted in their heads. I had hoped that other members of the military, navy guards, or medics who'd witnessed events the night of the detainee deaths, would reach out to me and put many of my questions to rest, but none had. I had also made preliminary efforts to locate Lisa, my friend who'd been on duty at the clinic on June 9 and 10, but did not follow through. I already knew the costs of coming forward, and I didn't feel comfortable exerting personal influence on a friend to speak out. I believed that witnesses should be moved to speak by their conscience, not by me, and that they should be given protection by the proper investigative authorities.

I could tell immediately that this caller was different, though. He had a decisiveness I didn't associate with the kooks who'd reached out to me in the past. But he wasn't a navy guard, either. The caller said he'd gotten my number from a high-ranking intelligence officer I knew of.

The still-unidentified caller said, "There are some people in the intelligence community who like the work you're doing, Joe." Then he added, "Some of us thought you might want to know how long the NCIS took to conclude its investigation."

It was a strange offer. "Uh, everybody already knows the NCIS investigation took about two years," I said.

"Want to bet on that?"

"What's that supposed to mean?" I asked, genuinely puzzled.

"They knew what they were going to say in that NCIS report before they ever released it," he said.

"I find that hard to believe."

"Look, how about if I can show you the real timeline of events?" he offered.

My source, who requested anonymity, directed me to a PDF copy of a memo from Admiral Harris buried deep within the Department of Defense website. About the time that the NCIS made its report on the detainee deaths public, the Pentagon quietly released thousands of other documents from Gitmo. Most of these came from the Staff Judge Advocate's (SJA) Office at Gitmo, which was responsible for running the detainee trials. The SJA had assigned some of its investigators on the island to look into the detainee deaths, just as the army's CID had done. The SJA and the CID had been pulled from the investigation within days, and only some of the documents compiled by their investigators had made it into the final NCIS report. The other documents had been released separately. Neither Denbeaux's student researchers nor I had ever thought to search through the hundreds of files released by the SJA for more information. The SJA files had been released under Freedom of Information Act requests made by lawyers who had been primarily concerned with the commission's trial process. They hadn't noticed the memo, either.

The military had released the SJA files in a manner about as organized and easy to sift through as the NCIS had done with its own report. Many of the SJA files were mislabeled. Those that were clearly labeled appeared to be records of humdrum administrative matters. But buried in this veritable electronic mountain of files was a small treasure.

It was a memo dated June 22, 2006, and had been dictated and signed by Admiral Harris twelve days after the detainees had allegedly died in their cells. The memo was addressed to General John Craddock, who at the time headed Southern Command, based in Miami, and was therefore Admiral Harris's direct superior.

In the first paragraph of the memo, Admiral Harris recounted a conference call that he had a day earlier with Thomas A. Betro, director of the NCIS; Paul C. Ney Jr., the acting navy general counsel; Bruce E. MacDonald, the deputy navy judge advocate general, or JAG; and lawyers from the Department of Justice. According to Harris, Director Betro and his staff from the NCIS "indicated that their suicide investigation was largely complete . . . [T]hey had concluded that the three deaths were suicides as a result of hanging undertaken solely by the victims themselves."

The first paragraph of the memo was by itself a shocker. NCIS did not arrive on the island until the fourteenth of June, so if its investigation was "largely complete" by June 22, that meant the entire investigation had lasted only eight days. Had the head of the NCIS really told Admiral Harris that the investigation was nearly complete just eight days after it began? City police departments typically required weeks to conclude even simple crime investigations. For the NCIS to have wrapped up its investigation of three simultaneous suicides in under eight days at a remote military base must have set a new record for government efficiency. That the NCIS concluded the suicides had been "undertaken solely by the victims themselves" was even more impressive given the number of witnesses: from guards, to medical personnel, to the dozens of Arab-speaking detainees housed in proximity to the three dead men.

"This is crazy," I told my source.

"Keep reading," he said. "It gets worse."

In the memo's second paragraph, Admiral Harris informed General Craddock that the NCIS, despite having reached its conclusion that the suicides were undertaken "solely by the victims themselves," was willing "to investigate whether the suicides were in furtherance of a larger plot or had been encouraged or ordered by other detainees." Though the memo did not state who suggested that the NCIS pursue that line of investigation, it seemed clear that the admiral was behind the idea.

Harris explained that the NCIS would initiate this new front in the investigation—and potentially reverse its finding that the acts were "undertaken solely by the victims themselves"—but only if a request came from General Craddock. The admiral asked Craddock to make the call, suggesting that the NCIS should search for evidence of "past, ongoing, or future plots for detainees to commit suicide" that involved "other detainees or third persons."

Clearly, Admiral Harris was not a disinterested party to the NCIS investigation. As the commander of Joint Task Force Guantánamo, he was ultimately responsible for any unnatural, violent deaths that occurred on his watch. Suicides that took place in heavily guarded prison cells automatically gave rise to questions of negligence. Three men able to cut up and braid their sheets into ropes, hang themselves, and go undetected for several hours in open wire-cage prison cells might perhaps as easily have cut through the wire walls, escaped, and wreaked havoc in the camp. The deaths, however they occurred, represented a major screwup on Admiral Harris's command. He and everyone under him, including my men, ought to have been targets of the NCIS's investigation.

The NCIS was an independent agency within the navy, headed and staffed by civilians in order to shield its investigations from influence by navy officers. The primary purpose of the NCIS was to investigate negligence or deliberate wrongdoing among navy personnel. Admiral Harris's memo to General Craddock appeared to be an unvarnished attempt to influence an investigation in which he was, or at least ought to have been, a target.

As I read the memo, I wondered if Harris's motive had been to deflect blame. Raising the specter of a grand plot—perhaps Al Qaeda!—sounded a lot better than the idea that the admiral's guards negligently allowed three desperate men to kill themselves. In fairness to Admiral Harris, I also wondered if perhaps he wanted the NCIS to investigate a wider suicide plot because he legitimately feared a rash of them taking place. The detainees had been waging fierce hunger strikes. They'd rioted in May. Maybe he believed that cell hangings were going to be the next disruptive trend.

But weighing Harris's memo with the benefit of hindsight, I had my doubts about the purity of his motives, as well as those of the NCIS. It's 2008 press release appeared to borrow heavily from the admiral's memo, with its references to a "larger conspiracy" and unidentified persons "directing detainees to commit suicide." The NCIS flogged these ideas even though its report contained not a shred of evidence to substantiate them.

Later that night, I couldn't sleep. Admiral Harris's memo kept turning me in circles. If he had redirected the NCIS to an outside plot in order to deflect blame, when the NCIS found that no plot existed, why had it not found negligence among the guards or other personnel in Harris's command? This was the question that Denbeaux's students kept raising since they had first read the NCIS report. We still had no answers. If anything, the memo I discovered with the help of my source complicated matters. Leaving aside the impropriety of Harris's effort to redirect the investigation, why had the NCIS wrapped up its investigation in only a few days? Whatever the admiral was up to when he wrote the memo, the speed with which the NCIS rushed to classify the violent deaths of three men as suicides—despite the improbable circumstances necessary for those acts to have occurred—suggested that the NCIS had a specific agenda even before the memo was written.

Like so much else that Denbeaux's students and I had uncovered, the memo raised suspicions about the integrity of the NCIS's investigation. It also led indirectly to two pieces of evidence that not only exposed more flaws in the NCIS report but also described explicitly an effort to fabricate evidence of the detainees' suicides. It was no surprise that these two pieces of evidence were cut from the NCIS's final report.

The surprise was where I found them.

CHAPTER 23

Missing Pages

THE SJA's office existed to deal with legal and criminal matters, so it was not completely out of the ordinary that a memo dealing with a criminal investigation had been filed with it. But after spending several days studying Admiral Harris's memo—and sharing it with Denbeaux and a handful of his student researchers—I noticed that something was missing from it: the SJA itself.

Though the SJA's office at Gitmo had sent investigators to look into the detainee deaths immediately after they occurred, the NCIS took over on the fourteenth. SJA investigators and army CID had been pulled from the case. And Admiral Harris's memo didn't appear to pertain to the SJA at all. The NCIS was the only investigative body referred to, and General Craddock was the sole recipient. So why was the memo filed with SJA documents? In the memo, Harris did refer to a conference call with the head of the NCIS and the acting general counsel of the navy, as well as representatives from the Department of Justice, the Department of Defense's General Counsel's Office, and an unidentified deputy navy JAG. It's possible that the deputy navy JAG was affiliated with the SJA's office at Gitmo, but it was unlikely. As I studied these details, I wondered why a critical document pertaining to the NCIS's investigation of the detainee deaths did not make it into the final NCIS report.

Ever since Kelli Stout and Meghan Chrisner assembled the NCIS report into a sequenced order, Denbeaux's students had suspected that some documents were missing. In several spots, witnesses referred to other personnel who appear to have never been interviewed. In addition, there were several places in the report where the page numbers skipped. Denbeaux's students suspected that sections of it had been pulled prior to its release.

I wondered if Admiral Harris's memo was the only document related to the NCIS's investigation that had found its way to the SJA's files. The SJA's office at Gitmo had released its files into a publicly accessible area of the Department of Defense website that contained over two hundred thousand files. It was a Pentagon-wide dumping ground for documents released under the Freedom of Information Act. Like the documents in the NCIS report, these were heavily redacted, dumped out of sequence, and hidden away in mazes of directories and subdirectories that appeared to have been labeled with random numbers or words. The files in them were not searchable by keywords or subjects in a search engine. I had to click through them by hand, a grinding and tedious job.

I spent three weeks combing through the DOD website. While I did this, Kelli and Meghan searched the site from their computers in New Jersey. Our communication was terse during this time. "Nothing." That's the word we traded back and forth in our emails and text messages. My hands hurt from clicking and typing. My eyes were sore. I promised myself I would stop after one more day.

Then, on what I had intended to be my final night of research, while flipping through the PDF files of another obscure subdirectory, I saw a series of ghost-like letters that spelled out "Formerly NCIS form 01604-81." In darker bold at the bottom of the page were letters spelling out "SJA GITMO 178." I felt a shiver of anticipation. This was a document from the NCIS's investigation that for some reason had been moved into the SJA's files.

Admiral Harris's memo had not contained any markings from the NCIS, meaning that it might never have been in the custody of the NCIS. But the page I found on the DOD website was not only marked according to the NCIS's filing system but also was an investigation report authored by an NCIS agent. Over the next week, I found three more associated pages in the SJA files. The four pages contained statements made by two witnesses to NCIS agents after the deaths of the detainees. One witness statement had NCIS page numbers on it that corresponded to a gap in the NCIS report. How these pages made it into an obscure subdirectory of the SJA files was a mystery.

Both of these witness statements directly contradicted key assertions made in the NCIS report. One statement in particular caught my attention. After weeks of "Nothing," I sent a text to Kelli and Meghan: "I think I've found our smoking gun." We finally had evidence of a cover-up.

The first report I found was a single-page transcription of a statement taken on June 10 by a navy officer identified as the "SMO"— senior medical officer—at the navy hospital. This officer said that he had attended detainee 093, al-Zahrani, who was brought to the hospital via ambulance at 1:11 a.m. on June 10. In the report, the SMO stated that at 1:50 a.m. he pronounced al-Zahrani dead. He noted that al-Zahrani had arrived at the hospital with "red marks on his neck from a ligature" but that these "impressions in the neck tissue were not extensive enough to indicate mechanical asphyxiation." The SMO listed the cause of death as asphyxiation caused by a blockage of the airway, a result of cloth inserted through al-Zahrani's oral cavity into the windpipe. The SMO confirmed what I had been told by my medic friend Lisa and by Colonel Bumgarner. Al-Zahrani, at least, had died as a result of choking on material stuffed down his throat.

Why had the SMO's statement been left out of the NCIS report? The SMO was a senior physician and had pronounced one of the detainees dead. Certainly his statement was essential to a thorough investigation. The fact that it had been left out of the final NCIS report was damning but still not evidence of wrongdoing. After all, he merely expressed a contradictory medical opinion.

The other report I found buried among the SJA documents seemed to offer proof not just that the NCIS's narrative was wrong but also that evidence had been fabricated to support it. This report, hidden away in the SJA file cache, had never before been made public. Originally it had been placed as an exhibit in pages 999 to 1001 of the NCIS report. But in February 2008, some six months before the report was released, it had been taken out, and—in an apparent effort to cover over its removal—the gap was filled with three random pages copied from a different section of the report, renumbered, and inserted in its place. The crude effort worked. Denbeaux's students had noted the repetition of identical pages in the report but chalked them up to its overall sloppiness. After analyzing the page numbering in the report, I discovered amid the SJA files that a switch had been deliberately made. Someone responsible for finalizing the NCIS investigation didn't want those three missing, incriminating pages read.

CHAPTER 24

What's the Motive, Joe?

T HE smoking gun report came from a navy petty officer, third class (MA3), a master-at-arms, or military policeman, one rank below that of sergeant. This MA3 was assigned to an escort unit tasked with transporting detainees. Like the drivers of the white van—who also were escorts, but assigned to a secret detail—his unit was responsible for moving detainees throughout the camps.

The night of June 9, he was called to assist medical personnel treating and transporting al-Zahrani. Four days later, on June 14, 2006, he described what he witnessed in a three-page sworn statement taken by an NCIS agent. His account of al-Zahrani's last hour on earth differed in key respects from those presented by witnesses in the NCIS report. To understand how his report countered the NCIS's version required following what the NCIS's primary witnesses said about al-Zahrani the night of his death.

The primary witnesses all said that the five guards on duty in Alpha block found al-Zahrani hanging in his cell at 12:30 that morning with his hands and ankles bound with white cloth. They claimed to have cut him down, removed the cloth that bound him, and finally cut the noose off his neck. Rigor mortis was noticeable in his fingertips, but they put cuffs and leg irons on him before placing him on a stretcher.

All five guards carried al-Zahrani down the walkway to the medical clinic. Once inside, Zahrani was pronounced dead at 1:05 a.m. I was thirty feet from the walkway in Tower 1 and neither saw nor heard any of this movement.

The MA3 escort made his statement as a "free and voluntary" declaration four days after al-Zahrani's death. He did so under oath and reread and signed his testimony on June 14, 2006. MA3's statement filled nearly three pages with dense, single-spaced typing.

On the night of the deaths, the MA3 was on his second tour at Gitmo, having been deployed there more than a year earlier as a guard in Camps 2/3. On his current tour, he had worked as a guard in Camp 4, the compliant camp, before moving to an escort team in April 2006.

In his report, he stated that on June 10 he was on duty, standing by at the Detention Operation Center (DOC), the command post located in Building 1, about fifty feet from the clinic. Sometime between 12:30 and 12:45, he and his partner were told by their control officer to respond to a medical emergency in Camp 1. The MA3 explained that the emergency was classified according to a "medical brevity code" that indicated a detainee was "having life-threatening symptoms, such as chest pains," though he added that it was not the highest code, and during hunger strikes, it was frequently called for detainees who grew faint from lack of nourishment.

He was careful to state this to make clear an additional fact: a suicide in progress, or a detainee showing no life signs, would have triggered a higher medical brevity code. In other words, the escort received a code that did not indicate a suicide was in progress.

After receiving the code, he and his partner were to proceed to the location where the detainee was held and meet up with medics dispatched from the clinic to assist in securing and transporting the ill detainee. But the MA3 pointed out that there was a problem with this order. He explained, "The specific block [where the sick detainee was located] was not indicated." Instead, they were ordered to head to Camp 1 to look for the platoon leader of the guards. He and his partner walked to the gate into Camp 1. A navy guard just inside the gate said the detainee was at the clinic. As the escort explains in his statement:

I was surprised to hear the detainee was already in the clinic, because he was not supposed to be moved from his cell without an escort team. For this reason I had a feeling something was wrong. From my experience, the usual response [to the medical code that was called] involves the Block Guard calling the Block Sergeant who will call the Sergeant of the Guard (SOG). The SOG then calls the DOC, and the DOC contacts the medical and escort teams to respond to the detainee's cell prior to removal . . . When detainees are out of our cells it is our responsibility to look after their well-being and ensure the safety of the detainee and those around him.

To most people outside of the military, reading the escort's recitation of the SOP may have been tedious. To me it was refreshing. Few of the witness statements, summarized or direct, in the NCIS report included specific references to the SOPs we operated under at Gitmo. Therefore, when civilians and members of the media read accounts of the detainee deaths, they weren't aware how out of bounds so much of the guards' behavior had to be in order for the NCIS story to be true.

The escort stated that he and his partner entered the clinic at about 12:45 that morning and saw "ISN 093"—al-Zahrani:

The first thing I noticed about the detainee was his blue feet. I also noticed that the detainee was limp. We asked medical if we would be going to the Naval Station Hospital, and they said we would, so I called back to control to have someone bring over a full set of [leg] shackles and the ID card used for ISN 093 because this is the standard procedure. I also recall a more senior medical person telling a junior corpsman to "stick him with something or start chest compression," but I never saw any medical staff perform chest compressions on the detainee . . . Medical advised the Camp 1 guards to remove the handcuffs that were on the detainee [al-Zahrani] so they could put the IV in him.

According to the navy escort's timeline, he and his partner entered the clinic at nearly the same time that clinic personnel claimed that al-Zahrani arrived. His description of al-Zahrani's blue feet was echoed in another clinic personnel statement. But his assertion that al-Zahrani was "limp" went against every other witness from the clinic, as did his claim that no one performed chest compressions. The MA3 seemed to be saying that al-Zahrani was alive—corpses don't get IVs—when he entered the clinic, but the life-saving measures clinic personnel undertook weren't as extensive as they later claimed.

The MA3's mention of "handcuffs" revealed another fact that contradicted SOP.

Cell block guards did not use handcuffs. They carried only flex cuffs, although for restraining detainees' feet, cell block guards had access to shackles. Navy escorts were the only personnel who carried handcuffs.

Who had put handcuffs on al-Zahrani? The MA3 did not speculate. I knew that navy escorts assigned to the white van carried handcuffs, and that I had seen navy escorts remove three detainees in handcuffs from Alpha block hours before al-Zahrani showed up dying at the clinic. What happened in between was still unclear. But the fact that al-Zahrani arrived at the clinic in handcuffs certainly lent support to what I saw. If three detainees were removed from Alpha block in handcuffs, it explained why al-Zahrani showed up cuffed hours later.

What the escort described next in his sworn statement was explosive:

> After the handcuffs were removed [from al-Zahrani], I observed a Corpsman wrapping an altered detainee sheet, that looked like the same material ISN 093 used to hang himself, around the detainee's right wrist. The other side of the material was bound to the detainee's left wrist with approximately a foot of cloth in between. The cloth was not on the detainee's wrists when the Camp 1 guards removed the handcuffs a few minutes earlier.

If true, the MA3 was asserting that the corpsman planted evidence on al-Zahrani in order to support the claim that he was found with his wrists bound. The escort highlighted this by repeating that he did not see the cloth on al-Zahrani's wrists earlier. Was he asserting that he had witnessed a war crime—an American military person fabricating evidence in connection with the violent death of a detainee—or was he merely pointing out an anomaly?

After seeing the second detainee being carried in, the MA3 stated:

> I moved back over to ISN 093, and noticed that FC1 [two names redacted] Combat Camera from DOC was filming ISN 093. Then the commanding officer of Joint Detention Group [Colonel Bumgarner] arrived . . . Another two Combat Camera personnel also arrived to begin filming the other two detainees with digital Cam Corders. I do not know how much of a chance they had to film . . . because Colonel B [Bumgarner] told them to stop fairly quickly.

I read this more than a year after the NCIS had claimed "no video evidence was available" in its report. Mark Denbeaux's students and I had always wondered what happened to the footage from the security cameras inside Alpha block. But none of us had ever considered that the navy's Combat Camera Unit, let alone one of its teams, had filmed al-Zahrani. They probably hadn't gotten much footage before Colonel Bumgarner shut them down, but it made me wonder if Bumgarner was also responsible for the footage from the security cameras becoming "unavailable."

The MA3 referred to two of these four combat cameramen by name, but the NCIS report contained no witness statements from any of these four men. As I read this section of the report, I became enraged. Here were two key witnesses who had been disregarded, just as the Justice Department had ignored most of my witnesses. Now there were four combat camera personnel thrown out of the clinic by Colonel Bumgarner, and their footage lost. One frame of the video footage of al-Zahrani could have potentially answered every question about him. What did he look like when they started filming? Did he have on handcuffs, bindings on his wrists and feet, or a noose? Were any of those items brought in with him on the backboard? Were there bruises on his neck? If so, how extensive were they?

The MA3 had provided his observations with a level of detail missing from other statements included in the NCIS report. Why had the NCIS cut his statement? If the escort had lied, there would have been a paper trail of evidence to dispute his claims. He also could have been charged with making a false statement. But there was no record of any of that. Nor was there one for the similarly excluded senior medical officer's determination that al-Zahrani died not from hanging but from "asphyxiation caused by a blockage."

The MA3 had noted of the ambulance ride to the clinic:

> When I pulled ISN 093's head back again the corpsman and I noticed the detainee's neck was swollen, puffy and was a purple color. As the corpsman pushed on the detainee's neck, the corpsman seemed surprised to see that the detainee still had a piece of material wrapped tightly three or four times around his neck. The corpsman tried to put his finger between the cloth and the detainee's neck, but the material was too tight . . . I know that the material was an altered sheet that was ripped into strands . . . The cloth was knotted around the detainee's neck in front, and appeared to have been cut just above the knot. The material was not braided but was bunched up. The corpsman cut the "rope" a bit to loosen it, but did not cut it all the way through, and it remained on the detainee's body. We continued CPR all the way to the hospital and on into the Detention/Detainee Advanced Care Unit.

The escort seemed to suggest that al-Zahrani was left to die at the clinic, with no examination or treatment other than an IV. Despite the man's clear difficulty breathing, chest compressions were not performed, and the makeshift rope was not cut away until the EMTs had arrived to take al-Zahrani away from the clinic.

His account proved that the clinic staff had lied about treating the unfortunate detainee. The NCIS report contained a detailed account of how al-Zahrani's hands had to be restrained on the floor of Alpha block while a "responder" cut the noose off his neck. If that was true, why would the noose have been cut off a second time in the ambulance?

Is it possible that the escort made up the story of finding the noose on al-Zahrani's neck in the ambulance? Why would he do so knowing that an NCIS agent could have interviewed the EMTs? As I asked these questions about the MA3's testimony, I had to ask the same of the guards and the medical personnel. Why would they have lied about having seen no evidence of a noose at the clinic? Perhaps the guard lied in order to prove that the detainee had been given competent medical attention when, in fact, he had not. But this seemed unlikely. In my experience, military medics tended to be aggressively proactive in treating injured or sick personnel, be they American, foreign, or enemy combatants. After reading the MA3's account, I felt I'd found the real reason.

Given the totality of contradictions, gaps, and outright absurdities in the NCIS report, it seemed most likely to me that the cell block guards lied about finding the detainees hanging in their cells and cutting nooses off their necks because the men hadn't been in their cells. The detainees who died were the same three men I saw removed from Alpha block earlier in the evening at the start of my shift. They died not by hanging but as a result of asphyxiation at a remote site, Camp No. Their deaths may have been accidental, perhaps during a punishment session intended to break the hunger strike. When the detainees were brought into the medical clinic by escorts from the white van, the escorts may have enlisted help from Camp 1 guards on duty but not assigned to cell blocks. The escorts who brought in the men may have believed they were all dead, or, in the case of al-Zahrani, nearly dead. If the medical clinic staff lied, it was simply about a call regarding the detainees having come from the cell block and the extent of care they rendered. In this scenario, whoever tied ropes on al-Zahrani's wrists at the clinic also tied one around his neck.

I called Denbeaux and told him all this.

"Joe, it sounds far fetched."

"Why do you say that?" I asked.

"Something like what you've laid out would require the silence and complicity of at least five guards, not to mention several members of the staff at the clinic. It's like a crazy conspiracy theory."

"Look, can you take a closer look at the MA3's report?" I pleaded.

"Okay, we'll look at it," Mark said before he hung up.

Over the next few weeks, Mark and his students began to feel that maybe there was some merit to my "conspiracy theory," but as I discussed it with him over the phone, he ended every call with a simple question: "But what's the motive, Joe?"

———◆———

CHAPTER 25

The Mefloquine Motive

MARK'S question about motive was a two-parter: Why were three men subjected to an ordeal outside their cells, and why would this have been covered up? Denbeaux's students had established early on that the three deceased detainees were among the last holdouts of the hunger strike that had begun after the May riot. Shaker Aamer, another die-hard hunger striker, claimed in his statement to his attorney that on the night the three men from Alpha block died, he was taken from his cell by navy military police, strapped to a chair, and beaten, choked, and gagged until he believed he would die. Perhaps the same thing had happened to the three who had actually died. What if the detainees were simply taken from their cells and beaten by sadistic guards who lost control of themselves?

It seemed that anger and revenge were obvious enough motives. I had witnessed guards commit sporadic acts of violence in the cell blocks. After the riot, I had seen Colonel Bumgarner and other officers allow navy guards to beat the prisoners we'd pulled from the communal cell on Whiskey Block. Hunger strikes made everyone's jobs more difficult and put all of us in a toxic mood.

I could imagine guards, if given the chance, beating detainees and going too far. But under no circumstances could I imagine a bunch of guards executing a complex scheme to remove detainees from their cells to punish them. The acts of sadism I saw always took place within the bounds of the SOP. Guards riled up the detainees and then, in a heated instant, retaliated. Other acts I'd seen guards commit, like the Frequent Flier drills they practiced on the prisoners, were done under the guise of "training."

Answering the second part of Denbeaux's motive question baffled me. There was a human instinct in the military to hide screwups. Whether you were a private or a general, nobody wanted to look bad. So, yes, I could imagine Colonel Bumgarner throwing out camera-carrying personnel from the clinic simply for fear that video evidence might make his command look bad. It made sense that in Admiral Harris's first press statements, he blamed the detainees for their own deaths, not failures in his command. His subsequent effort to blame a broad suicide plot—for which he offered no evidence— seemed an understandable attempt to draw attention away from the gross lapses in SOPs that would have been necessary for suicides to have occurred.

But I could not see why the NCIS investigators would ignore all the vague and nonsensical statements made by their witnesses. I wondered who in the NCIS had supervised or approved of the decision to not interview key witnesses or to remove the testimony of others. The NCIS's report was so tainted as to suggest that the investigation itself was compromised, but this made no sense to me. The NCIS would have no stake in protecting a few bad guards.

The white van seemed to be the missing piece of the puzzle. Though the movements of the van were outside the bounds of our normal SOP, the van's operations in the camp were routine. I wondered: What if the NCIS hadn't been motivated to protect a few bad guards at Gitmo—or the reputation of commanders like Admiral Harris—but to keep routine operations secret? What if it was normal to beat or suffocate detainees to within an inch of their lives at Gitmo, but in this particular instance three men happened to die?

I had no direct proof of this, but when I looked at all of the evidence, it seemed like both the command and investigative bodies were covering up something larger. By the time the NCIS report had been released in 2008, dark secrets of the military and intelligence establishments had already been made public. Topics such as renditions, waterboarding, and the bizarre abuses committed at Abu Ghraib were almost passé. What else could the government possibly be hiding?

I found my first clue in materials already released in the NCIS report. Denbeaux's students and I had probably read over the detainee autopsy reports released by the NCIS a thousand times. But one night, sitting at my kitchen table, I picked up a stack of NCIS documents to move them out of the way for my dinner plate when on top I noticed the medical intake form for Ali Abdullah Ahmed, the twenty-six-year-old Yemeni. It was a standard checklist form of treatments given to all detainees upon entering Gitmo.

The checklist noted that when Ahmed entered the camp on June 18, 2002, a medic had given him a 750-milligram dose of the antimalarial medication mefloquine, followed by another 500 milligrams twelve hours later. Denbeaux's students and I had casually skimmed over this passage because mefloquine, made by Hoffmann–La Roche and sold under the name Lariam, had been commonly used by the US military since the late 1980s.

I recalled a conversation with a friend of mine from a National Guard unit who was deploying to Afghanistan in 2009. "Watch out for malaria," I had told him.

"You know they're switching us from Lariam to doxycycline," he said. "Some of us aren't happy about that."

"Why?" I asked.

"Well, you only have to dose with Lariam once a week. You have to take the other stuff every day." Remembering this comment, I wondered why Ahmed had been given two doses within twenty-four hours.

Leaving my dinner untouched, I ran to the computer. I went to the website of the US Food and Drug Administration and looked up information on mefloquine. Sure enough, the prescribed dose was just once a week. Even more puzzling, the dose was not to exceed 250 milligrams.

Medics at Gitmo had given Ahmed five times the recommended dose. I searched for the medical histories of the other two detainees in the NCIS report, but these had not been included—typical, I thought, of the seeming haphazardness of the NCIS's work.

As my friend had mentioned, the military had been transitioning away from giving mefloquine to troops because of its adverse side effects. After more than a decade of use by the military and the general public, FDA-approved studies revealed that mefloquine sometimes produced anxiety, hallucinations, depression, insomnia, and suicidal thoughts. Studies showed that as many as 67 percent of those who took the standard dose experienced some degree of negative side effects. Just over 10 percent of those taking the drug were completely incapacitated by it. Hoffmann–La Roche stopped marketing Lariam in the United States in 2009, but generic mefloquine remained widely available. The military banned its use by troops in 2013.

I searched online through open sources and discovered that mefloquine was derived from quinoline, a chemical that was also used to manufacture pesticides and herbicides. Mefloquine was a diluted form that was somewhat safe for human consumption but toxic to malaria in the bloodstream. However, a Senate report from 1977 showed that in addition to identifying its antimalarial properties, government researchers had classified diluted quinoline as a "hallucinatory and psychotomimetic drug"—meaning that it not only produced hallucinations similar to those from LSD but also induced a mental state identical to that of psychosis. The Senate report sprang from a subcommittee investigation of CIA research into quinoline drugs that often used unwitting subjects as part of Project MK-Ultra, a program in the 1950s that experimented with behavioral engineering. According to the Senate report, the CIA concluded that quinoline and its related family of drugs were more powerful and dangerous than LSD because of their psychotomimetic properties. The agency worried that "an adversary service could use such drugs to produce anxiety or terror in medically unsophisticated subjects unable to distinguish drug-induced psychosis from actual insanity."

I spent that night reading about the CIA's MK-Ultra research into quinoline, wondering if there was a connection between its findings in the 1950s and Ahmed's high dosage some fifty years later. With the morning sun peeking through my window, I began to question my own judgment. I worried I was going down a conspiracy theorist's rabbit hole. "This is crazy," I thought. I nearly jumped out of my skin when the phone rang.

It was Mark Denbeaux. "I was just calling to check in," he said. "Have you found anything new?"

"No," I lied. The path I was going down seemed too nutty to lay out to the professor.

I had to be sure my findings were solid before I brought them to Denbeaux. I noticed in his medical history that Ahmed was given mefloquine before he had even been tested for malaria. Ahmed had also been in American custody in Afghanistan for more than forty days before being sent to Gitmo. During that time, he'd received medical care, but there was no indication that he had tested positive for malaria then, either. Other medical research suggested that if he had been infected with malaria, mefloquine was the wrong antimalarial treatment for people in the Afghanistan-Pakistan region where Ahmed had been captured. The US Centers for Disease Control and Prevention (CDC) recommended other drugs such as chloroquine, sulfadoxine-pyrimethamine, and amodiaquine as being more effective. On top of all that, malaria had been eradicated at Gitmo and throughout Cuba decades earlier, so there was no way he could have caught it on the island. No one in my squad had been given antimalarial medicine before going to Gitmo or after we arrived.

Why had they given it to Ahmed? And why had they given him five times the normal dose? All the research I found suggested that administering mefloquine was wrong and extremely dangerous at the levels Ahmed had received. But all of these conclusions were based on my own research, not expert medical opinions.

To get a better sense of what I was seeing, I called several doctors and university professors who specialized in malaria or pharmacology.

All of them expressed concern over the dosage given to Ahmed, but it was Dr. Remington Nevin who really helped me understand. Dr. Nevin, an active-duty army major previously attached to Walter Reed Army Medical Center, was then researching the dangerous side effects of mefloquine at the Johns Hopkins University Bloomberg School of Public Health.

I called the doctor and introduced myself. I told him I was trying to find out about the antimalarial drug. "What's your medical opinion of a twelve-hundred-fifty-milligram dose, Doctor?" I asked.

There was a sort of stunned silence on the line. "Twelve hundred fifty milligrams?" he asked. "Of mefloquine?"

"Yes. Would that ever be medically sound?"

"That would be a massive overdose," said Dr. Nevin. "Not sound treatment at all. Even at its recommended dosage, mefloquine is the wrong drug to give people from Afghanistan because it's not that effective against the strain of malaria common to that part of the world."

"So what would the effect of such a large dose do to a person?" I asked.

"In layman's terms, it would make them wacko," he said. "Mefloquine has a forty-day half-life and is fat soluble. That means that even after forty days, anyone given a twelve-hundred-fifty-milligram dose would still have several times the levels of a standard dosage in their system."

He then said something that sent a chill down my spine: "Administering a dose that high would induce terror in most subjects that would persist for a month or longer. It's the equivalent of psychological waterboarding."

The NCIS report didn't include the medical histories of the other two men who died on June 9, so I contacted their attorneys. I also spoke to more than ten attorneys representing other detainees. None could release his or her client's medical histories, but each said that Ahmed's treatment was consistent with other clients' records. Several added that in the weeks after their clients' arrival at Gitmo, the detainees had experienced what their attorneys described variously as "mental breaks," "hallucinations," "severe depression," or "psychotic episodes."

I was ready to call Mark Denbeaux and tell him I had something new and significant, but I still didn't know where it was leading. I needed his help.

Denbeaux's students did their work, tearing through all available data. Their research confirmed that mefloquine at the dose given to detainees caused extreme anxiety and often symptoms of psychosis. In Ahmed's medical history, there was a note made by an unidentified military doctor or medic who interviewed him on July 2, two weeks after he'd been given the massive dose of mefloquine. At the interview, Ahmed reported a loss of appetite and suicidal thoughts. Two days later, he was interviewed again. This time he noted that he was having auditory and visual hallucinations of "voices and the ceiling coming down," and also reported sleep "broken by nightmares" and decreased appetite and concentration. In addition, Ahmed told his interviewer that he was still having thoughts of suicide but indicated that such an act was "against my religion."

It's likely that the NCIS released these notes about Ahmed's suicidal ideations in 2002 because they seemed to show that his death in 2006 was self-inflicted. The notes on Ahmed's psychological complaints in 2002 make no reference to mefloquine, but the symptoms he complained of were all FDA-reported side effects of the drug. They also reflected the hallucinatory and psychotomimetic properties that the CIA had discovered in its tests of mefloquine's precursor quinoline drugs decades earlier.

Denbeaux's students noted that the SOP for processing all detainees at Gitmo called for each one to be placed in isolation for a minimum of thirty days after his arrival. This was a detail I had not known while working there. We were aware that newer detainees were held in the isolation cells in Camp 5 but did not know that it was SOP to put them there. The SOP stated that the purpose of placing new arrivals in isolation was to "enhance and exploit the disorientation and disorganization felt by a newly arrived detainee in the interrogation process." According to the SOP, new detainees could be held in isolation for a longer period—or indefinitely—if the head of the Joint Intelligence Group (JIG) and the interrogators deemed it appropriate for his "behavior management plan." When Denbeaux's students brought this to my attention, I felt the first shiver of what ought to have been an obvious truth.

The Joint Intelligence Group, which oversaw interrogations, had complete authority over where detainees were placed and how they were treated at Gitmo. This was not illogical. Presumably the people brought to Gitmo were enemy combatants or terrorists who might possess vital intelligence. It made sense that our intelligence personnel played a central role in dealing with them when they arrived. But JIG had total control. The blanket policy of thirty days' isolation violated standard Geneva Conventions regarding captured enemy personnel, as did other facets of the policy. Newly arrived isolated detainees were denied religious items such as the Koran and any contact with Red Cross representatives. Were high dosages of mefloquine and its neuropsychiatric side effects part of this program?

"Joe," Denbeaux said on one of our calls, "there's a paper trail on this that stretches back for miles. The students have found stuff from the CIA, even the White House." He explained some of their findings to me. In the 1977 Senate report on the CIA's use of quinoline, its authors had worried that enemy forces would use such drugs on captured American personnel. At Gitmo, we were giving that same drug in more than adequate doses to achieve the effect of drug-induced psychosis on all who arrived. But we didn't just isolate people after they were given the mefloquine. All of them arrived after having been in the custody of US forces in Afghanistan, or in the custody of allied security services, such as those of Pakistan, often for as long as thirty days or more. Most, if not all, were subject to strenuous interrogations at those prisons before being shipped to Gitmo. On their flight to Gitmo, they were subjected to sensory deprivation. As called for by our SOP, they had black goggles placed over their eyes, noise-cancelling headphones secured over their ears, and filtration masks placed over their mouths and noses. During their seventeen-hour flights from Bagram Air Base in Afghanistan—where most originated—they were shackled to the floor of the military transport planes. This treatment by itself was a formula for inducing panic and mental breakdown. To then administer the mefloquine and lock them up alone for at least thirty days constituted a long-lasting neuropsychological assault, especially in light of the fact that the damaging effects of mefloquine remained active for a minimum of thirty days.

Even John Yoo, the White House counsel infamous for drafting memos justifying use of "enhanced interrogation techniques" such as waterboarding, wrote in those same memos that any drugs that "penetrate to the core of an individual's ability to perceive the world around him, substantially interfering with his cognitive abilities, or fundamentally altering his personality" would qualify as torture. In another such memo, "Military Interrogation of Alien Unlawful Combatants Held Outside the United States," dated March 14, 2003, Yoo described such banned drugs as any that cause "brief psychotic disorder" or "delusions or hallucinations" lasting an entire day or longer. He also wrote that drugs that pushed "a person to the brink of suicide, particularly where the person comes from a culture with strong taboos against suicide," should not be used. The man who argued that waterboarding was acceptable seemed to say, in his legal opinion, that a drug like mefloquine constituted torture.

"So, by Yoo's own definition, Ahmed's suicidal feelings and hallucinations constituted torture, but only if the military health professional who took the notes linked these symptoms to the mefloquine he'd been given?" I asked Denbeaux.

"Looks like it," he said. "Yoo's memo left a huge out for the US government." Yoo wrote that administering such drugs met the legal standard of torture only if those giving it "specifically [intended] to cause such prolonged harm."

Nowhere in the SOP or in any statements did any official state that mefloquine was administered to produce psychological effects. The intake forms prescribed the massive doses of mefloquine in conjunction with malaria tests. But none of the detainees whose medical histories were released had tested positive for malaria. Indeed, the results of their tests were never entered into the records. Denbeaux's students were unable to find evidence that a single detainee at Gitmo had ever tested positive for malaria while there.

In the Seton Hall report on mefloquine that Denbeaux and his students eventually released in December 2010, they noted, "[I]t does not appear plausible from the available evidence that mefloquine was given to treat malaria" in any detainee who arrived there. The Seton Hall report went on to state, "This suggests a darker possibility: that the military gave detainees the drug specifically to bring about the adverse side effects, either as part of enhanced interrogation techniques, experimentation in behavioral modification, or torture for some other purpose." But the report also stated that its authors—Denbeaux and his student researchers—could "not reach a conclusion about the actual motives for" giving high-dose mefloquine to detainees.

As a lawyer, wedded to hard evidence, Denbeaux chose a cautious response. It seemed clear that personnel at Gitmo had administered mefloquine overdoses to break down detainees, and such use would constitute torture according to the Bush White House counsel's own legal definition. But because mefloquine could theoretically be used to treat malaria, and Denbeaux's students found no statements or records that Gitmo personnel intended any other purpose for it, his Seton Hall report held back. Privately, Denbeaux told me that the administered dosage of five times the recommended one was what he called prima facie evidence—that is, legally sufficient to establish a case—that the drug was knowingly given to produce its dangerous side effects, but he wanted to err on the side of caution.

The same day the Seton Hall report was published, investigative reporter Jason Leopold and psychologist Jeffrey Kaye published a much less cautious article about mefloquine and the detainees at Gitmo. Their article, "Controversial Drug Given to All Guantanamo Detainees Akin to 'Pharmacologic Waterboarding,'" in *Truthout*, a daily online newsletter, pointed out something I had noticed earlier: no military personnel stationed at Gitmo received mefloquine or any other type of malaria drug when arriving there. It went on to explain that none of the third country nationals who worked as support personnel on the base had received malaria drugs upon their arrival, either. This was particularly notable, since some of those people came from countries like the Philippines, where the risk of malaria was high.

Leopold and Kaye had also discovered that of the fourteen thousand Haitian refugees housed at Gitmo between 1991 and 1992, none received mefloquine to prevent malaria.

It appeared that the only people ever to be prescribed mefloquine at Gitmo were the detainees.

Not long after issuing the Seton Hall report on mefloquine, one of Denbeaux's students found documentary evidence that would lead the group to its next report, this one revealing unequivocal evidence that the entire purpose of Gitmo was to practice new interrogation techniques on detainees, regardless of any information they may or may not have possessed. From this research, it became clear that not only was mefloquine administered as part of this program, the deaths of the three detainees likely occurred under the shadowy operations of something called a special access program (SAP)—and it had to be kept secret at all costs.

———◆———

CHAPTER 26

America's Secret "Battle Lab"

W ITH the mefloquine motive in our hands now, we needed to trace the narrative of a special access program at Gitmo, identify the personnel involved, and define its objectives and practices—which, given the mefloquine angle, seemed to be solely about creating an environment in which human beings could be broken down with the greatest efficiency.

It wouldn't be easy. An SAP was a higher-than-top-secret operation that could be approved only by a few high-ranking officials in the executive branch of government. Most SAPs were so secret that they did not have congressional oversight. Military SAPs were sometimes referred to as "black operations." Even personnel connected to them may not have known the aims of the entities they served. Therefore, if we were lucky, when called to testify before Congress or when releasing routine government reports, they would sometimes inadvertently expose secrets. Just as Ahmed's revealing medical history had probably been released in the NCIS report to buttress claims that he was suicidal, numerous details about the SAP program were leaked by people who were probably unaware of what they were leaking. During the six years that Denbeaux's students and I took to establish that an SAP program existed at Gitmo, the wall of secrecy around it had been more like a sieve.

The problem was that the information dripped out into a vast ocean of data. In this ocean, law student Brian Beroth found an army CID report investigating a Fort Bragg sergeant on temporary assignment to Gitmo who was accused of stealing prayer beads from a detainee. The investigation documents showed that the sergeant was part of a training program known as SERE—short for Survival, Evasion, Resistance, and Escape—which had come to Gitmo to develop and fine-tune new interrogation techniques. Originally established by the air force at the end of the Korean War, SERE's existence wasn't a secret, but it was our first hint that something unusual was going on. However, to understand what the SAP was, we needed to find several hundred more such drops of information. The fifteen law students from Seton Hall who threw themselves into the task soon gathered buckets of data. Tips I received from sympathetic sources in the intelligence community also helped. At the end of our process, a clear picture emerged of the SAP program, its supremacy in the chain of command, its relevance to the deaths of the three detainees, and its successful co-opting of the detainee medical teams at Gitmo not just to administer mefloquine but also to stand by as participants during torturous interrogation sessions. We just had to fit together all the pieces.

Joint Task Force (JTF) 160 was established in the mid-1990s at Gitmo to process Cuban and Haitian refugees. However, after 9/11 and the invasion of Afghanistan, JTF-160 was put in charge of running a new prison camp to be built at Camp X-Ray, where refugee housing had previously been located. American armed forces and intelligence units began to capture—or, more commonly, acquire through bounty hunters and other foreign intelligence entities of dubious merit—the men who would fill Gitmo.

Five weeks after Gitmo accepted its first twenty detainees, President George W. Bush issued a secret executive order—an SAP—designating a new task force, JTF-170, to take charge of interrogations at Gitmo. The executive order has never been declassified or published, but the content of the order was accidentally revealed in an email that Linda Watt, a US Southern Command official, sent to the US State Department in February 2002.

Watt's email explained that as part of this executive order, JTF-170 would be "responsible for the worldwide management of interrogation of suspected terrorists detained in support of us [*sic*] military operations."

The email also stated that Major General Michael Dunlavey was to become head of JTF-170 and chief of global interrogation efforts. In sworn testimony he later provided to the Senate, Dunlavey stated, "I got my marching orders from the president of the United States. I was told by the SECDEF [Secretary of Defense Donald Rumsfeld] that he wanted me back in Washington, DC, every week to brief him."

Despite JTF-170's important role in global interrogation efforts, JTF-160 still had day-to-day physical control of the detainees housed at Gitmo. This soon caused tension between the two task forces. In March 2002 General Rick Baccus assumed command of JTF-160, telling troops under him that they were to carry out detention operations in accordance with the Geneva Conventions. All of them, he stressed, "must recognize the fact that you need to treat the detainees humanely" and understand that when "anyone lays down their arms, our culture has been to treat them as noncombatant and humanely."

Baccus's approach put him at odds with personnel from JTF-170. He later told a reporter that JTF-170 pressured him to institute "environmental stimulus changes" at the camps intended to foster greater cooperation from detainees, such as enclosing individual cells with materials to create total darkness inside—what he called "sensory deprivation" cages. Baccus told a reporter in a 2005 PBS *Frontline* TV interview that he would occasionally find occupied cells that had been completely covered over. When he confronted his cell block guards to ask, "Who ordered this?" they would respond, "We don't know. We found it like that." In the same interview, he added, "It was constant. You had to go around and constantly police the situation to make sure that nothing was out of hand."

While Major General Baccus was patrolling the camps trying to undo efforts by unknown personnel, higher-ups in JTF-170 were codifying a plan of aggressive interrogation techniques—the SAP—that would affect the treatment of every detainee held in Gitmo. Colonel Stuart Herrington, a senior officer at JTF-170, wrote a memo stating one of the goals of the SAP:

> To effectively carry out its intelligence exploitation mission, [J]TF-170 and its interagency collaborators need to be in full control of the detainees' environment. Treatment, rewards, punishment, and anything else associated with a detainee should be centrally orchestrated by the debriefing team responsible for obtaining information from that detainee.

A new interrogation plan was developed under the leadership of Major General Dunlavey, who later said, "The SECDEF [Donald Rumsfeld] said he wanted a product and he wanted intelligence now. He told me what he wanted; not how to do it."

Within days of his arrival at Guantánamo, Dunlavey created the position of Interrogation Control Element chief—the "Iceman"—to manage and facilitate interrogations. But the how-to part of conducting the interrogations fell to the Behavioral Science Consultation Team (BSCT), which had been created as an offshoot of JTF-170. Members of this group, led by psychologists, Special Forces operators, and SERE personnel, arrived at Gitmo at about the same time that Dunlavey did in March 2002. Their joint goal was to develop interrogation techniques that could be applied across all theaters in the global war on terror. Their recommendations were sent directly to Donald Rumsfeld and the White House, whose Office of Legal Counsel used the recommendations to help draft the "torture memos" under the leadership of John Yoo. Within two months of the BSCT's arriving at Gitmo, the medical staff would begin administering its 1,250-milligram overdoses of mefloquine to incoming detainees under the guise of treating malaria, but actually as part of the SAP's goal of extracting information.

Many of the BSCT's recommendations stemmed from the expertise of its members who came from the military's SERE program. SERE's techniques drew upon experiences of American soldiers who'd been subjected to interrogations, torture, and behavior modification—sometimes referred to as brainwashing—while in captivity during the Korean and Vietnam Wars. The program had initially been created to train military personnel to withstand and survive such practices. But at Gitmo, according to Major Paul Burney, a member of the BSCT, the interrogation plan was developed largely by reverse engineering the SERE program. As he told a Congressional staffer in 2007, BSCT's recommendation came mostly from SERE, but "other approaches were simply made up by the BSCT" on the spot at Gitmo.

The SERE techniques were not endorsed by everyone. Lieutenant Colonel Morgan Banks, the army's senior SERE psychologist, wrote an email to Major Burney in the BSCT outlining his concerns. He noted, "The training that SERE instructors receive is designed to simulate that of a foreign power. I do not believe that training interrogators to use what SERE instructors use would be particularly productive."

In particular, Banks was concerned that SERE's use of "physical pressures"—including hitting entrants to the program, waterboarding them, applying pain to their joints and muscles, caging or chaining them in uncomfortable positions—would be adopted by interrogators. He later testified in writing to the Senate: "Because of the danger involved, very few SERE instructors are allowed to actually use physical pressures . . . everything that is occurring [in SERE school] is very carefully monitored and paced . . . Even with all these safeguards, injuries and accidents do happen. The risk with real detainees is increased exponentially."

Though Major Burney appeared to share some, if not all, of Banks's views, other members of the BSCT believed that adopting SERE tactics to use against detainees at Gitmo was a good idea.

In October 2002 Burney authored a memo detailing the progress of the BSCT to date. According to the memo, the BSCT proposed, "What's more effective than fear based strategies are camp-wide, environmental strategies designed to disrupt cohesion and communication among detainees . . . [The] [e]nvironment should foster dependence and compliance . . . We need to create an environment of 'controlled chaos.'" When I first read this, I began to wonder: Could the chaotic conditions at Gitmo have been a small part of that plan?

For the more compliant detainees, the BSCT proposed an interrogation regimen—to be implemented at the discretion of each detainee's assigned interrogation chief—that included: isolation for up to thirty days; food deprivation for up to twelve hours; back-to-back twenty-hour interrogations once a week; removal of comfort items, including religious items; forced grooming (shaving of beards, often accompanied by cold showers); use of handcuffs; and placement of a hood over the detainee's head during questioning or movement. Several of these recommended measures would be applied to all detainees entering Gitmo.

According to the major's memo, for more resistant detainees, who were "suspected of having significant information pertinent to national security," the BSCT recommended: daily use of twenty-hour interrogations; strict isolation without medical visitation or access to the International Committee of the Red Cross; food deprivation for up to twenty-four hours once a week; use of scenarios "designed to convince the detainee he might experience a painful or fatal outcome"; and the use of noninjurious physical consequences such as removal of clothing and exposure to cold weather or water.

In the memo, Major Burney stated that by the fall of 2002, "there was increasing pressure to get 'tougher' with detainee interrogations but nobody was quite willing to define what 'tougher' meant." Burney noted that the BSCT was under "a lot of pressure to use more coercive techniques."

Major Burney further stated that he and at least one other member of the BSCT "were not comfortable with" the recommendations they were given to interrogate detainees. The memo was made all the more interesting by the fact that it was dated October 2, 2002, the same day the BSCT produced the minutes of a wide-ranging and apparently contentious meeting of the BSCT group and other staffers with JTF-170.

The meeting was labelled the "Counter Resistance Strategy Meeting." Held at Gitmo, it included Major Burney and several other members of the BSCT, as well as Lieutenant Colonel Diane Beaver, a representative from the SJA office who was on hand to assess the legal implications of proposed BSCT techniques.

The minutes noted that Lieutenant Colonel Beaver advised that all interrogation techniques recommended by the group were legally acceptable, but that some of the techniques should be hidden from the International Committee of the Red Cross to avoid what she called "a lot of negative attention."

Following a discussion about the possibility of administering experimental drugs on the detainees, such as something the attendees called "truth serum," the session came to a close. Major General Dunlavey and Lieutenant Colonel Beaver authored memos to their superiors requesting that all the techniques proposed at the meeting be approved.

But Mark Fallon, a member of NCIS posted to Gitmo as an official observer to BSCT's activities, wrote an email two days after the meeting to an unidentified Department of Defense staffer in which he expressed his concerns about the recommendations. He worried that the techniques would taint future legal proceedings involving the detainees, adding that some of them were "the stuff Congressional hearings are made of."

Fallon, who attended the meeting, attributed several quotes to Lieutenant Colonel Beaver that were not included in the official minutes. According to Fallon, Beaver said of harsh techniques, "If the detainee dies, you're doing it wrong." She also allegedly warned the BSCT that "medical personnel should be present [at all harsh interrogations] to treat any possible accidents." Fallon wrote that such measures "seem to stretch beyond the bonds of legal propriety."

But Fallon's most intriguing comment came at the end of his email, where he wrote, "Talk of a 'wet towel treatment' which results in the [victim] reacting as if he is suffocating, would in my opinion, shock the conscience of any legal body looking at using the results of the interrogations . . . Someone needs to be considering how history will look back on this."

Shortly after the memos were sent, Donald Rumsfeld approved the "enhanced interrogation techniques," in a public memo he signed on December 2, 2002.

Unfortunately for Rumsfeld, representatives from the air force expressed "serious concerns regarding the legality of many of the proposed techniques." The navy recommended that "a more detailed interagency legal and policy review be conducted. The Marine Corps's legal experts "disagree[d] with the position that the proposed plan is legally sufficient," and the army's legal analysts found that some of the recommended techniques "appear[ed] to be clear violations of the federal torture statute."

Following a veritable mutiny among his top commanders, Rumsfeld issued a follow-up memo on January 15, 2003, withdrawing his authorization for the use of harsh techniques at Gitmo, except in specific instances where he approved them. Rumsfeld also ordered the creation of a Detainee Interrogation Working Group based at Gitmo and gave them two weeks to come up with alternatives to the harsh techniques.

This "new" group appeared to include several members of BSCT who had created the previous set of recommendations. David Becker, later identified in a 2007 Senate report as the Interrogation Control Element chief—the Iceman—took the lead in writing the new group's proposed guidelines. Becker doubled down on its past recommendations. He argued for the efficacy of SERE techniques and others that he described as the "most aggressive and controversial."

In a separate memo from that same time, Becker said, possibly referring to his recent experience as the Iceman, that "the use of a wet towel and dripping water were very effective," as was "water-boarding." Yet there was no mention of waterboarding or wet towel practices in Becker's new official memos. Their use and legality remained murky.

The murkiness surrounding approved interrogation practices at Gitmo was not improved by Rumsfeld's order that the new working group come up with better practices. The memo this new group sent back to Rumsfeld's office in March 2003 expressed its support for the previous recommendations with only one significant change. Whereas the old group had titled its proposed interrogations guide as the *Gitmo*

SERE Interrogation Standard Operating Procedure book, the new group changed its title to the *Gitmo Management Interrogation Standard Operating Procedure* book. A handwritten note on a previous copy of the book (that I obtained with the help of an intelligence source) states, "All Reference to SERE will be removed as per Lt. Col. Moss."

Rumsfeld did not respond in writing to the new recommendations. His earlier January 15 memo deauthorizing the harsh interrogation techniques stood in the official record. But the actions taken at Gitmo and other battlefronts suggested a harsher regimen was being implemented as part of the secret SAP.

General Baccus, who believed that detainees should be treated according to the Geneva Conventions, was removed from his command of JTF-160. A short while later, JTF-160 was absorbed by JTF-170, which became JTF-GTMO. Major General Dunlavey was replaced by Major General Geoffrey Miller, a hard charger who was also given authority over interrogations done at Abu Ghraib prison in Iraq.

I interviewed Major General Janis Karpinski, who commanded the military police unit at Abu Ghraib that participated in abuse of detainees there. She told me, for the record, that in August 2003 Major General Miller arrived at Abu Ghraib accompanied by Lieutenant Colonel Beaver to inform her that he would be directing interrogations and detainee management at Abu Ghraib from Gitmo, and that he was acting on directions given him by Donald Rumsfeld. This seemed to indicate, again, that an SAP specifically designed to ruthlessly extract information from detainees was in place. Years later, during the trials indicting soldiers for abusing detainees at Abu Ghraib, several witnesses stated that General Miller, while on a tour of the prison, had personally advised them to use attack dogs to intimidate detainees.

At Gitmo, General Miller continued the practice of administering high-level doses of mefloquine to incoming detainees and codified the SOP of isolating new entrants, denying them Korans and comfort items such as blankets and mattress pads, and using "forced grooming." But the SOP still made no mention of waterboarding or similar practices, despite subsequent admissions by administration officials that three detainees at Gitmo were subjected to the practice during Miller's tenure as commander there.

The disconnect between stated procedures and actual practices at Gitmo extended to other areas of the facility as well. In the summer of 2003, at a time when President Bush and others in his administration were repeating to the American public that Gitmo held the "worst of the worst," Donald Rumsfeld was saying something else entirely. In a private email he sent to air force general Richard Myers, the chairman of the Joint Chiefs, Rumsfeld wrote, "We need to stop populating Guantánamo Bay (GTMO) with low-level enemy combatants."

If the cell blocks and isolation units at Gitmo were filled with low-level nobodies as Rumsfeld essentially described them—and which was supported by detailed analysis carried out by the Seton Hall group in 2006—what was the point of developing harsh treatments and interrogations aimed at all of them? Why were all of them dosed with a drug likely to produce mental breakdowns, locked in isolation without bedding for thirty days or more, and then subjected to harsh interrogations?

Why were men of little or no value kept under these conditions, and even repeatedly interrogated, months or years after they'd been taken into custody? Even if they'd had any intelligence when they came in, what relevance would it have years later? What would be the value of interrogations on such men?

One answer seemed to lie in the description that Major Generals Dunlavey and Miller both applied to Gitmo. They called it "America's battle lab." The SOP that Miller later approved for interrogations at Gitmo included a motivational blurb for its readers:

> History is being made with the Interrogations Operations taking place at Guantánamo Bay. Operationally, it breaks new ground. The Command, [redacted], Analysts, Service and Support elements, and Military Police are daily being asked not just to do the jobs they were trained for, but to radically create new methods and methodologies that are needed to complete this mission in defense of our nation.

Colonel Britt Mallow, commander of the army's Criminal Investigative Task Force based at Gitmo, later testified to the Senate, "I personally objected to the implied philosophy that interrogators should experiment with untested methods, particularly those in which they were not trained." But that was the SAP.

Some degree of experimentation was to be expected, given the new challenges posed by violent, religiously motivated, stateless actors. But most detainees were of low intelligence value and low threat. The desire to simply use them as test or training subjects stuck out. Even the FBI, which later rejected many of the interrogation techniques adopted at Gitmo, initially embraced the "battle lab" potential of Guantánamo. T. J. Harrington, deputy assistant director of the FBI Counterterrorism Division, called the interrogations "the perfect opportunity to get my agents and analysts in the box with a bad person to build their competence." The FBI sent 530 agents to observe or participate in interrogations at Gitmo during the first eighteen months that it was open.

During this period, the FBI was part of a flood of more than 120 other intelligence entities that observed or participated in interrogations at Gitmo. Among these were dedicated units such as the BSCT or officers representing various interests of the CIA, from field interrogation teams to members of its Enhanced Interrogation Psychopathology Unit from the Directorate of Science and Technology. But many more visitors were "TDYers," a military term for those traveling on temporary duty.

Major General Miller later stated, "[Private] contractors probably made up roughly fifty percent of the personnel."

It was not always easy to distinguish who was who in what appeared to be a free-for-all spying atmosphere. Scott Gerwehr, a RAND Corporation analyst and CIA contractor who in 2007 complained to the CIA's inspector general about alleged detainee abuse he witnessed during interrogations, said that when he was attached to an interrogation team at Gitmo, he adopted a cover by dressing in the uniform of a low-ranking navy guard.

An unidentified ICE chief who served during this period described his job overseeing interrogations, saying that when an intelligence entity wanted to interrogate a detainee, it "would have to make a 'reservation' like at a hotel."

The ICE hotel front desk was managed from a command center in Camp Delta—a trailer-like office across from the medical clinic. An ICE chief named Ted Moss wrote the first draft of the interrogation manual developed by the BSCT in early 2002. At that time, the ICE chief had a supervisory role overseeing interrogation teams and booking them with detainees, but the head of JTF-GTMO—first Major General Dunlavey and then Major General Miller—had command responsibility for the interrogations.

In late 2003 the structure changed. A man named Esteban Rodriguez, an interrogation specialist with the Defense Intelligence Agency, an espionage organization under the Department of Defense, was made the Joint Intelligence Group director. Rodriguez later described his position as being "responsible for managing and overseeing interrogation operations" at Gitmo. He appeared to serve under the head of JTF-GTMO and in a supervisory role above the ICE chief.

But Rodriguez's position came with an unusual twist. According to testimony he provided the Senate in 2007, although he served under JTF-GTMO, he reported directly to Secretary of Defense Donald Rumsfeld when determining how to proceed with certain interrogations. According to his testimony, "tiger teams"—his term for interrogation teams—would draft interrogation plans that the ICE chief would approve. But for reasons Rodriguez did not specify, the ICE chief determined that some plans needed special approval. These Rodriguez would present directly to Rumsfeld. If the defense secretary did not respond within a week, then Rodriguez would "instruct the tiger team to proceed with an approach determined by the ICE chief and myself."

This meant that Rodriguez and the ICE chief operated as a semi-independent cell. The JTF-GTMO commander was cut out of the decision loop regarding interrogations, and if Rodriguez's testimony was to be believed, he and the ICE chief were sometimes left to make decisions on their own, completely outside the chain of command.

Rodriguez, who appeared to have attained the rank of army captain, and the ICE chief still had independent discretionary power over the interrogations program when Admiral Harris assumed command of JTF-GTMO in 2006. Harris was boxed out of the most sensitive program in his command.

The unacknowledged SAP program added an additional level of compartmentalization to the operation. Though Rodriguez testified that he and the ICE chief approved the work done by tiger teams before they started interrogations, the existence of the SAP program added further unknowns to the equation.

A secret executive order is one way to create an SAP. Major General Dunlavey's assertion, made to a Senate committee in 2007, that he got his "marching orders from the president" and that Rumsfeld required him to come to Washington "every week to brief him," indicated an extraordinary level of oversight from the executive branch—more so than General Tommy Franks had when commanding the initial combat operations in Afghanistan, or General David Petraeus during the surge in Iraq.

When I arrived at Gitmo with my unit, I believed we were guards protecting America from the worst of the worst. But by the time I'd gathered and sifted through all the relevant documents, I realized that all of us who arrived there, even Admiral Harris, had entered an intelligence operation in which no normal military rules or codes applied.

Instead of order and discipline, the authorities behind it aimed to create "controlled chaos." The people we were guarding weren't just suspected jihadists or enemy combatants, but men who'd been given drugs by our medical personnel intended to make them believe they were insane when they arrived. We were required to stop our commanding admiral for jogging without a proper safety vest, but we could not stop or question navy petty officers driving an unmarked white van with a windowless steel box in the back for carrying out the men we were supposed to be guarding. Interrogations, the most sensitive and potentially dangerous operations at the camp, were run by a pair of midranking officers who consulted directly with the secretary of defense. It was a place where three detainees died in one night—an event that caused headlines around the world—but none of the guards or their commanding officers tasked with protecting them was ever punished for negligence or any other infraction.

When we deployed to Gitmo, without knowing it, all of us had checked into a strange, opposite land outside of normal military rules.

We had checked into the Iceman's hotel.

I suspect that the deaths of the three detainees were accidental—the result of a punishment session that went too far—but they occurred in the midst of operations that were routine for Gitmo. As I came to understand the command structure, I could see the elements of a cover-up were built right into it. Whether or not the deaths occurred as part of the SAP, the compartmentalization, the deniability, and the lack of accountability were key to the design of the Iceman's hotel.

AFTERWORD

In the *Adweek* article that questioned my credibility, NBC Pentagon correspondent Jim Miklaszewski was quoted as saying, "I devoted a lot of time to [Hickman's allegations], and my conclusion was that it just didn't seem possible that that many people could have been involved in a conspiracy and to have [it] remain secret. It stretched all credulity, I thought."

Of all the critical comments made about me, Miklaszewski's was the only one that bothered me. It bothered me because it seemed so reasonable. I had said the same thing myself when I heard from my commanders about the deaths and, later, reading the NCIS account. I thought that no conspiracy could contain this many actors.

The whole idea seemed implausible. But the problem I faced, even before finding the hidden reports cut from the NCIS investigation, was equally unbelievable. Each thread of the report unraveled into nonsense. As I delved deeper into Denbeaux's students' research, it became clear that the only conspiracy theory was the one spun by Admiral Harris about the mysterious suicide plot.

So what really happened to those three men? They were close in age, ranging from twenty-two to twenty-six. They were Arab—two Saudis and a Yemeni. They were middle class and educated. Al-Utaybi, twenty-one, was enrolled at university when he was picked up in Pakistan. Ahmed was a university graduate, active in a charity but also suspected of being a militant when he was snatched from a car in Pakistan with other men who were suspected of having trained at a terrorist camp. Al-Zahrani was seventeen when he was captured in Afghanistan, but he had attended a good high school in Saudi Arabia and was the son of a mid- to high-ranking Saudi official. They all leaned religious, toward jihad, and had gravitated to a part of the world that attracted such young men.

None had been captured by American forces, and in the roughly four years each had been held at Gitmo, the US military had failed to make a strong case against any of them. For a time, Ahmed had been suspected of having links to midlevel Al Qaeda members or of using his charity as a cover for jihadist activities. But no proof of that ever materialized, and the charity Ahmed was affiliated with had never been put on the US's watch list. In fact, it had been deemed an organization that attracted "moderates."

Al-Zahrani's father had hired lawyers in Saudi Arabia and sent numerous letters to him along with a video asking him to cooperate with the Americans, but none of these was passed to him.

Al-Utaybi's lawyer, a volunteer, had made numerous attempts to meet with him during the previous year, but camp officials had turned him down. Al-Utaybi's name was spelled at least two different ways in the intelligence files used by authorities at Gitmo, and the officials couldn't be sure that the lawyer was attempting to contact the correct detainee. But as Josh Denbeaux pointed out to me later, by the same logic, how could the authorities be sure they had the right al-Utaybi?

Despite the fact that al-Zahrani was barred from receiving communications from his father—or sending mail, according to a letter that the NCIS described as a suicide note—authorities at Gitmo had already decided to release him within the month. There is no indication in the letter he wrote or in any records that he was told this.

If there was anything that united the three men, it was their participation in numerous hunger strikes, possibly going as far back as 2003. Al-Zahrani's letter was mostly about hunger strikes. Like the short suicide notes all three of them allegedly wrote, al-Zahrani's letter made few religious references other than a couple of general comments about the United States killing Muslims in Iraq. A note written by an unidentified interrogator released with the NCIS report stated that al-Zahrani described himself as a jihadist when he was captured in Afghanistan, and was so devout that he'd "memorized the Koran." Nowhere in al-Zahrani's writings was there a single verse from the Koran.

Was it possible that during his captivity al-Zahrani forgot his religion? Was this why his letter seemed no more religious than one I would have written? Was his boast about having memorized the Koran bluster from a seventeen-year-old who'd come to Afghanistan to join the Taliban? Or was this fact simply made up by any of the dozens of Afghans and Americans who had handled him since his capture by anti-Taliban forces in late September 2001?

I wondered if al-Zahrani had ever been at war with America. He'd entered Afghanistan three months before the 9/11 attacks. American intelligence files made no mention of his having any contacts with Al Qaeda. He had tried to join a band of Taliban fighters in what was a relatively tranquil area until the 9/11 attacks and the US military response. Had that seventeen-year-old believed he was going to get into war at all, or had he entered as a summer adventure; a rebellion against his police officer father?

His letter, the alleged suicide note, his last testament of any length, not only failed to say much about Islam but also failed to express any particular hatred for America other than for its war in Iraq, which had begun nearly a year and a half after he was captured. Al-Zahrani made no negative references to Israel, Jews, or American culture that one might expect from a jihadist days away from committing what Admiral Harris called his "act of asymmetrical warfare."

His writing seethed with anger, but it was all directed at the administration of the prison, the forced feedings, and the fact that authorities had destroyed a letter he'd previously written to a loved one on the outside. This, too, didn't quite fit with Admiral Harris's characterization of him and his group: "They have no regard for life, either ours or their own."

The only thing that seemed to strongly define al-Zahrani in his letter was his defiance in the face of ongoing forced feedings. He came
off as a fiery resistance fighter, but not against Christianity or America,
just against the prison's regime.

The other two men did not leave any significant written letters, but
Ahmed's medical record, which showed that some five months before
his death, in February 2006, he'd required surgery to repair damage to
his nose caused by feeding tubes during an earlier hunger strike, was a
testament to his commitment to this form of resistance.

In any case, the records showed that the three men were all put into
the isolation unit on June 4. Typically, such punishment would not
have been meted out to three individuals who'd ceased striking and
were, by definition, on good behavior.

Early on the morning of June 8, they were all released from the
isolation unit and placed in Alpha block. An entry in their records
stated that their cells were to be "kept apart" and they were to have
"no communication with each other." As per these directions, the
men were placed in three cells as far apart from each other as was
possible within the block, and the cells on either side of them were
kept empty.

Were they kept apart because they were known coconspirators?
There was no record of the three having colluded in the past, ex-
changed illicit communications, or been called out by other detainees
as plotters in any other schemes. Given Admiral Harris's statements
after their deaths, as well as his memo requesting that NCIS search
for a plot, if such records existed from their four years in Gitmo, they
likely would have been released.

There was no note in their records, either, as to why the three
detainees were put into Alpha block under mild isolation. Records
of whether they were subjected to forced feedings on June 8 or 9, or
whether they ate meals in their cells, ought to have existed, but they
were never released.

Based on what I saw, I believed the three men taken from Alpha
block were the same ones who died later on. The statement that
Shaker Aamer made to his lawyer on June 9 about being taken from his

cell and beaten and choked both corroborated and complicated what seemed to have happened to the other three.

Aamer asserted that he was beaten because of his ongoing participation in the hunger strike. The beating, he believed, was intended to persuade him to stop.

Camp authorities hated hunger strikes. From a command standpoint, they made the authority of the camp, and America itself, look bad. Media was ever present. Fox News's Bill O'Reilly had just left the day before the deaths. A CNN or network reporter was present most days just outside of Camp Delta. Though they were kept away from the cell blocks, when the strikes were large enough, they could see detainees being driven to the forced-feeding area. The handful of lawyers who trickled in and out sometimes got word of the strike from their clients.

The camp administration fought hunger strikes like low-intensity battles. As per previous agreement with the Red Cross, Gitmo authorities said that they would not conduct interrogations on striking detainees, but most other punishments—sleep deprivation, isolation, stress positions—were all encouraged. So were the three men punished because of a hunger strike or to prevent one?

Either way, I believed that the three men from Alpha block were taken to the off-site facility, Camp No. Based on (1) the witnesses at the clinic who described two of them as arriving there hours later with fabric in their mouths, (2) the senior medical officer's suppressed finding that al-Zahrani's cause of death was asphyxiation by blockage, as well as (3) the refusal of US authorities to release their neck organs, which would show definitively whether hanging played a part in their deaths, I believed the three men had socks, gauze, or similar forms of cloth put in their mouths as gags.

Inserting cloth into the men's mouths could have been a punishment in its own right, or a precursor to "wet-toweling": the simple form of waterboarding in which a cloth gag is dribbled with water, in conjunction with blocking the victim's nose, to induce the sensation of drowning. This form of punishment was discussed as a possible SOP to employ in interrogations not long after Gitmo opened.

On October 12, 2011, Tony Bartelme, a reporter at the *Charleston (SC) Post and Courier*, published an expose on the treatment of Ali Saleh al-Marri, a Qatari arrested in December 2001 in Illinois on suspicion of abetting Al Qaeda through credit card fraud, a charge to which he pleaded guilty in 2009. Al-Marri was one of three terrorist suspects held in the navy brig in Hanahan, South Carolina. Until his plea deal, he had spent more than six years in solitary confinement. Bartelme reported that after al-Marri pleaded guilty, he "told his attorneys that interrogators stuffed a sock in his mouth and taped his lips shut with duct tape . . . When he started to choke, the interrogators ripped off the tape." Though the military denied that al-Marri was tortured, Bartelme reported, "Logbooks and other information obtained by al-Marri's Charleston attorney, Andy Savage, revealed that Defense Department and CIA agents interrogated Al-Marri for months, and at one point wrapped his head in duct tape and stuffed his mouth with a gag, a tactic Savage called dry boarding."

If al-Marri had been interrogated by CIA and military officials between 2002 and 2005, he would have most likely been handled by interrogators who reported to JTF-GTMO. His story suggested that personnel associated with JTF-GTMO employed various forms of gagging in addition to the more elaborate and classic form of waterboarding.

Would interrogators at Gitmo have punished and gagged three detainees simply because they refused to eat? I liked to think not, but given the evidence, the scenario seemed plausible. In his June 2 letter, al-Zahrani appeared to bring up the idea:

> The American government has ordered the administration of the camp to stop the strike by any means. It is true after that most of those who were in hunger strike have stopped, except for a hand full of people which are still undergoing different sorts of pressure methods until this day.

What did he mean by "stop the strike by any means" and people "undergoing different sorts of pressure methods"? In context, his meaning seemed clear. The reference to "different sorts of pressure methods" was written by a man who seven days later was wheeled into the medical clinic "with what appeared to be a sock in his mouth"—according to the second witness interviewed from the clinic in the NCIS report. Did al-Zahrani describe the motive and manner of his murder?

Most civilians assumed that an interrogator's sole job was to obtain information. But the SOP at Gitmo, as well as numerous statements and documents created by its architects and operators, emphasized again and again that an additional goal of the "interrogators" and the techniques they used was to bring about "behavior modification."

Persuading a hunger striker to eat was a prime example of such a modification goal. Particularly defiant strikers may have even represented a welcome challenge to a team of interrogators eager to prove its skill or try out new techniques.

But there were a couple of facts I couldn't account for. Why would three men be subjected to treatment at the same time? The logistics of moving, controlling, punishing, and watching three men seemed daunting. Wouldn't it have been simpler to completely isolate the men and break them one at a time, or was there a clinical or instructional benefit to practicing harsh techniques on three at the same time? Would the three have been dealt with in the same room, or would they have been isolated from one another?

The biggest question I had was why would the interrogators let three men die?

In 2006, reporters from *Time* magazine obtained logs kept by interrogators at Gitmo that describe some of the techniques they practiced on detainee Mohammed al Qahtani, believed to be the "twentieth" 9/11 hijacker (who missed his flight that morning).

Al Qahtani was chained in uncomfortable positions for twenty hours a day and questioned nonstop. This went on for months. When he started to fall asleep, interrogators forced him to move around. They forced him to take enemas. On another occasion, they used IV drips to pump him full of fluids and then refused to let him use a toilet. When he urinated in his pants, they made him wear them for hours.

The logs noted something else: during one short period of his ordeal at Gitmo, al Qahtani had his blood drawn to check his kidney function, underwent an electrocardiogram, CT scan, and ultrasound, and had his pulse checked fifteen times (occasionally multiple times per day). He was tended constantly, it seemed from the logs, by medics and a doctor. Like the mefloquine given detainees, some of this medical attention may have been a twisted form of punishment or even torture.

But it was also clear from the statements made by the architects of SERE and the interrogation programs at Gitmo that harsh techniques were to be accompanied by close medical supervision to prevent unwanted injury or death. A 2003 memo from the CIA's Office of Medical Services warned that among the dangers of waterboarding, "for reasons of physical fatigue or psychological resignation, the subject may simply give up, allowing excessive filling of the airways and loss of consciousness."

Torturers were generally not supposed to kill. Given the number of interrogation entities active at Gitmo, it was possible that an incompetent team got into the system. Could a team practicing harsher techniques without full authorization have waived off medical supervision to ensure that a session stayed off the books? Possibly. But it was difficult for me to imagine how three detainees undergoing punishment could have died at the same time.

While I couldn't be sure exactly how the three men died, I was certain of how they did not die. As several of Denbeaux's students concluded after studying the NCIS report—long before they met me—they did not die in their cells. That much I was sure of.

I tended to look at conspiracies through the mental lens of Hollywood movies. I imagined kooks spinning tales about Roswell, New Mexico; and the moon landing. Such conspiracy theories were usually premised on the idea that everybody involved understood the common goal—assassinating a person or faking a terrorist attack—and that they all worked together to carry it off.

But I realized, after reading the MA3's statement, that wasn't the case. The MA3 gave a scathingly honest account of what he witnessed up until he was asked about the hangings. Then he'd been vague. He didn't know the ultimate goal, but he had stayed in his lane.

Don't ask, don't tell. Gitmo was structured to enforce that maxim. Not only were we supposed to keep our names and assignments secret from people outside our squads, we weren't supposed to ask anybody for his or her information, either. Compounding the secrecy were the private contractors who operated outside military law. Contractors were outside the chain of command, the uniform code of military justice, and not subject to transparency laws such as the Freedom of Information Act. Specialized contractors, like interrogators, who cost on average three times as much as their government counterparts, were typically used to add another level of deniability.

When I came forward to tell my story, I had to give up my career in the military to speak freely. There have been thousands of news stories about Gitmo and about the treatment of detainees. After I spoke to Scott Horton for his article in *Harper's*, I didn't take it personally that people attacked my credibility. The only thing that hurt was when a Pentagon spokesman told reporters that I was "disrespecting the troops."

I *was* a troop. I served proudly at Guantánamo, with some of the finest soldiers I have ever known since my military career began in the Marine Corps. I was not a whistle-blower. It was the duty of every sworn member of the United States military to report wrongdoing. I followed every proper channel to do so.

I wrote this book in the spirit of what I learned in the Marine Corps. After a mission, I was trained to sit down with my unit and discuss what happened, what we could do better, what we learned. It was called an after-action report. I did the same here. I wrote this account to provoke further research and informed debate, so that hopefully we may do a better job with our detention program.

It is my informed opinion that there were three wrongful deaths at Gitmo on June 9, 2006, while I was on duty. I believe that my command, including Colonel Mike Bumgarner, Admiral Harry Harris, who today serves as assistant chairman to the Joint Chiefs of Staff, and Secretary of Defense Donald Rumsfeld participated in a cover-up. In

the very best case, the investigations that took place under their command were grossly incompetent.

These are strong opinions. I have been as transparent as possible
about how my opinions have been formed. I encourage people who
question my analysis of the NCIS report to go and read it themselves.
I wrote this book while soldiers were still serving in Afghanistan. As an
American soldier, I support their mission. I believe in American justice.
And I believe that the truth about June 9 must be revealed.

ACKNOWLEDGMENTS

The following people were invaluable to the completion of this book and I thank them deeply for their contributions. Seton Hall University School of Law, especially, deserves praise for its support of this project, particularly Professor Mark Denbeaux for his guidance, belief in my story, and his tireless efforts to make sense out of a dense and tangled narrative. I'd also like to thank Josh Denbeaux for being a fantastic attorney and a great friend who has always had my back. A big debt of gratitude is owed to those Seton Hall research fellows who spent many sleepless hours fueled by coffee and pizza while poking holes in the NCIS story to arrive at the truth. My eternal thanks to Sara Ben-David, Brian Beroth, Alex Bregman, Scott Buerkle, Sean Camoni, Meghan Chrisner-Keefe, Ed Dabek, Adam Deutsch, Kieran Dowling, Jesse Dresser, Doug Eadie, Bahadir Ekiz, Michael Fish, Christopher Fox, Ryan Gallagher, Erin Hendrix, Marisa Hourdajian, Sean Kennedy, Ed Kerins, Adam Kirchner, Marissa Litwin, Christal Loyer, Michael McDonough, Eric Miller, Emma Mintz, Michael Patterson, Kelly Ross, Shannon Sterritt, Kelli Stout, Nick Stratton, Kelly Ann Taddonio, Paul Taylor, Philip Taylor, Lauren Winchester, Chris Whitten, Joshua Wirtshafter, and Haoyang Zhu. I'm proud to have had the honor of working with them. I am also thankful for Gwenda Davis at Seton Hall Law School for her support throughout this entire project. Richard Marek deserves my warm appreciation for writing the book proposal that got the ball rolling on this project. Major thanks to my literary agents, Stu Miller and Jim Kellem, who believed in my story from the beginning and never wavered during the long process of completing it. Finally, a tip of the hat to Thomas LeBien and Brit Hvide at Simon & Schuster for their patience, guidance, and perseverance throughout the writing of this book.

INDEX